SECULAR SABOTAGE

SECULAR SABOTAGE

How Liberals Are Destroying Religion and Culture in America

BILL DONOHUE,
President of the Catholic League

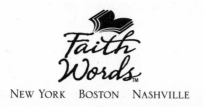

NEW YORK   BOSTON   NASHVILLE

FaithWords
Hachette Book Group
237 Park Avenue
New York, NY 10017

Visit our website at www.faithwords.com.

Printed in the United States of America

First Edition: September 2009
10 9 8 7 6 5 4 3 2 1

FaithWords is a division of Hachette Book Group, Inc.
The FaithWords name and logo are trademarks of
Hachette Book Group, Inc.

Library of Congress Cataloging-in-Publication Data

Donohue, William A., 1947
    Secular sabotage : how liberals are destroying religion and culture in America / William A. Donohue.
        p. cm.
    Summary: "America's cultural traditions are under attack in the name of tolerance and our heritage will be lost unless we dare to fight back"—Provided by the publisher
    ISBN 978-0-446-54721-5
  1. Christianity—United States. 2. Liberalism—United States.
3. Christianity and culture—United States. 4. Christianity and politics—United States. I. Title.
    BR515.D66 2009
    277.3'083—dc22   2009012148

Book design by Charles Sutherland

For Tara

CONTENTS

ACKNOWLEDGMENTS   ix

CHAPTER 1
Revenge of the Nihilists   1

CHAPTER 2
Multicultural Sabotage   8

CHAPTER 3
Sexual Sabotage   35

CHAPTER 4
Artistic Sabotage   61

CHAPTER 5
Sabotaged by Hollywood   83

CHAPTER 6
Sabotaged by Lawyers   117

CHAPTER 7
Democratic Sabotage   137

CHAPTER 8
Self-Sabotage: Catholicism   163

CHAPTER 9
Self-Sabotage: Protestantism   200

CHAPTER 10
The Perfect Cultural Storm   218

NOTES   223

ABOUT THE AUTHOR   259

ACKNOWLEDGMENTS

Many thanks to my family and friends for supporting me at every stage of this book. Always interested in the latest update, they were a steady source of affection and inspiration.

What would I do without my agent, Loretta Barrett? She is more than an agent—the former senior editor knows every facet of her trade. She guided the book from what started out as an oversized and uncoordinated work and turned it into something much more focused. And from there she persuaded me to seize on the material that might interest readers most. Her advice, along with the initial input from Michelle Rapkin, proved to be determinative.

It took no time at all before I hit it off with Harry Helm, associate publisher at Hachette; he edited the book step by step. He is a brilliant and amiable person, and his strong interest in the book gave me the drive needed to meet deadlines and make the necessary adjustments. Any author would be fortunate to have him in his corner.

Irving Louis Horowitz, the founder of Transaction Press, must also be acknowledged. He is much more than a dear friend: his interest in publishing my first book on the ACLU, and subsequent volumes, helped craft my career. Hence, were it not for Irv, this book would never have been published.

Finally, there is the Catholic League community: the staff; the board of directors; the board of advisors; and the members. Both boards are important, but it is the staff that brings the Catholic League to life. And without the members—the best in the world—none of this would have been possible.

SECULAR SABOTAGE

CHAPTER 1

Revenge of the Nihilists

- A college student is threatened with expulsion because she prayed on campus for her ill professor.
- Radicals bust up a Mass and spit the consecrated Host on the floor.
- An artist is awarded first prize for drawing a picture of a priest performing oral sex on Jesus.
- A professor predicts violence will follow a movie about the death of Jesus and cops are ordered into theaters to monitor the situation.
- A civil rights organization protests a statue of Jesus found on the ocean floor.
- A religious outreach adviser to a political party signs a brief trying to excise the words "under God" from the Pledge of Allegiance.
- An organized group of nuns files a brief in support of abortion.
- A prominent minister implores the faithful to reject Christianity.

All of these incidents, and many more, are discussed in this book. The secular assault on the Judeo-Christian ethos is not happening because of accident or whim. It is happening because disaffected men and women have deliberately set out to upend tradition. Indeed, they are hell-bent in their determination to tear down the traditional norms, values, and institutions that have undergirded American society from its founding. The cultural debris that these secular saboteurs have created will take decades to clean up, but we people of faith have no other alternative save moral decomposition.

All of us know people who are nonbelievers, and most of them are decent human beings. Many of them wish they could believe but find it difficult to do so. They may be secularists, but they are not a problem. Nor are liberals of a moderate bent. The problem group are radical secular activists out to disable America.

What bothers these men and women more than anything is the Judeo-Christian heritage that marks Western civilization. That tradition stresses virtue and places a premium on the family and the sanctity of human life. It emphasizes sobriety and moderation, shunning excess and debauchery. It understands that there is a moral hierarchy and acknowledges the existence of truth. It recognizes sin and evil, but it also believes in redemption. And it professes a strong belief in God, the Creator of the universe. All of this makes radical secularists sick.

No part of society is off-limits to these extremists. It is not just the dominant culture that is under assault—left-wing activists have sunk their secular claws into Catholicism and Protestantism as well. The goal is not reform: it is an attempt to gut core beliefs and practices. And to a disturbing extent, the secularists have succeeded in turning things upside down and inside out.

Jews are at one another's throats as well, and indeed tensions are so bad that Columbia University professor Samuel G. Freedman says that a "civil war" has broken out between raging factions.[1] But the situation with Jews is different: there is a secular-religious divide, but it tends to run along parallel denominations and associations. As such, there is nothing analogous in the Jewish community to the kind of sabotage that Christians have experienced. Moreover, radical secularists rarely target Judaism—it is Christianity they want to sunder.

What exactly motivates them? They started as egalitarians. Now they are mostly anarchists. In other words, their passion for equality across the board—class, race, ethnic, gender—has fizzled, leaving them angry and dismayed. Whatever might be said of the Marxists, they had a blueprint for the future. Sure, before they could achieve communism, capitalism had to collapse; so it made sense to try to rally the urban working class against the bourgeoisie. But they were not levelers for the fun of it. To give them their due, the Marxists, although completely wrong, at least had a game plan, a clear but distorted vision of what the new society would look like. They were not anarchists happy to search and destroy everything in sight. No, they wanted to start de novo, building a new society on the soil of the old one.

This is not what we are faced with today. What we are faced with is nihilism. Today's secular extremists more resemble bratty kids throwing a temper tantrum than they do revolutionaries: they want to knock the house down. Having witnessed their left-wing hopes go up in flames with the crash of the Berlin Wall, the Soviet Union, and all the other Marxist wonderlands, they are in a state of despair. That they have absolutely nothing to offer in the way of an alternative social order not only reveals their intellectual bankruptcy, it explains their rage. This is the revenge of the nihilists.

At work is envy, not jealousy. The jealous want what others have; the envious want to deprive others of what they have. Yesterday's revolutionary really believed he could deliver Utopia; today's nihilist is content with upending the status quo. To put it differently, the radicals of old wanted to steer the bus along paths never envisioned. Today's radicals want to run the bus off the road.

If the secular saboteurs really believed in diversity, they

would evince a laissez-faire attitude and go their own way. They might even be inclined to accept their status as a subculture. That's what diversity is all about—pluralism. But to live in a plural society implies tolerance, and that is one virtue the saboteurs sorely lack.

To accomplish their world without hierarchy, they are prepared to use every trick in the book. In this regard, they do resemble the Marxists of old: they hold to the principle that the truth is that which serves the cause. Honesty, as Lenin made plain, was for chumps. Similarly, today's nihilists use deceit, demonization, and coercion as their weapons. "Come the revolution, everyone will eat strawberries," the comrade said. "But I don't like strawberries," said a dissenter. "Come the revolution, everyone will like strawberries."

In other words, radical secularists have become cultural nihilists, or what might be called secular saboteurs. Essentially, what is being described is a highly politicized segment of the population that has seen its ideals crushed and has set its sights on destruction.

Those who challenge the radical secularists have been, and continue to be, demonized in a manner that knows no ethical boundaries. Unlike thoughtful liberals who are motivated by a sincere commitment to the common good, the extremists want to subvert everything associated with our Judeo-Christian heritage. For them, what counts is winning, and if that means winning without rules, so be it. Everything is on the table. Indeed, they have perfected the politics of personal destruction. Unlike reform-minded liberals and conservatives seeking to amend the social order, secular saboteurs seek its demise.

Religion is the cultural nucleus of society, so it is not surprising that the nihilists would pay special attention to its influence. It is not easy to decide which religion—Catholicism or Protestantism—has been hit the hardest; both have had the wind knocked out of them. Those doing the damage are not seeking reasonable changes. It is one thing to gently push the envelope here and there, hoping to open the eyes of those who prefer the status quo. It is quite another to jam a pair of scissors in their eyes.

For all the talk about how multicultural our society is, the United States is still only .4 percent Hindu, .6 percent Muslim, and 1.7 percent Jewish; approximately 8 in 10 Americans are Christians. It stands to reason, then, that the radical secularists must sabotage Catholicism and Protestantism if they are to be a success. And that they have done. The most cherished beliefs and practices of Christianity are routinely trashed by those who have laid anchor in both the Catholic Church and the mainline Protestant churches; this includes some who teach in the seminaries and divinity schools. They could move on to some other religion, but they choose to stay where the action is.

Princeton's Robert George believes that the real clash of civilizations is less between the world's major civilizations than it is "between those who claim the Judeo-Christian worldview and those who have abandoned that worldview in favor of the 'isms' of contemporary American life—feminism, multiculturalism, gay liberationism, lifestyle liberalism." Lumped together, they constitute what George calls "the secular orthodoxy." When it comes to the central issues involved in the culture war, George notes that for the most part we are dealing with "sexuality, the transmitting and taking of human life, and the place of religion."[2]

Driving the nihilists is a tortured vision of sexuality that is so unhinged from reality as to be maddening. Libertinism is too kind a word to describe what they want. And to reach their state of perpetual ecstasy, they need to take down Christianity, especially Catholicism: it is restraint that the secular purists find most objectionable. Make no mistake about it, what they desire is nothing less than full-blown genital liberation. They want it all—with whomever they want—and they want it now. To deny them is to kill them. Indeed, they'd rather be dead than utter the dreaded words "Thou Shalt Not."

Christian holidays make secular nihilists sick. Which explains why they are relentless in their quest to censor Christmas and cast eternal doubt on the biblical account of Easter. They have no use for believing Jews as well, but they know they are too few to matter. Muslims scare them—in more ways than one— but right now they are prepared to give them a pass. No, it is Christianity that dominates, and it is therefore incumbent on them to bring it down.

Influenced by Antonio Gramsci, the Italian Marxist, today's secular saboteurs have worked hard to grab control of the cultural command centers. Their tireless efforts to use and abuse the arts and the entertainment industry are testimony to their cause. And their cause is nothing less than the public flogging of Christianity. From scatological art exhibits to perverse plays, shows, and movies, it is evident that the obscene tracks the blasphemous. Indeed, nowhere is nihilism more fashionable than among the cultural elite.

At the intellectual level, a militant atheism has surged, firing a cadre of hate-filled activists who go for the jugular. Richard Dawkins and Christopher Hitchens are not content to dissect religion—they want to annihilate it. At the level of pop culture, comedians like Bill Maher are not satisfied to lambaste religion— they want to insult, demean, and disparage believers; his assaults on Catholicism are so vicious and relentless as to be pathological. Consumed with rage, these nihilists are on a mission, and they are in fact more dogmatic in their beliefs than the most fundamentalist of the faithful.

No victory would be complete without a radical reconstruction of the Constitution. The First Amendment, in particular, is under siege precisely because it affects so much of the way we live. Ideologically driven law professors, legal activists, and judges have delivered a rendering of the Constitution that would make the Framers wince. Their goal has less to do with advancing liberty, properly understood, than with tailoring the First Amendment to serve their agenda. They are aided and abetted in this process by many in the Democratic Party. They do not seek to propose anything—their objective is to impose their will on the masses.

The American experiment was never supposed to be a celebration of unbounded liberty. On the contrary, it was supposed to be a mission in service to the good society, one where justice and happiness triumphed. To do this required ordered liberty. But for cultural nihilists, ordered liberty is an oxymoron. Ironically, even the Marxists knew that to have a communist society there had to be social stability. But that's because Marxists were in the business of societal reconstruction. Today's radicals are more like termites than revolutionaries.

Have the moral anarchists won? No, but if they are not stopped, they will. The only force capable of defeating them is a strong coalition of religious conservatives. For this to happen— and it is already happening—religion's conservatives will have to put aside their theological differences. Traditional Catholics, evangelical Protestants, and Orthodox Jews, as well as most Orthodox Christians, Muslims, and Mormons, share a core set of moral values that are antithetical to the moral wasteland of those out to destroy them. To prevail, the conservatives have to be bolder than ever, and that means they have to be prepared for assaults on their character and their religion.

Most Americans do not want to lock horns in the culture war, but it is clear that their sentiments are not with the nihilists. It is up to religious conservatives, at least the activists within this camp, to make sure that radical secularists do not succeed in their quest to sabotage our culture.

CHAPTER 2

Multicultural Sabotage

Multicultural Madness

If a benchmark of the good society is the way racial, ethnic, and religious minorities are treated, then the United States is deserving of high marks, at least in recent decades. Unfortunately, genuine concern for the welfare of minorities often becomes a highly politicized exercise. Worse, it becomes unhinged from reality. Take Native Americans.

Over the past quarter century, high school, college, and professional sports teams have jettisoned the use of Native American mascot names, all in the name of sensitivity. Led almost exclusively by white liberals, those who pioneered this effort never bothered to learn whether their hypersensitivity was reflective of the sentiment in the Native American community. They just assumed it was. And they assumed wrong: polls show that while Indian elites may agree with white liberals, most Native Americans are not offended by Indian mascot names.[1]

At face value, it sounds so nice: we should respect all cultures and heritages, embrace diversity, and practice inclusion. But the fact is that most cultures have delivered nothing but savagery and slavery and are worthy of unqualified condemnation, not respect. Moreover, diversity and inclusion are polar opposites and cannot possibly exist simultaneously: if everyone is to be included, there can be no diversity. Besides, those who typically invoke these notions have an agenda: they hate Western civilization and its Judeo-Christian ethos. The irony is that *all* the ideas and institutions that have made Western civilization the greatest success story in the history of the world—as measured in terms of liberty and prosperity—find their roots in the Judeo-Christian heritage.

Ideological isms have caused some of the greatest catastrophes in history, and in the past few decades, none has been more pernicious than multiculturalism. Yet to secular saboteurs, multiculturalism is a godsend. It gives them all the justification they need to attack our Judeo-Christian roots. Here's how they operate.

They begin by saying that our nation, and the world itself, is becoming increasingly diverse. Then they say that it behooves us to make a twenty-first-century adjustment and prepare the way for all these diverse peoples. In other words, we'd better get used to a changing world. We can begin by burying our religious traditions and practices, they instruct. This is not just an idea that secularists have—it is dogmatically enshrined in their heads. So much so that they no longer need to think: words like tolerance, diversity, and inclusion constitute a mantra. They are the holy trinity of multiculturalism.

The fact of the matter is that the United States now contains more Christians than any other nation in history.[2] "Surprising though it may seem," writes Dinesh D'Souza, "the total number of non-Christians in America add up to less than 10 million people, which is around 3 percent of the population." D'Souza has more bad news for the secularists: "In terms of religious background, America is no more diverse today than it was in the eighteenth and nineteenth centuries." This is because most of the immigrants are coming from south of the border, and almost all of them are Christians.[3] In fact, the U.S. is more Christian today than Israel is Jewish.[4]

Moreover, the world is becoming *less* multicultural: the world's largest religions—Catholicism, Protestantism, Islam, and Hinduism—have expanded at a rate that exceeds global population growth. At the beginning of the twentieth century, exactly 50 percent of the world was Catholic, Protestant, Muslim, or Hindu. At the start of the twenty-first century, their combined numbers total 64 percent, and by 2025 it is estimated that these four religious groups will constitute close to 70 percent of the world's population.[5]

When presented with this evidence, secularists are unfazed: they accept the mantras of multiculturalism with dogmatic certainty. Indeed, if they had to admit that all their assumptions about the present and the future are built on faulty data, their whole world would collapse. Better to play make-believe. They do it so well because they've had so much practice at it. For example, we all know that America was founded on Judeo-Christian principles and that Christianity has been the foundational structure of American history. Yet there are still some, like Garry Wills, who claim this is a "right-wing fiction."[6] Others persist in seeing secularism as our founding edifice.[7] But no amount of wishful thinking can get in the way of historical facts.

Conservative writer and chronicler of the American experience M. Stanton Evans does not exaggerate when he says of America's Founding Fathers that "virtually all of them were professing Christians, affirmed their faith in God, and expressed this faith in public statements." It is precisely because "a teeming record" shows this to be true that Evans says that "the notion that America's founders were 'secular liberals' . . . is absurdly false."[8]

In *The Theme Is Freedom*, Evans quotes George Washington imploring his troops "to live and act as becomes a Christian soldier." Similarly, he quotes John Adams's remark that the United States was established on "the general principles of Christianity."[9] Can anyone imagine Washington urging his troops to act like good atheists? Or Adams saying that America was based on "the general principles of secularism"? As for Jefferson, it is worth recalling his prescience: "Can the liberties of a nation be thought secure when we have removed their only firm basis, a conviction in the minds of the people that these liberties are of the gift of God?"[10]

Secularists get angry when they hear someone say that "this is a Christian nation." But this is exactly what the United States Supreme Court said in 1892.[11] Today, two-thirds of Americans say the U.S. is a Christian nation,[12] and most still look to religion as a remedy to personal and social problems. This does not sit well with the Anti-Defamation League, the nation's most influential Jewish civil rights organization. For instance, it has tried to censor the words "The true Christian is the true citizen" from a courthouse in Riverside, California (the words belong to Teddy Roosevelt);[13] it also wants to censor the words "under God" from the Pledge of Allegiance.[14]

Religious Jews, of course, do not feel that they are represented by the ADL. Rabbi Daniel Lapin, the founder of Toward Tradition, a Jewish group that espouses traditional values, says the question should not be "Is America a Christian nation?" but "Should America be a Christian nation?" To which he says, "As a non-Christian myself, I still insist the answer must be yes." That's because he sees, as do many other Jews, that "the choice is between a benign Christian culture and a sinister secular one."[15] Don Feder agrees: "The choice isn't Christian America or nothing, but Christian America or a neo-pagan, hedonistic, rights-without-responsibilities, anti-family, culture-of-death America."[16] As devout Jews, Lapin and Feder are not about to convert to Christianity. All they are saying is that it is in the best interests of Jews to nourish Christianity, not secularism.

Richard Bernstein, a Jewish writer not associated with religious conservatives, is as critical of multiculturalism as Lapin and Feder. For Bernstein, it is the "narrow orthodoxy" that marks multiculturalism that is most disconcerting. He even goes so far as to say that the bureaucracy that has grown up around multiculturalism is run by people like Robespierre. Now, today's nihilists may not be responsible for a Reign of Terror, but their resort to punitive measures against those who cross them is real. There are important differences: Robespierre was executed; today's brutes get federal grants. "It is an ardently advocated, veritably messianic political program," Bernstein says, "and, like most political programs that have succumbed to the utopian temptation, it does not take kindly to true difference."[17]

In 1994, Bernstein chose to title his book *Dictatorship of Virtue: Multiculturalism and the Battle for America's Future*, and 11 years later Joseph Cardinal Ratzinger, just before he became Pope Benedict XVI, chose the words "dictatorship of relativism" to describe the fruits of multiculturalism. He used this term to describe the reigning idea that each individual is capable of possessing his own morality. This popular view, it must be said, is not only sociologically illiterate—no society in history has ever survived without a moral consensus—it leads inexorably to moral anarchy.

Moral truths, which are central to Christianity, must be accepted by the masses lest chaos prevail. Ironically, it was the pope's fellow Germans who gave us the diabolical idea that moral absolutes are nonsense—nihilists such as Nietzsche and Nazi enthusiasts such as Heidegger. It is not a matter of speculation what happens when truth is discarded. "There is no such thing as truth, either in the moral or in the scientific sense." Those words were penned by Adolf Hitler.[18]

Pope Benedict XVI rightly observes that multiculturalism has bred not only a contempt for the moral truths that adhere to the Judeo-Christian ethos, it has led to "a peculiar Western self-hatred that is nothing short of pathological."[19] Hudson Institute president Herb London agrees, noting that multiculturalism "paradoxically assumes that non-Western cultures are somehow more equal, more worthy, than their Western counterparts." He nails it just right when he says, "This Orwellian phenomenon preaches the gospel of equality, but proceeds as much from self-loathing as from egalitarianism."[20] We saw this attitude on display in the late 1980s when Jesse Jackson led students at Stanford University in their successful campaign to abolish a Western Culture program. They chanted, "Hey, hey, ho, ho, Western Culture's got to go."

The same sentiment was evident in the 1990s when Yale University gave up $20 million given to them by Lee M. Bass: he wanted the money to be spent on efforts to expand the Western civilization curriculum, but highly politicized members of the faculty wanted to replace it with a multicultural program. The faculty won and Bass got his money back.[21] Yale may have been exceptional in this regard, but the multicultural assault on Western traditions was anything but exceptional. For example, in 1992, five hundred years after Columbus discovered America, radical faculties in high schools and colleges took the occasion to bash Columbus as a Christian oppressor. Yet it wasn't Columbus, as Robert Royal points out, who introduced the Indians to human sacrifice, cannibalism, slavery, and torture.[22]

No one has done a better job of chronicling the ideologically skewed nature of the multicultural curriculum than Diane Ravitch. The prolific author, who has taught at Columbia and New York University and served as Assistant Secretary of Education in the first Bush administration, investigated assigned textbooks used at all levels of education. What she found was a disturbing agenda. "The textbooks sugarcoat practices in non-Western cultures that they would condemn if done by Europeans or Americans," she writes. As she puts it, "Textbook after textbook tells the story of the 'spread' of Islam. Christian Europe invades; Islam spreads." Unlike Christianity, which is subjected to microscopic criticism, "The treatment of Islam, for example, lacks any critical analysis." The spin is so wildly dishonest—Islam is "tolerant and egalitarian"—as to verify the pope's charge that multiculturalism in practice constitutes self-hatred on the part of its Western proponents.[23]

Further proof was afforded in 2008 when the American Textbook Council issued a disturbing report, *Islam in the Classroom: What the Textbooks Tell Us.* The report focused on ten widely adopted junior and senior high school history textbooks. The bias is startling: "Islam is featured as a model of interfaith tolerance; Christians wage wars of aggression and kill Jews. Islam provides models of harmony and civilization. Anti-Semitism, the Inquisition, and wars of religion bespot the Christian record." The Crusades, according to this propaganda, were not a reaction by Christians to Muslim violence, rather they were "religious wars launched against Muslims by European Christians." In short, "While Christian belligerence is magnified, Islamic inequality, subjugation, and enslavement get the airbrush."[24]

As Ravitch learned, there are "bias" guidelines for testing that amount to censorship. One of the subjects that teachers are told is "sensitive" is religion. For example, they are instructed to avoid talking about religion, including holidays—even Thanksgiving! The "language police," as Ravitch properly calls them, are not above tampering with the words of authors. For example, in one textbook, the novel *The Ox-Bow Incident* was reprinted, but many passages were redone: "By the Lord God" was switched to "By heaven"; "By God" was changed to "By gum"; "My God" became "Hey!"; and in another instance was altered to read, "You don't mean it."[25] None of this was done to protect kids—it was done to censor any reference to religion or God.

It's not just in textbooks that Christianity is mistreated—it's also in the classroom. "On America's elite campuses, today," writes Yale law professor Stephen Carter, "it is perfectly acceptable for professors to use their classrooms to attack religion, to mock it, to trivialize it, and to refer to those to whom faith truly matters as dupes, and dangerous on top of it." Carter rightly concludes that if similar things were said about other groups in society, it would be called "bigotry."[26] Camille Paglia goes further by arguing that an honest multicultural program would constitute "a core curriculum based on the great world religions." As only she can say, "I'm coming at this as an atheist—I believe that every single religion is saying something truthful about the universe."[27] But to accept all religions would be to accept Christianity, and that's where the problem begins. The secular saboteurs will have none of it.

Some college officials are totalitarians. No other word can be used to accurately describe what happened at two California colleges in 2008, Yuba and the College of Alameda. The president of Yuba College told a 20-year-old student, Ryan Dozier, that he had better stop handing out gospel booklets or face disciplinary action. Believe it or not, Yuba has a free speech zone on campus and it is limited to two days a week for one hour. Dozier faced possible expulsion for simply distributing Christian literature without a school permit, and campus police informed him he might be arrested for violating the college's policy. At the College of Alameda, Kandy Kyriacou was caught praying on campus. When the student found out that her professor was ill at Christmastime, she prayed for her. Though her professor had no problem with the prayer, another professor, Derek Piazza, did. He reported the student to the administration, which quickly sent her a retroactive "intent to suspend" letter accusing her of "disruptive or insulting behavior" and "persistent abuse of" college employees. If she persisted with praying on campus, she was told she could be expelled.[28]

The multicultural industry, which includes academia, publishing houses, and the whole of array of diversity consultants in the workplace, is so wealthy and so influential that its antireligious views have penetrated virtually every institution in society. When the Red Cross bans high school kids from singing "God Bless America" and "America the Beautiful" at its luncheons, it is positive proof that delirium has become normality. This almost happened in 2002, save for pressure from the Catholic League.

The problem began when the Red Cross Orange County Chapter in Santa Ana, California, banned students from Orange County High School of the Arts from singing the two patriotic songs at one of its events. When the American Red Cross issued a news release defending the gag rule, the Catholic League called on over a hundred organizations to drop their support for the Red Cross. Four hours later, the two conditions we demanded were met: the decision to censor the songs was reversed and an apology was granted.[29]

Censoring Christmas and Easter

It's a close call who gets more excited each year about Christmas: the 96 percent of Americans who celebrate it or the secular crusaders who want to censor it. Knowing that they lack the ability to ban Christmas altogether, the next best thing the secularists can do is neuter it. That is why they push so hard to promote every conceivable holiday that occurs in December, including Boxing Day (which isn't even an American holiday), so that they can nullify Christmas celebrations. It's all so contrived. Take Hanukkah and Kwanzaa, for example. As the proportion of Jews has declined significantly in the past 50 years, the prominence of Hanukkah, a minor holiday for Jews anyway, has skyrocketed (it is easier to get a menorah displayed in the schools than a crèche). Kwanzaa, which has nothing to do with Africa—it was invented in 1966 by an ex-con who served four years in jail for ordering the beating of a woman[30]—is celebrated by only 2 percent of Americans, or about 15 percent of African Americans;[31] yet Kwanzaa celebrations in the schools are ubiquitous.

Secularists such as Frank Rich of the *New York Times* and *Salon*'s Michelle Goldberg are angry at those who are fighting back against attempts to censor Christmas. Rich agrees with Goldberg that the war on Christmas is "a burgeoning myth," maintaining that the grievances constitute nothing more than "anomalous idiocies and suburban legends."[32] This dismissive approach is not shared by Adam Cohen of the *New York Times*. In an editorial, he lashed out at the Catholic League and others, accusing them of promoting a "campaign to make America more like a theocracy, with Christian displays on public property and Christian prayer in public schools."[33] But if what Cohen says is true, it follows that America was a theocracy up until recent times: before the 1960s there was prayer in the schools and nativity scenes were everywhere. If this is what a theocracy looks like, no one in the United States seems to have noticed.

Irving Kristol says that when he was growing up, "there were practically no Jews" who cared about what Christians did at Christmastime. "I went to a public school," he writes, "where the children sang carols at Christmastime. Even among Jews who sang them, I never knew a single one who was drawn to the practice of Christianity." Even the performance of a nativity play didn't bother most Jews, Kristol says, and there was "no public 'issue' until the American Civil Liberties Union—which is financed primarily by Jews—arrived on the scene with the discovery that Christmas carols and pageants were a violation of the Constitution."[34]

Burt Prelutsky is a Jewish writer who agrees with Kristol. In a piece he titled "The Jewish Grinch Who Stole Christmas," Prelutsky wrote that "I blame my fellow Jews. When it comes to pushing the multicultural, anti-Christian agenda, you find Jewish judges, Jewish journalists, and the American Civil Liberties Union, at the forefront." Regarding the latter, he says, "It is the ACLU, which is overwhelmingly Jewish in terms of membership and funding, that is leading the attack against Christianity in

America." He concludes by saying, "This is a Christian nation, my friends. And all of us are fortunate it is one."[35] It is for reasons like this that comedian Jackie Mason joined Don Feder, Rabbi Aryeh Spero, and me in a press conference on the steps of St. Patrick's Cathedral in 2005 proclaiming, "Jews Say It's Okay to Say 'Merry Christmas.' "[36]

Rabbi Lapin adds that "Secular fundamentalism has successfully injected into American culture the notion that the word 'Christmas' is deeply offensive." But he does not shy from chastising Jews in Palm Beach from tolerating discrimination against Christians: if a menorah is allowed on public property, he advised his fellow Jews, a nativity scene should be permitted as well.[37] Jeff Jacoby, who writes for the *Boston Globe*, says it bothers him as a Jew as he watches in disbelief every year the many attempts to turn "Christmas" events into "holiday" ones. For him, "suppressing the language, symbols, or customs of Christians in a predominantly Christian society is not inclusive. It's insulting." He adds that it is also discriminatory: Hanukkah menorahs are never called "holiday lamps."[38]

All of these writers are correct to say that secular Jews are disproportionately represented in the war on Christmas. But there aren't enough secular Jews to pull this off by themselves. That's why it makes more sense to speak of this as an assault by radical secularists. As I wrote in 2006 in an op-ed page ad in the *New York Times* on this subject, "it is important to recognize that the few who are complaining [about Christmas celebrations] do not belong to any one religious or ethnic group—there is plenty of diversity among the ranks of the disaffected."[39] Don Feder gets it right when he says that "the secularist assault on Christmas" is something that is "unwittingly aided by the perpetually aggrieved and sensitivity-whipped."[40] There is, unfortunately, a sizable number of Christians who have such a deep-seated need to prove to the world that they are not bigots that they are prepared to sell out their own religion in an effort to validate their bravery.

A survey taken in 2006 disclosed that approximately 7 in 10 Americans say that "liberals have gone too far in keeping religion out of schools and government."[41] In 2008, a poll commissioned by the ADL found that 61 percent of Americans say they believe "Religious values are under attack in this country."[42] One reason so many feel this way is the annual banning of crèches, but not menorahs, from the public schools. The situation got so bad in New York City that I arranged for the city to be sued.

In 2001, I learned that New York City schools allowed menorahs and star and crescents in the classroom, but not nativity scenes (the former were—erroneously—declared secular symbols). A letter from Schools Chancellor Dr. Harold Levy explaining the discriminatory treatment proved to be classic. "The Supreme Court has previously refused to permit erection of a nativity scene on public property," he said.[43] I quickly corrected him about the high court's rulings—it never said any such thing—and noted the following irony: New York City allows me to put a crèche on public property every year, namely in Central Park, and that's because I get a permit from the Parks Department (Orthodox Jews get a permit to put up "the world's largest menorah" every year, and Muslims occasionally display their symbol).

With the help of the Thomas More Law Center, a suit was filed against New York City. On February 18, 2004, United States District Court Judge Charles Sifton ruled against us. He maintained that the menorah and star and crescent had a secular dimension while the nativity scene was "purely religious." Best of all was his remarkably revealing comment: he said the holiday displays "must be reviewed as perceived by the children, Christian children in particular, but not one hyper-sensitive Catholic child."[44]

On appeal, the Second Circuit said New York City was wrong to say that the menorah and star and crescent were not religious symbols, but it balked at ordering the crèche to be displayed (as long as some holiday symbol was allowed, it reasoned, there was no discrimination). Importantly, the court did not say the display of a crèche in the schools was unconstitutional. It explicitly said, "We do not here decide whether the City could, consistent with the Constitution, include a crèche in its school holiday displays."[45]

In a stunning rebuke to Christians, the ADL, which was not a litigant in this case, filed an amicus brief arguing that it was okay to have a menorah but not a nativity scene, in the schools. It said "displaying the crèche carries with it the potential risk of an excessively religious message."[46] When questioned about this, ADL spokeswoman Deborah Lauter said that "A symbol that is pervasively religious gives the appearance that it's an endorsement by the school of one religion over the other."[47] She did not say how the government was able to distinguish between a "pervasively religious" symbol and just an ordinary one. No matter, as I have said many times, if nativity scenes were allowed in the schools and menorahs were not, I would demand equal treatment and push for the display of the menorah. The ADL does not speak for many Jews, and that is why Jewish activists like Rabbi Yehuda Levin of Jews for Morality and Beth Gilinsky of the Jewish Action Alliance have been so critical of it over the years.

In 2007, the United States Supreme Court refused to hear the case. Because the Second Circuit decision left the door open to the display of a nativity scene, the Catholic League then asked the New York City Council to direct the Department of Education to do so. In 2009, I testified before the Education Committee of the City Council asking for parity: if Jews and Muslims are allowed to display their religious symbols, Christians should be afforded the same treatment. Only one person who testified opposed a resolution by New York City Councilman Tony Avella to do just that, and that was a representative from Americans United for Separation of Church and State. She said, without a trace of evidence, that it was "emotionally disturbing" for children to see some religious symbols in the schools. Interestingly, there's no evidence that she ever complained all those years that the menorah and star and crescent were permitted—it was only when the nativity scene stood a chance of being included that she got upset.

Some of the assaults on Christmas are right out of the *Twilight Zone.* For example, in 2003, Central Michigan University and Indiana University went off the deep end with their alleged sensitivity to non-Christians. The affirmative action office at Central Michigan listed a calendar, available online, that mentioned Christmas, Hanukkah, Kwanzaa, and Las Posadas as holidays in December. But there was an asterisk next to Christmas that was priceless: It read, "Warning of Holiday Decorations." By clicking on the "Warning," it was possible to access a document titled "How to Celebrate Christmas Without Offense." Since none of the other holidays merited an asterisk or a warning, it must have meant that Jews, African Americans, and Latinos possess an ability that Christians who celebrate Christmas obviously lack— they are able to party without ticking others off. Either that or anti-Christian bigotry was at work.

The instructions found in the document were gems. "It is inappropriate to decorate things with Santa Claus or reindeer or 'Christmas' decorations." Given this cast of mind, it makes one wonder what the multicultural gestapo would do if they stumbled on a nativity scene—smash it with clubs? The document included advice on what to do: "Good ideas for decorations during this time are snowflakes, snowpeople, poinsettias to give people a feeling of the winter."[48] Yes, snowpeople have a way of doing just that.

At about the same time, Florence Roisman, a professor at Indiana University Law School, was upset about a Christmas tree on campus and succeeded in getting it removed. She said that the 12-foot tree celebrated Christmas, and that as a Jew she found it problematic: "To honor one religion and not honor others is exclusionary." It is important to note that the tree had no religious ornaments on it. The dean of students, Tony Tarr, acceded to her demands and had the tree replaced by two smaller trees, along with a sleigh stuffed with red and green poinsettia plants. He declared the first tree the "denominational" tree and the new ones "a normal Indiana scene." Roisman objected to the new display as well. All of this was carried out by men and women who work in higher education.[49]

Here's another example of secular lunacy. In December 2006, Olympic skater Sasha Cohen was skating at a rink in Riverside, California, when a high school choir started singing "God Rest Ye Merry Gentleman." Immediately, a government employee went into orbit, summoning the police to institute a gag rule. The cop promptly told the choir to knock it off. The offense? Cohen, the bureaucrat advised, was Jewish and would be upset by the Christmas carol. Not that it should matter, but the fact is Cohen was never asked what she thought. When she got the chance to speak, she said it didn't matter at all what the choir was singing.[50] Such paternalism, as well as bigotry, is a hallmark of the sensitivity police.

The hatred of Christmas is so strong in some quarters that a song doesn't even have to be religious to get the censors' juices flowing. In 2008, a woman from North Carolina objected to the song "Rudolph, the Red-Nosed Reindeer." Her problem? The words "Santa" and "Christmas" are mentioned. When she failed in her effort to censor the song, she pushed to get Hanukkah songs included in the holiday program. In other words, she really didn't object to religious songs being sung in the schools— just ones that reminded everyone of Christmas. Even worse that year was Clair Ebel, head of the New Hampshire ACLU. If nativity scenes are allowed in the parks, she instructed, it is permissible to have "a display of satanic ritual."[51] Perhaps the ACLU has one to loan.

To demonstrate how multicultural madness is truly multicultural, consider what happened in England in 2008. Muslim preacher Anjem Choudary branded Christmas "evil," causing hardly a stir. Perhaps he was assimilating what he learned from the Brits: his damning of Christmas occurred at the same time it was announced that the words "bishop," "chapel," "monk," "nun," etc., were to be forever banned from the Oxford Junior Dictionary.[52] All this from those who gave us the King's English.

The effects of multiculturalism are so deep and wide that they even reach megastores like Wal-Mart, often cited as a bastion of American traditionalism. In 2005, at the start of the Christmas season, a customer relations employee, responding to complaints that Wal-Mart was dumbing down Christmas, sent an e-mail to a woman on the pagan origins of Christmas; the recipient forwarded the note to the Catholic League. When it was brought to the attention of the top person in public relations, he agreed with the mind-boggling statement. It said that Christmas has roots in "Siberian shamanism" and that the colors red and white "are actually a representation of the aminita mascera mushroom." Similarly, Santa, mistletoe, the Yule log, the tree, etc., have non-Christian roots.[53]

That made me curious. After kicking around the Wal-Mart Web site, I discovered that there was a Hanukkah and Kwanzaa section but no Christmas one (there was just a "Holiday" section). Thus, a pattern of discrimination was emerging. That was it. The Catholic League called for a boycott and contacted 126 religious organizations spanning seven faith communities. Within 48 hours, Wal-Mart issued an apology, changed its Web site, and fired the customer relations employee.[54] In 2006, Wal-Mart received many kudos for its totally pro-Christmas promotions. It admitted that it had learned a valuable lesson the year before.[55]

What is particularly disturbing about all this is the rank hypocrisy involved. It is said that we should be careful about celebrating Christmas in the schools and at work because not everyone is Christian. But to be excluded is normal. Mother's

Day, Father's Day, Veterans Day, Black History Month, Gay Pride parades—they all exclude someone. So, too, do the Olympics: they are a showcase of segregation—men are barred from participating in women's sports—yet not even radical feminists object. Moreover, if a white student said he felt excluded during Black History Month and wanted it canceled, would we seek to educate the bigot or allow him to veto the celebrations? If the answer is obvious, why do we tolerate different rules when it comes to the bigots who hate Christmas?

Why is it that we are so busy celebrating diversity during December instead of January? Why don't we give the same amount of attention to the First of Muharram and Ashura as we do to Martin Luther King Jr.'s birthday? After all, they fall in January. The reason is obvious: it would have the effect of diluting the overriding significance of Martin Luther King Day. This is exactly what is at work when we seek to hype every holiday that falls in December—the goal of the secular saboteurs is to neuter the significance of Christmas.

While nothing gets the secularists more angry than Christmas, they bring their multicultural agenda to bear against Easter as well. Hardly a year goes by without a major weekly like *Time*, *Newsweek*, or *U.S. News and World Report* running a story that questions the authenticity of New Testament accounts of Jesus' death and resurrection. PBS and NPR can similarly be counted on, as can the networks' magazine shows like *20/20* and *Dateline*. No other religion is ever submitted to such scrutiny, and indeed the more primitive the religion, the more respect it is shown.

The most absurd attack on Christianity to take place at Eastertime came in 2007 when James Cameron of *Titanic* fame teamed up with TV director Simcha Jacobovici to offer a Discovery Channel documentary—it was really a docudrama—claiming that they had found the Jesus family tomb.

Israeli archaeologists take great pride in their work and have little patience for charlatans. That is why they were up in arms with the extravagant claims being made. Amos Kloner, for example, was in charge of the 1980 investigation of the tomb that Cameron and Jacobovici seized upon 27 years later when they made their allegations. "The claim that the burial site has been found is not based on any proof, and is only an attempt to sell," Kloner said. "With all due respect," he offered, "they are not archaeologists." Indeed, he said their claims were "impossible" and "nonsense." What Kloner said was backed up by virtually all the experts, but this did not stop the *Titanic* fraud from being hawked. However, when even Ted Koppel of the Discovery Channel, who moderated a discussion on the claims, was unpersuaded, the station's officials backed away from the movie and said they would not rerun it.[56] To top it off, when the book on the subject appeared, it contained not one endnote or citation of any kind.[57] That's what happens when there is no evidence.

If Lent of 2007 started with Cameron's scheme, it ended during Holy Week with a Chocolate Jesus being nixed by the Catholic League. The Roger Smith Lab Gallery of the Roger Smith Hotel in New York City was set to display a six-foot-tall anatomically correct sculpture of Jesus in milk chocolate; the figure was depicted as crucified. Artist Cosimo Cavallaro titled his work *My Sweet Lord* and invited the public to eat his creation of Jesus, genitals and all. This pushed me to challenge the hotel's president and CEO, James Knowles, to substitute Muhammad for Jesus and display him during Ramadan. For some reason, he wasn't interested. The Catholic League then contacted approximately five hundred allied organizations, asking them to boycott the hotel.[58] It was this kind of public pressure that forced the hotel to cancel the exhibit. When the artist asked me on TV where he should display his work, I answered, "In New Jersey—that's where New Yorkers put their garbage. There's a big sanitation dump."[59]

Deference to Muslims

There are those who say that secular saboteurs do not target Christianity more than other religions. But the evidence does not support this. Take Islam, for instance. The deference shown to Muslims is simply not shown to Christians. To wit: in 2007, the U.S. House of Representatives voted 376 to 0 in favor of a resolution giving tribute to Ramadan and Islam, but a similarly worded resolution giving tribute to Christmas and Christianity found 9 members voting against the resolution, 10 who simply voted "present," and 40 others who didn't vote at all.[60]

Bad as things are in the United States, they are even more insane in Britain. In 2008, a Scottish police force postcard was pulled because it featured a German shepherd puppy advertising a new nonemergency police phone number. The offense? Muslims complained that dogs are regarded as "unclean." The year before, the kitchen staff at a British hospital was told not to serve hot cross buns to patients at Easter because it might "upset non-Christians."[61]

What is even more amazing is that, after 9/11, there are indications that Muslims are being given preferential treatment. Consider what happened at Sharon High School in Sharon, Massachusetts, a month after the United States was attacked.

At a Halloween costume party, first prize was awarded to three boys: two were dressed as pregnant nuns and a third was dressed as the impregnating priest. It was the faculty that granted the award. Following complaints from Catholic students and the Catholic League, officials at the high school confessed that they were as perplexed about what happened as anyone. They said that they had gone out of their way that year not to offend Muslims. But their sensitivity meter obviously didn't apply to Catholics. To top it off, instead of inviting someone from the Catholic League to address the student body, a representative from the ADL was invited. He talked to the students about bigotry and chose as his subject the Holocaust.[62]

Two years later, an equally appalling thing happened at Princeton University. The Woodrow Wilson School of Public and International Affairs hosted Ricanstructions, an art exhibit by Juan Sanchez. Included in the exhibit was a display called *Shackles of the AIDS Virus*, a 1996 work by the artist that features such devotional items as scapulars and images of the Virgin Mary arranged in a circle. Another display showed naked female torsos arranged in the shape of a cross; it was labeled *Crucifixion No. 2*. There was also a display of torn-up images of the Sacred Heart of Jesus. Dean Ann-Marie Slaughter defended the anti-Christian art for its alleged "educational value." This was hardly exceptional—it's what deans are programmed to say. What was surprising was her honesty: she said that a display that offended Islam would not be tolerated on the campus.[63]

The Danish cartoon controversy seals the argument being made here: the media show Islam more respect than Christianity.

Whenever the Catholic League criticizes a work of art, cartoon, movie, or TV show, we are told that we're the intolerant ones; what is offensive is in the eye of the beholder; art is supposed to make people uncomfortable; no one can criticize something unless he's personally seen it; protests have a "chilling effect" on free speech; it's not real anyway; get over it. But when an inoffensive depiction of Muhammad is objected to by Muslims, the same rules don't apply. Their sensibilities are respected, the cartoon is not shown, and none of the criticisms thrown at the Catholic League are voiced. Worse, the media lie. With the singular exception of the *Boston Phoenix*, which admitted that it was fear that persuaded the paper not to print the cartoons, the media refused to admit that their unusual act of self-censorship was driven by primordial self-interest. They were afraid of being beheaded.

Why, according to the *Washington Post*, did European newspapers reprint the cartoons? It was "not their love of freedom but their insensitivity—or hostility—to the growing diversity of their own societies." The *Los Angeles Times* said it would not reprint "these insensitive images." The *Miami Herald* boasted that it "must take great care not to offend." The *New York Times* said it was wrong to publish "gratuitous assaults on religious symbols." The *San Francisco Chronicle* announced that "insulting or hurting certain groups" is wrong. Both CBS and NBC said it wasn't necessary to show the cartoons in order to report on them. CNN even went so far as to say that it "has chosen not to show the cartoons out of respect for Islam."[64]

All of these remarks are fabulously ludicrous, but the grand prize goes to the *New York Times*. In his piece on this subject, Michael Kimmelman recalled how the Catholic League protested the 1999 Sensation exhibit at the Brooklyn Museum of Art that featured a "collage of the Virgin Mary with cutouts from pornographic magazines and shellacked clumps of elephant dung." He further said that in contrast to irate Muslims, "No protester torched the museum or called for beheading anybody." This was all fine and good, save for one thing: on the same page where it was noted that the *New York Times* would not reprint the Danish cartoons—out of respect for Muslims—it reprinted the offensive art from the Sensation exhibit. Evidently, some have a hard time connecting the dots at the Old Gray Lady.[65]

An episode at the University of Oregon in 2006 was just as bad. The March edition of the *Insurgent*, the university's student newspaper, contained a large graphic cartoon depicting a naked Jesus on the Cross with an erection; there was also a graphic titled *Resurrection*, which showed a naked Jesus kissing another naked man, both sporting erections. The entire issue was replete with the most egregious examples of hate speech directed at Christians. For example, there were several cartoons of Jesus—including Jesus crucified—that were so gratuitously offensive that only the most depraved would defend them. All of this occurred during Lent, at a state institution. What made it even more insane was that this obscene explosion was a response to a decision reached by one of the *Insurgent's* rivals, the *Commentator*, to publish the 12 Danish cartoons that had inflamed the Muslim world. An *Insurgent* editorial said that because the *Commentator* published the Danish cartoons so as to "provoke dialogue," they had a right to bash Christians as a way of provoking dialogue.[66]

South Park creators Trey Parker and Matt Stone played the same game. When Comedy Central refused to show some of their work lambasting Muslims, Parker and Stone answered by delivering an all-out assault on Christians, just to show how hypocritical the station's managers were. But at least they didn't lie. "That's where we kind of agree with some of the people who've criticized our show," Stone told ABC, "because it really is open season on Jesus. You know? We can do whatever—we can do whatever we want to Jesus. And we've had him say bad words, we've had him shoot a gun, we've had him kill people. And you know, we can do everyone. But Mohammad, we couldn't just show a simple image."[67] Parker is just as blunt: "We rip on absolutely everyone, in really horrible, terrible ways. And if you're saying this is the one thing we can't do, because they're threatening violence, well, then, I guess that's what everyone should do. If the Catholics don't want us ripping on Jesus anymore, they should just threaten violence and they'll get their way."[68]

Theocracy

Over the past few decades, religious conservatives have forged an alliance to confront the unremitting secular assault on the nation's Judeo-Christian heritage. Unfortunately, whenever the conservatives fight back—usually to maintain or restore the status quo, for example, to keep "under God" in the Pledge of Allegiance—they are demonized for doing so. In fact, demonization is one of the most popular weapons in the arsenal of those out to annihilate our culture. The most common accusation holds that traditional Catholics, evangelical Protestants, and Orthodox Jews desire nothing less than a theocracy in America.

Norman Lear's organization, People for the American Way, is second to none in its vigilance of religious conservatives. Since its inception, it has considered them a serious threat to democracy. Indeed, it was one of the first secular organizations to brand religious conservatives Nazis; that occurred in the 1980s.[69] Now such labeling has become commonplace. Nicholas von Hoffman, for example, sees no difference between Christian activists and Muslim terrorists. "Like the Islamists, with whom they are brothers under the skin," he writes, "they are intent on imposing a Christian form of sharia on believers and non-believers alike."[70]

John Dean of Watergate infamy says that "Christian Nationalists" are running the Republican Party, but that not everyone is aware of this coup. Using tactics "not unlike those American Communists once used," he observes, "Christian nationalists often operate by stealth." For instance, he says, when President Bush sought to appoint William Pryor and Janice Rogers Brown to the federal bench, few knew that standing right behind them "lurked the hand of the Christian nationalists."[71] Less sensational is Andrew Sullivan, who prefers the term "Christianist" to refer to those who blend politics and religion, but unlike other commentators—and it is a credit to him—he makes it clear that the term "is in no way designed to label people on the religious right as favoring any violence at all."[72]

In 1994, Christian conservatives took a double-barreled hit when the American Jewish Committee and the ADL issued separate reports blasting them for promoting hatred. The first group was upset because Christians "adamantly oppose social acceptance of homosexuality as an alternative lifestyle." Notice that

Christians weren't being blamed for rejecting homosexuals, but for refusing to accept the gay lifestyle. What is striking about this is that none other than homosexual activist Larry Kramer has called the so-called gay lifestyle a death style,[73] yet this is exactly what the American Jewish Committee implored Christian conservatives to accept. No wonder Rabbi Lapin branded the report, *The Political Activity of the Religious Right in the 1990s*, "biased and bigoted."[74]

The ADL's volume *The Religious Right: The Assault on Tolerance and Pluralism in America* was a similar broadside. It was so over the top that Midge Decter, who has a long record of fighting anti-Semitism, said that the ADL had "become guilty of the one bigotry that seems to be acceptable these days—bigotry against conservative Christians."[75] Her criticisms, however, were to no avail. In 2005, the ADL unleashed another attack.

At the end of that year, Abraham Foxman, national director of the ADL, and Rabbi Eric Yoffie, president of the Union for Reform Judaism, held a private meeting to discuss what they said were plans to "Christianize America." Speaking of religious conservatives, Foxman said, "Their goal is to implement their Christian worldview. To Christianize America. To save us." He specifically mentioned Focus on the Family, the Alliance Defense Fund, the American Family Association, and the Family Research Council, all staffed mostly by evangelicals. Foxman's demagoguery was outdone by Yoffie, who compared the evangelicals to Nazis. "We cannot forget when Hitler came to power in 1933, one of the first things that he did was ban gay organizations."[76] If these were the remarks that were made publicly, God only knows what Foxman and Yoffie said about religious conservatives behind closed doors.

A year later, Foxman sounded the alarms again, this time accusing the "Christian Supremacists" of engaging "in an aggressive campaign to transform America into a theocracy ruled by their warped biblical law."[77] This isn't the discourse of disagreement—it's speech designed to shut down debate. What is most incredible about Foxman's remarks is that this was the way he introduced his comments on the subject "The Threat of Islamic Extremism." One Jewish writer, Zev Chafets, had the guts to take Foxman on directly. "No mainstream secular Jewish leader had ever taken such a confrontational line against conservative Christians," he said. He accused Foxman of arrogance, maintaining that what he had done was "an act of self-confidence not likely to be undertaken by the spokesman of a genuinely endangered minority."[78]

Michelle Goldberg, author of a highly critical book on Christian conservatives, calls them "Christian nationalists" and accuses them of wanting to impose a "totalistic ideology" on America. She really believes that "the ultimate goal of Christian nationalist leaders isn't fairness." So what is it? "It's dominion," she answers. According to her, these Christians are hell-bent on ruling. "That doesn't mean nonbelievers will be forced to convert," she says reassuringly. However, "They'll just have to learn their places."[79] While she wants us to understand that we are not "on the cusp of totalitarianism," this is no time to drop our guard. That's because "there are totalitarian elements in the Christian nationalist movement," and already "it is changing our country in troubling ways." Worse, "its leaders say they've only just begun."[80] So where are we headed? "The influence of Christian nationalism in public schools, colleges, courts, social services, and doctors' offices will deform American life, rendering it ever more pinched, mean, and divided."[81]

Goldberg comes across tame compared to what Rabbi James Rudin has to say. Having engaged him in conversation on the perennial fight over Christmas, I found Rabbi Rudin to be a reasonable representative of the secularist point of view. His book on the subject, however, is not reasonable. Indeed, the very title, *The Baptizing of America: The Religious Right's Plans for the*

Rest of Us, suggests that religious conservatives are up to no good.

Rudin calls Christian conservatives "Christocrats" and says that their pursuit of a Christocracy is now "a clear and present danger" to America. With dramatic flare he announces, "I am not reassured that the Cross will not ultimately dominate and control the Eagle."[82] He feels this way because he thinks "Christocrats believe it may even be necessary to destroy democracy in order to save the American people from the perils of secular humanists" and others. He cites no examples, but he does offer plenty of conjecture.

If religious conservatives win the culture war, Rudin writes, "all manifestations of public homosexual or lesbian acts—including holding hands or kissing—would be subject to a fine and a jail sentence."[83] Additionally, "All government employees—federal, state, and local—would be required to participate in weekly bible classes in the workplace, as well as compulsory daily prayer sessions."[84] He does not lack for specifics: "I am convinced they seek to control what takes place in every room of the American mansion: the bedroom, the hospital and operating room, the news and press room, the library room, the courtroom, the schoolroom, the public room, and the workroom—the major facets of American society."[85] What is most unbelievable about all this is that Rudin and millions of secularists really believe this stuff to be true.

Perhaps the most humorless account of what religious conservatives are supposed to be plotting comes from Sam Harris. A few pages into his book *Letter to a Christian Nation*, he congratulates himself for setting out "to demolish the intellectual and moral pretensions of Christianity in its most committed forms."[86] What bothers him is America. After citing survey data indicating that most Americans believe that God had a hand in creation, Harris erupts. "Among developed nations," he says, "America stands alone in these convictions." This is not good news. "Our country now appears," he laments, "as at no other time in her history, like a lumbering, bellicose, dim-witted giant."[87]

It seems that there is nothing about religion, especially Christianity, that this man likes. It is responsible for our lackadaisical attitude toward animal suffering[88] and, of course, for the Holocaust.[89] Harris's contempt for Christianity can only be called blind hatred. How else does one describe someone who blames the Bible for not containing a chapter on mathematics, and for not discussing electricity, DNA, or a cure for cancer?[90] Nor does it contain a recipe for chocolate pudding.

Ross Douthat, after having been given the assignment to read all these Christian-bashing books for *First Things*, opened his review by saying, "This is a paranoid moment in American politics."[91] I can sympathize with him—I had to read the same books just to write this one. Pulitzer Prize–winning historian Gordon Wood agrees: "The modern notion that we're being overtaken by a theocracy and that evangelical Christians are running amok—I think that's just kind of a madness that comes from people who have no historical perspective."[92]

Stanley Kurtz sees the secular assault as "a systematic campaign of hatred directed at traditional Christians."[93] Even someone not enamored of religious conservatives, Nicholas D. Kristof of the *New York Times*, blames authors like Harris for launching an "acerbic assault on faith." Writers like Harris may scream all they want about Christian zealots, Kristof argues, "Yet the tone of this Charge of the Atheist Brigade is often just as intolerant—and mean. It's contemptuous and even a bit fundamentalist."[94]

CHAPTER 3

Sexual Sabotage

Secular saboteurs not only seek to destroy the public role of Christianity, they seek to sabotage the Judeo-Christian understanding of sexuality. "Orthodox secularist moral belief portrays personal morality as being essentially concerned with extrinsic constraints upon appetite or passion," writes Robert George.[1] An "everything goes" attitude is part and parcel of the secularist mind-set: if two guys want to get married, let them do so, and if another lover shows up, there's nothing wrong with a threesome. Procreation is not important anyway, and may even be a problem. What counts is the right of every individual to satisfy his sexual appetites—no matter how perverse—and to do it now. Any precept that teaches restraint must be annihilated, and doubly so when the teachings are religiously grounded.

It is difficult to think of a more radical departure than this from what all the major world religions have embraced. In 1968, Will Herberg got it just right when he said, "Today's culture comes very close to becoming a nonmoral, normless culture."[2] Two decades later, Leszek Kolakowski would ask, "To put it crudely, shall we say that the difference between a vegetarian and a cannibal is just a matter of taste?"[3] The everything-goes mentality brooks no compromise, treating infringements on instant gratification as positively tyrannical. Nowhere is this delirium more evident than in sexual expression.

Delirium is not too strong a word to describe what happened on August 15, 2002, in New York's St. Patrick's Cathedral. At around four in the afternoon, in a church packed with men, women, and children—it was a holy day of obligation for Catholics—a man and a woman had sex in the pews while Paul Mercurio provided a detailed description of what they were doing on the radio show *Opie and Anthony*. The radio station, WNEW (an Infinity Broadcasting outlet), offered a prize to a couple having sex in the riskiest location. The complaint I filed with the FCC resulted in the two shock jocks getting canned (they later apologized, a gesture I found sincere; we are now on friendly terms).[4] But the larger issue remains: why do those who practice reckless sex typically lash out at Christianity, especially Catholicism? Are they that driven by guilt?

In the United States, if there is one man who epitomizes the nihilistic assault on the Christian sexual ethics, it is Larry Flynt, publisher of *Hustler*; he seeks to pulverize Christianity and all those who stand in his way. For instance, when Flynt had had enough of Reverend Jerry Falwell's moralizing, it wasn't sufficient to condemn him. Flynt had to create an ad showing Falwell discussing his first sexual encounter while he was drunk with his mother in an outhouse. Similarly, when asked to give a lecture at Georgetown University, Flynt went on a rampage against the Catholic Church, saying, "The Church has had its hand on our crotch for 2,000 years."[5] When he set his sights on Bill O'Reilly, Flynt actually asked his fans to participate in a National Prayer Day, August 5, 2003, calling for O'Reilly's death. Flynt's prayer asked God "to afflict Bill O'Reilly with a brain aneurysm that will lead to his slow and painful death. O, Lord, may his blood vessels bulge out of his head and explode without mercy."[6] Where are the exorcists when we need them?

Virtually all the diabolical secularists in Western history have strongly rejected the Judeo-Christian belief in the necessity of sexual restraint. The Marquis de Sade, for instance, not only celebrated every sexual perversion imaginable, he loved to portray nuns and priests fornicating. In *120 Days of Sodom*, he portrayed a scrawny and weak bishop who had a passion for anal sex with girls and women. In addition to depictions of incest and torture, Sade created a character who had sex with nuns while watching Mass. The French atheist was so full of hate that he even paid a prostitute to trample on a crucifix; he was arrested for doing so, but it never changed his behavior.[7] In the United States, secular sexologists are fond of citing the work of Walt Whitman, an atheist whose free-love ambitions were matched only by his loathing of Christianity. Whitman was not without influence, and it would take more than a century before his 1855 classic, *Leaves of Grass*, would no longer provide shock value.

The assault on Christian sexual ethics has long been seen by secular saboteurs as integral to their radical political agenda. Wilhelm Reich, whose psychoanalytical writings are a blend of Freudianism and Marxism, was a prominent twentieth-century champion of this notion. For example, he argued, "There is no political revolution without first a sexual revolution." Reich sought a sexual revolution that abolished traditional Christian morality and the family.[8] According to Catholic author E. Michael Jones, "Reich noticed a simple fact. If you changed the sexual behavior of idealistic young Catholics in the direction of social liberation . . . then the idea of God simply evaporated from their minds and they defected from the Catholic Church, and the way to successful revolution was clear."[9] It is for reasons like this that Reich has been called the Father of the Sexual Revolution.[10]

The Hungarian scholar Georg Lukács, who did more to promote Marxism in the West than almost anyone, shared Reich's contempt for Christian sexual ethics. Like Reich, he wanted to annihilate Christianity altogether, advocating "demonic ideas" in the spread of "cultural terrorism." To accomplish this task, he established a curriculum for students in which they learned the wonders of free love and the horrors of monogamy. Lukács particularly focused on women and children, knowing that if he could sell libertinism to them, the big loser would be Christianity.[11]

These Christian-hating revolutionaries often seek cover by pointing to the various studies produced by social scientists. And of all the disciplines that have long sought to cast Christianity as the devil that must be defeated, psychology is among the leaders. Freud, of course, was the most prominent exponent of the "Catholicism = sexual repression" school of thought. Self-described as "a godless Jew," "a wicked pagan," and "totally non-religious," Freud made it clear that "my real enemy" was "the Roman Catholic Church."[12]

Jung felt the same way. "Jung's entire life and work were motivated by his detestation of the Catholic Church," writes clinical psychologist Richard Noll, "whose religious doctrines and moral teachings he considered to be the source of all the neuroses which afflicted Western man." Noll cites Jung's *New Paths of Psychology* as his definitive work on the subject. "Jung wrote that the only way to overthrow the neuroses inducing Judeo-Christian religion and its 'sex-fixated ethics' was to establish a new religion—the new religion of psychoanalysis," he writes. "Jungians understand that they must do everything in their power to eliminate the traditional understanding of Roman Catholicism."[13]

The founders of psychotherapy certainly gave it their best shot. Rollo May said Christianity was for "weaklings," and Eric Fromm made palpable his disdain in *The Dogma of Christ*. More recently, Raymond L. Lawrence has given us *Sexual Liberation: The Scandal of Christendom*, which employs psychoanalytic tools to understand how Christianity has "perversely demonized" sexual pleasure. Not surprisingly, this Director of Pastoral Care at the New York Council of Churches ends his book by seeming to be making light of pedophilia. "Man/boy love has never been my cup of tea, but in recent times its harmful effects on personality development have been exaggerated beyond reason or evidence."[14] Though the secularists don't want to admit it, this defense of child rape is the direct consequence of sexual nihilism. Strip away the Christian cultural influence from sexual ethics and what's left is moral anarchy.

It was in the 1960s that the work of men like Norman O. Brown and Herbert Marcuse opened up a double-barreled assault on the Christian ideal of sexual reticence. Brown's trumpeting of sexual liberation and Marcuse's vision of a "non-repressive civilization" were swallowed whole by libertines like Gore Vidal. He envisioned a time when "it is possible to have a mature sexual relationship with a woman on Monday, and a mature sexual relationship with a man on Tuesday, and perhaps on Wednesday have both together."[15] Singing this tune were people like Kate Millett, a feminist whose idea of women's rights meant obliterating all sexual taboos.

Perhaps no one hated the Christian idea of sexual restraint more than Mary Daly. She taught her students at Boston College for decades that Christianity is a form of "phallicism" and oppression. When the theological feminist was told in 1999 that she could no longer ban men from taking her classes, she quit.[16] Today, there is no better exponent of the "life-denying brutality of traditional values" than A. C. Grayling. The British writer sees Christianity's call for sexual moderation a "crime against humanity," traceable to St. Augustine.[17] Augustine clearly regarded lust to be a serious sin, but Grayling's crude characterization of him is positively slanderous.

In the United States, no name is more associated with the secular worldview of human sexuality than Alfred Kinsey. He was so extreme that it once led anthropologist Margaret Mead—no sexual prude herself[18]—to say that in Kinsey's view, there was no moral difference between a man having sex with a woman or a sheep.[19]

Judith A. Reisman has spent a good part of her adult life tracking Kinsey's work, and what she has found is sickening. Dr. Reisman maintains that in his quest to prove how natural sex is, Kinsey sexually abused over 300 children. Infants as young as two months old were sexually stimulated to trigger orgasms, and in some cases were stimulated nonstop for over 24 hours. Kinsey biographer James H. Jones does not validate everything Reisman says, but he does admit that children were masturbated and penetrated by at least one pedophile.[20] One of Kinsey's informants, "Mr. X," kept a record of his sexual achievements: when he wasn't busy sexually abusing children (600 boys and 200 girls), he managed to find the time to have intercourse with 17 blood relatives, including his own grandmother.[21] Now it is one thing to note that Kinsey himself was a sadomasochistic, child-abusing, voyeuristic pervert, quite another to understand why. Fortunately, we have enough evidence to adequately answer the question.

Kinsey rebelled against what he saw as his puritanical Methodist upbringing, and he particularly rebelled against his father. According to Joseph Epstein, Kinsey was so enamored of his hedonistic beliefs that he blamed Christianity, not libertinism, for the breakdown of the modern family. Furthermore, he labeled celibacy, delayed marriage, and asceticism, but not pederasty, as "cultural perversions."[22] It was his assistant Wardell Pomeroy who shed the most light on this issue.

In 1972, in the *American Journal of Psychiatry*, Pomeroy wrote that Kinsey "knew a great deal about the Judeo-Christian tradition, and he was indignant about what it had done to our culture. He often cited the inaccuracies and paranoia in which he asserted it abounded."[23] His daughters admitted that he was totally opposed to religion, so much so that he couldn't tolerate a moderately religious secretary working for him. Ever the hostile atheist, Kinsey even pronounced that "the whole army of religion is our central enemy."[24]

After Kinsey died in 1956, his work was given new life by the Sex Information and Education Council of the United States (SIECUS). With seed money from the Playboy Foundation,[25] Kinsey associates like Pomeroy went to work arguing that "laws against child molestation were relics of the Victorian Age and that incest was just another outdated taboo, like adultery, homosexuality and sadomasochism."[26] Indeed, he even maintained that incest "can sometimes be beneficial."[27] What Pomeroy was doing was hardly under the radar of SIECUS officials: cofounder Lester Kirkendall looked forward to a day when adult-child sex was legal. It is worth noting, too, that these charges are not the stuff of right-wing ascetics. Edward Eichel, who coauthored *Kinsey, Sex and Fraud*, holds to a liberal and secular worldview.[28]

In 1991, SIECUS issued its recommendations for sex education. "Guidelines for Comprehensive Sexuality Education: Kindergarten—12th Grade" instructed kids in kindergarten to understand that "A woman faced with an unintended pregnancy can carry the pregnancy to term and raise the baby, or place the baby for adoption, or have an abortion to end the pregnancy." The tots were also told that "Some couples who love each other live together in the same home without getting married." Naturally, the guidelines were pro-homosexuality, pro-abortion, and wary of religion.[29] Kids as young as five were told that "it feels good to touch parts of the body" and that "some men and women are homosexual." Moreover, they were told that others like to "kiss, hug, touch, and engage in other sexual behavior with one another to show caring and to share sexual pleasure."[30] Kinsey would have been proud.

Planned Parenthood is another major organization that has long harbored ill feelings toward Christianity. Founded by birth-control advocate Margaret Sanger, Planned Parenthood was originally concerned about weeding out the "undesirables," by which it meant African Americans. "Many of the colored citizens are fine specimens of humanity," it boasted in 1932. "A good share of them, however, constitute a large percentage of Kalamazoo's human scrap pile." As Rod Dreher notes, that was written in *Birth Control Review*, a publication that ceased in 1940 "as Jews, Gypsies, homosexuals and others from humanity's 'scrap pile' were being herded into Nazi death camps."[31]

In one important respect, Sanger was different from today's Planned Parenthood activists—she was antiabortion. But like her successors, she was a Catholic basher; even her sympathetic biographer, Ellen Chesler, admits that Sanger was "rabidly anti-Catholic as she grew older."[32] Indeed she was. She regularly compared the Catholic Church to communist regimes and the Ku Klux Klan, even though she could teach the Klan a thing or two about racism. And she wasn't shy about unloading on Al Smith when the Catholic New Yorker ran for president. An editorial in *Birth Control Review* warned of "tyrannical intolerance and usurpation of power exercised by office-holders born and bred in the Roman Catholic faith."[33] Again, it was she who was the master of intolerance. She was so wildly anti-Catholic that she literally said that no Catholic "has any moral right to hold a position of authority for the State." The blacklist was necessary, she maintained, because Catholics "cannot help but give their first allegiance to the Church."[34]

Planned Parenthood is still anti-Catholic—its International Federation has supported efforts to oust the Holy See from the United Nations on ideological grounds—but the most viciously anti-Catholic organization in the abortion industry has long been NARAL (the National Abortion and Reproductive Rights Action Legal, more recently known as NARAL Pro-Choice). Organized in Chicago in 1969, NARAL was initially led by Lawrence Lader, an anti-Catholic bigot. We know this, in part, because of the testimony of Dr. Bernard Nathanson, one of NARAL's original members and a close confidant of Lader's (Nathanson later reversed course, became pro-life, and joined the Catholic Church). Nathanson has admitted that from the very beginning, anti-Catholicism "was probably the best strategy we had."[35]

When NARAL was founded, Lader referred to the Catholic Church as "our favorite whipping boy," making it plain that his goal was to "bring the Catholic hierarchy out where we can fight them. That's the *real* enemy." The Catholic Church was so nefarious that Lader called it "the biggest single obstacle to peace and decency throughout all of history." Indeed, Nathanson said that Lader's hatred of Catholicism was visceral. "It was a comprehensive and chilling indictment of the poisonous influence of Catholicism in secular affairs from its inception until the day before yesterday," he said. What this shows is that NARAL officials were not content to merely challenge Catholicism, they were out to annihilate it.

Nathanson admitted that, at that time, "I was far from an admirer of the Church's role in the world chronicle, but his [Lader's] insistent, uncompromising recitation brought to mind the *Protocols of the Elders of Zion*. It passed through my mind that if one had substituted 'Jewish' for 'Catholic,' it would have been the most vicious anti-Semitic tirade imaginable."[36] This is strong language given that the *Protocols* is a libelous anti-Jewish screed.

NARAL officials were conniving enough to exploit the media's distrust of the Catholic Church in the 1960s. In fact, Nathanson later explained that "it was an easy step to targeting the Catholic Church in its opposition to abortion as making opposition to abortion a pro-fascist, reactionary position."[37] The strategy worked. But by 1975, two years after abortion was ruled constitutional, Lader was forced out of his position as executive director of NARAL. However, that didn't stop him from setting up Abortion Rights Mobilization, an organization that will be remembered for its unsuccessful effort at stripping the Catholic Church of its tax-exempt status.[38]

By the late 1980s, Lader was still spouting his anti-Catholic propaganda. In his book *Politics, Power and the Catholic Church*, he wrote that "The development of Catholic power— the influence of its religious morality and political aims on American society—has followed a careful design. . . . By 1980, with the election of Ronald Reagan, the Catholic church achieved what it had only grasped for before: national power that gave the bishops more access to the White House than any other religion, and made them one of the most awesome lobbying blocs on Capitol Hill." But if the Catholic Church was so powerful, then why was *Roe v. Wade* decided over its objections? Indeed, as Robert Lockwood found, it was Lader's book *Abortion* that was cited favorably eight times in *Roe* by Justice Harry Blackmun—not any papal encyclical.[39] Thus does the nihilist agenda run deep. How the legal system has been penetrated by these saboteurs will be discussed in a later chapter.

When Lader died in 2006, feminist icon Betty Friedan rightly called him the father of the abortion-rights movement. While his obituary in the *New York Times* mentioned his battles with the Catholic Church, it said nothing about his unabiding bigotry.[40] To this day, NARAL remains profoundly anti-Catholic,[41] a proud recipient of money from the Playboy Foundation.[42]

NARAL's sister organizations are just as bad. For example, in 1987, the National Organization for Women protested Pope John Paul II's visit to the United States; demonstrators wore antipapal buttons. Joining in the protest was Eleanor Smeal, who would later head the Feminist Majority. She went one better and arranged to have herself arrested outside the Vatican embassy in Washington.[43] When the pope came to New York City in 1995, he was greeted once again by Catholic-bashing feminists. Sexual libertines of all persuasions showed up, many of them holding obscene posters of the pope and New York's John Cardinal O'Connor.[44]

What unites these champions of unbridled sex is anti-Catholicism. Count the radicals in the gay community among them. None of them has any stomach for any person or institution that counsels restraint, especially Catholicism. The sexual crazies love promiscuity and they don't want to be told otherwise.

Gay Saboteurs

Radical gays, in general, hate Christianity. They reject the idea that what they are doing is wrong and they cringe when others say their behavior is immoral. This is easily seen in the arts, where gays are disproportionately represented: much of their work constitutes hate speech directed at Christians, especially Catholics.

In many cases, gays were brought up in a Christian household and later rebelled against their religion. It is easy to verify this accusation by simply turning to the Catholic League's annual reports on anti-Catholicism; there are plenty of examples. Worse, some of the hate mongers are supported by the federal tax code. For example, the Sisters of Perpetual Indulgence, a group of Catholic-bashing gays who dress up as nuns, mock Jesus (every Easter they have a Hunky Jesus contest), and are awarded a tax-exempt status by the United States government for doing so. How is this possible? They give a few dollars to charities every year.

However obnoxious these people are, they are not a menace. The same cannot be said of ACT-UP. "ACT-UP is nihilistic. Completely nihilistic. It wants to destroy the authority of religion, but it has nothing to put in its place. That is the tremendous failure of the gay establishment to me."[45] These are not the words of a right-wing religious activist: those are the words of Camille Paglia, an iconoclastic lesbian atheist. She does not exaggerate. The following example speaks volumes.

What happened on December 10, 1989, in St. Patrick's Cathedral was an exhibition of cultural fascism. Hundreds of ACT-UP (AIDS Coalition to Unleash Power) members and supporters showed up to protest the Catholic Church's teachings on sexuality, targeting Cardinal O'Connor as the number one villain. Forget about the fact that no private institution in New York gives more money to fight AIDS than the New York Archdiocese—in fact, the Archdiocese opened the first AIDS nursing home in New York City the same year as the ACT-UP explosion[46]—and that no religious body worldwide gives more to help this cause than the Vatican. What matters to these hate-filled homosexuals is that Catholicism is to blame for their own self-inflicted maladies.

The week before the protest began there were posters all over the city that read, "PUBLIC HEALTH MENACE: CARDINAL O'CONNOR." On the posters were statements like these: "Cardinal O'Connor wants to force women to have children"; "Cardinal O'Connor opposes the teaching of safe sex in order to save lives"; "Cardinal O'Connor condones hatred and violence against lesbians and gays." It was paid for by ACT-UP and WHAM (Women's Health Action Mobilization), the groups that organized the demonstration.[47]

On the day of the event, dozens of protesters were arrested for blocking traffic by lying prostrate in the street; they were taken away on stretchers for refusing to stand up. Others carried signs: KEEP YOUR CHURCH OUT OF MY CROTCH; KNOW YOUR SCUMBAGS; KEEP YOUR ROSARIES OFF MY OVARIES; CURB YOUR DOGMA, PAPAL BULL, etc.[48] Here is how one reporter put it: "Several slender young men wearing gold-colored robes similar to clerical vestments hoisted a large portrait of a nude Jesus drawn in such a way as to appeal to the prurient interest of homosexual males."[49] But it was in the cathedral where the most grotesque activities took place.

Dozens made their way into St. Patrick's Cathedral by flinging condoms in the air, and chaining themselves to pews. They did this while Cardinal O'Connor was attempting to give his homily at the 10:15 Mass; he stopped and led the parishioners in prayer instead.[50] "In all my life," said Ray Kerrison in the *New York Post*, "I have never witnessed a spectacle quite like that which shook St. Patrick's Cathedral yesterday when radical homosexuals turned a celebration of the Holy Eucharist into a screaming babble of sacrilege by standing in the pews, shouting and waving their fists, tossing shredded paper and condoms into the air and forcing squads of cops lining the aisles to arrest them."[51] The absolute worst moment came when one of the maniacs literally spit a consecrated Host on the floor. An editorial in the *New York Times* called it "an act of desecration."[52] It could also be called satanic.

What happened that day was met with deserved condemnation from Protestants and Jews as well as Catholics. But not everyone objected, and some even got angry at those gays who branded what happened as sacrilegious.[53] Harriet S. Bogard, director of the New York Regional Office of the ADL, showed which side she was on when she attended the Mass. She explained her presence by saying, "I went because I felt it was the right thing to do."[54] Here she was, a Jewish woman paid to fight bigotry, enjoying Nazi-style tactics against Catholics. She must have been disappointed when Cardinal O'Connor said that future Masses in the Cathedral would be halted "over my dead body."[55] Rock star Madonna was displeased as well. When asked what she thought about the urban terrorists busting into St. Pat's, she said, "Sometimes you just have to go in and make a mess of things to get people to pay attention. I think they did the right thing."[56]

Five years later, St. Patrick's Cathedral would be the site of another gay eruption. It was time for Stonewall 25.

On June 27, 1969, seven New York City policemen raided a small Greenwich Village bar under the suspicion that the club was operating without a liquor license. Inside the Stonewall Bar the cops found boxes of illegal booze and an assortment of drag queens, transsexuals, and other sexual deviants. When the bust started, the transvestites and their homosexual friends attacked the police by trying to burn them alive by throwing lighter fluid and matches on them.

It was this queer event that started the gay rights movement. A quarter of a century later, Stonewall 25 took place, celebrating two and a half decades of what many homosexuals regard as liberation. Unfortunately, as a direct consequence of experiencing liberation gay style, many of those who basked in the libertinism of the 1960s, '70s, and '80s never made it to Stonewall 25.

What happened during Stonewall's silver jubilee in 1994 was more than unfortunate—it was one of the most obscene demonstrations of anti-Catholicism ever to take place in any American city. I personally observed much of what happened, and the pictures taken by a photographer I hired provide stunning evidence.[57]

On the last Friday of June, Dignity held a vigil across the street from St. Patrick's Cathedral. Dignity is comprised of renegade gay Catholics, but one would never know this by listening to "Father" Mallon and national president Marianne Duddy: they actually think of themselves as more Catholic than the pope.

James Mallon is a former member of the Institute of Charity, and he once worked in the Archdiocese of Philadelphia. He spoke at the evening vigil and, along with Ms. Duddy, placed a wreath on the steps of St. Patrick's; it was done to symbolize all those who had died from AIDS. Both speakers had the same message: there are two churches in the Catholic religion, the hierarchical or institutional church and the "real" church. It was their goal, they said, to "take back the church."

On Saturday they packed them in for a "High Mass" at St. Bartholomew's. This is when the ironies really began. St. Bart's is not a Catholic church—it's Episcopalian. The priest who presided over this "Catholic" service was an Episcopalian, Reverend Ronald E. F. Hoskins. Given the massive exodus of Episcopalians from their church (precisely for reasons like this), it was no doubt the biggest crowd that Reverend Hoskins had seen in some time. Fit for the occasion, a man wearing earrings, a necklace, and short, tight leather pants greeted the crowd with a program of the liturgy.

The Prayer of the Faithful had much to comment on, including this gem: "For the institutional Church and especially its hierarchy, grant them at least a little more wisdom and a great deal of mirth." Everyone was then asked to respond, "O God of laughter, our God, tickle them." And then there was this plea: "For all women called to ordained ministry, that the keys of the kingdom may be theirs." To which the crowd boomed, "Mother God, our God, send your Holy Spirit down upon them, that She may dwell with them." Most inventive was the gay version of the Lord's Prayer. It began, "Our Mother/Father in heaven, hallowed be thy name."

The biggest event of the week was supposed to be the Sunday parade up First Avenue, but it was trumped by another march up Fifth Avenue. The former was legal and well-behaved while the latter was illegal and vulgar. Both were lily-white, especially the illegal march, and both were clearly dominated by men.

Originally, there was only supposed to be one parade. But a rift between the organizers of the parade, most of whom were from out of town, and radical New York gays grew into a major divide. The initial organizers wanted the gay parade to be an international event, sending an appeal to every nation on earth that homosexuals deserve more rights. They chose to march up First Avenue because they wanted to process in front of the United Nations. But the New York militants weren't interested in challenging the U.N.—they wanted to attack the Catholic Church. That is why they demanded a parade up Fifth Avenue, home of St. Patrick's Cathedral. Though they lost in court, represented by the New York Civil Liberties Union, they marched anyway.

Before the parade began, there was a huge police presence, most of them in front of the cathedral. St. Pat's was under siege. So was the residence of Cardinal O'Connor. There were cops all over, waiting and watching. I nestled up close to the barrier, along with a sea of lesbians, gays, bisexuals, and transgender persons. The protesters were on their way.

Ironically, the cops kept telling us to stand away from the barriers. Here were police officers, all of whom were told not to arrest anyone except in cases of violence, telling me not to lean on the barrier while they patiently waited to watch an illegal march. The police commissioner showed up, casually dressed, securing a better spot than I did to watch the parade.

Finally, the illegal parade made its way to the cathedral, escorted—incredibly—by cops on scooters. The marchers were the strangest-looking people I had ever seen. There were men in white chiffon skirts doing pirouettes in the street. There were men (I think they were men) wearing red plaid skirts; others wore black platforms, blond wigs, and red lipstick. There were half-naked men wearing feathers and some who wore purple chiffon butterfly wings. Some simply wore their jockey shorts while others sported a preference for jockstraps. And dozens wore nothing but shoes. In a grand display of equality, there were dozens of bare-breasted lesbians (many of whom belonged to Dykes on Bikes) and some women who wore nothing at all.

My personal favorite was the guy who wore nothing but a jockstrap, with his entire body (face and head included) covered with what looked like paint. He was light green and was adorned with gold sparkles. My choice for the silver medal was the person whose hair and face (that is all I could see initially as my view was temporarily obstructed) looked exactly like a woman's. But when I looked down at her body I noticed that she wasn't wearing any clothes and then realized that that was no woman. The bronze went to the lesbians who had key rings, carnations, and the like hanging from their pierced nipples.

To get a sense of how the protesters behaved in front of St. Pat's, consider first that a contingent from the North American Man-Boy Love Association (NAMBLA) marched. NAMBLA had been banned by the international parade on First Avenue but was welcomed by the ACT-UP terrorists on Fifth. The child molesters (their motto is "Eight is too late") fit right in with the Radical Faeries, drag queens, and Leather Fetishists. What pulled them together more than anything was their hatred of the Catholic Church.

In front of St. Patrick's Cathedral, the crowd stuck their middle fingers at the church and screamed—on command—a two-word obscenity. They said it over and over again. They laid down in the street. They chanted, "Confess, Confess, the Cardinal Wears a Dress." The group Pagans and Witches did a witch dance. They dressed in scarlet robes as cardinals. They dressed as priests and nuns. They went nude. They masturbated in the street. And the cops, under orders, did nothing. I witnessed this live and have pictures to prove it. This was cultural nihilism gone off the deep end.

When a police captain was asked by a reporter why there were no arrests for parading in the nude, he said: "As long as they are peaceful and moving along, it's okay. We don't want another Stonewall." Better still was the response of Lieutenant Raymond O'Donnell, a police spokesman. He said that he would "have to check the penal law" to see if public nudity was a crime. But no one beat Deputy Mayor Fran Reiter, who hailed the illegal march as "great."

When Mayor Rudy Giuliani was asked about this collapse of authority, he replied that it would be too difficult to arrest 6,000 people. He never explained why he bothered to get a court order barring the march. In short, what happened on June 26, 1994, was not just a gay victory. It was a big win for Catholic bashing.

When it came time for the Gay Pride Parade in 1995, I put pressure on Mayor Giuliani to speak out about the events of 1994 and take measures to see to it that Catholics were spared a repeat performance.[58]

A couple of weeks before the Gay Pride Parade, I received a tip that the march was to begin at noon at 52nd Street and Fifth Avenue, just one block north of St. Patrick's Cathedral. On June 8, I wrote to Mayor Giuliani expressing my concerns. I wanted the starting point of the parade to begin at a point below St. Patrick's; I suggested 42nd Street and Fifth Avenue as a point of departure (the parade was going to head south to Greenwich Village). At first, he didn't reply, but when I wouldn't give up, he had to do something.

Giuliani did not meet with me but he did change his tune. One week before the parade, the best he could do was label some of the behavior in the 1994 march as "inappropriate," but by week's end he had raised his objections to "reprehensible." Indeed, Giuliani was now boasting that "Had I been there [on the street during the 1994 march], had I made the decision on the spot, I think these people should have been arrested." As for the 1995 parade, he knew he had to do something, so he decided not to march with gays past St. Patrick's but would join the march at 47th Street. This was similar to what the previous mayor, Ed Koch, had done. He said that he could not move the starting point of the parade because a police permit had already been granted.

I added to this pressure by contacting the U.S. Department of Justice and the New York State Attorney General's office requesting that federal marshals and state officials be dispatched to the steps of St. Patrick's, working the parade as observers. My point was that if lawlessness reigned and the police did nothing, then the role of the observers would be indispensable to the pursuit of justice in the courts. The mere fact that we made public our contact with these authorities was enough to stir the pot a bit more.

Four days before the parade, Mayor Giuliani held a press conference at City Hall explaining his position. When an NBC reporter called me requesting an interview at City Hall following Giuliani's statement, I agreed to come. But he warned me to meet him on the steps of City Hall as he did not want to be responsible for the "press riot" that might take place if I stepped foot into the same room with Giuliani.

On the eve of the parade, Giuliani offered a remarkable plea to the gay community: "It probably is better to keep your clothes on. Then you are not going to get in an area of ambiguity."[59] This was the best Catholics could get from a Catholic mayor who never stopped touting his law-and-order record. (By the way, nothing has changed since: in 2008, the registration packets that were sent to the Heritage of Pride organizers warned that "New York State has a law against public nudity below the waist and police enforce it."[60] There is no other parade in New York where the organizers tell the participants that they have to keep their pants on when they march. Moreover, the police do not enforce the laws on nudity. As reported by the *New York Times*, after the 2008 parade "about eight nude dancers—men and women alike—gyrated in the front window"[61] of a diner with impunity.)

Norman Siegel, executive director of the New York Civil Liberties Union, warned that any arrests of topless women might encourage other women to bare their breasts. Similarly, Manhattan Borough President Ruth Messinger said that the mere threat of arrest for going topless would tempt many women to take off their clothes. And all this was happening, so I was told by the press, because of me.

My favorite question came from Jane Furse of the New York *Daily News*. Furse told me that she had just spoken to a woman who was so irate at me that she was going to take off all of her clothes during the march. When asked to respond, I was dumbfounded: lots of people get angry at me, and many say some pretty mean things, but no woman has ever decided to walk around New York in the nude because she didn't like what I had to say. I was too embarrassed to ask what she might do if I really got her angry. Another reporter asked me, "What would you say to those lesbians who are threatening to go topless?" "Keep your blouses buttoned and your bras on," I replied. It was all so surreal.

On the day of the parade, 3,000 people jammed St. Patrick's for Cardinal O'Connor's Mass. As the faithful walked into the cathedral, they were given a pamphlet by Dignity; predictably, it blasted the Catholic League. Dignity was upset when I said, "To allow Catholic-bashing gays to begin a parade by St. Patrick's Cathedral is tantamount to allowing the Klan to assemble near a Harlem Baptist church or the Nazis to start near a Jewish synagogue." The gay group also carried anti-Catholic League signs during the parade.

At precisely noon on June 25, 1995, in front of St. Patrick's Cathedral, a police officer yelled into a bullhorn, "Anyone who takes off his clothes will be arrested." It was time for the Gay Pride Parade to begin.

When the parade began, St. Patrick's was sealed like a war zone. No one could get near it as the police barricaded the cathedral and the sidewalk across the street. All the usual suspects were there: drag queens, cross-dressers on Rollerblades, the Butch/Femme Society, the sadomacho brigade in black leather, Men of Discipline, and other lovely types. Commercialism was evident as about a third of the floats were sponsored by various gay bars and clubs. Though there were no signs indicating that the North American Man/Boy Love Association was there, they were listed in the program.

There were men dressed as women and bizarre-looking men on stilts. Hundreds of men wore nothing but jockstraps, shaking their bodies to the beat of the blaring rock music. Olympic diving champion Greg Louganis was one of the grand marshals, and pop singer Cyndi Lauper danced and sang her hit "Girls Just Wanna Have Fun." Strange-looking people were everywhere and often it was difficult to tell whether it was a man or a woman, and in some cases it appeared that it was both. And yes, some of the girls did bare their breasts (a few of them apparently spray painted their chests), but in all fairness it must be said that most of the girls managed to keep their clothes on. The police carried yellow blankets to cover the girls up but decided against using them. Following tradition, no one was arrested.

Most memorable was the same fat guy who showed up the year before dressed as the pope. He made it back, carrying a sign, MY CHURCH ORGAN IS BIGGER THAN YOURS. Then there was the car that passed by with a string of unrelated four-letter words and sexual terms on it. Some marchers wore shirts with various vulgarities inscribed on them. There were large pictures of men performing oral sex and there were several examples of men simulating oral sex live atop the floats.

The most flagrant anti-Catholicism came from Catholic Ladies for Choice. In this group, there were gay men and lesbians dressed as nuns carrying coat hangers and lesbians dressed as nuns carrying tambourines. Most incredible was the gay man who wore a black bra and a black jock strap with a habit on his head and a huge set of rosary beads around his otherwise naked body. There was also someone dressed as the pope with a banner that read, "The Catholic Church, a history of murder, lies, censorship, oppression and hypocrisy."

And what did Mayor Giuliani have to say about all this? He called it a "very dignified parade." Police Commissioner William Bratton agreed, saying that the march was "a very respectable parade, one that I think gays and lesbians could feel quite proud of."[62]

Following the 1995 parade, Bernadette Brady, vice president of the Catholic League, and I sat down with senior officials of the Giuliani administration to discuss what was going to be done about the 1996 parade. We made it plain that if nothing was done to curb the anti-Catholic bigotry, we would organize Catholics to rally against the event. What persuaded them to act was the set of photographs we showed them from the 1994 and 1995 parades. They couldn't believe their eyes. Thanks to Fran Reiter, Paul Crotty, and Peter Powers—three of Giuliani's most trusted aides—they intervened and successfully lobbied gay leaders to tame things down. While subsequent parades have not exactly been without incident, the worst excesses were eliminated.

Folsom Street Fair

What happened at San Francisco's Folsom Street Fair in 2007 easily matched what happened in New York City in the mid-1990s. To make matters worse, the Miller Brewing Company—the only national sponsor of the event—defiantly refused to pull its sponsorship or issue an adequate apology for the multifaceted outrages that took place. Until, that is, it was hit with a national boycott and a major public relations campaign advertising its delinquency (the Catholic League blanketed Milwaukee, Miller's home). In the end, justice was done, but only after six weeks of relentless pressure.

In late September 2007, the Catholic League contacted the Miller Brewing Company asking it to withdraw sponsorship of the Folsom Street Fair. What concerned us was an ad for the September 30 gay/leather event depicting half-naked homosexuals at a table mimicking the *Last Supper*. The sadomasochistic theme featured sex toys displayed on the table. Very quickly, Miller issued a statement ordering its logo removed from the ad. This might have been the end of the dispute except that I then learned that some of the monies being raised by the event were being funneled to the notoriously anti-Catholic group the Sisters of Perpetual Indulgence. Not only that, but the group was scheduled to hold a "Last Supper With the Sisters" days before the street fair; it was billed as a way "to prepare your mortal flesh for the kinkiest weekend on Earth" (its emphasis). Miller, to my surprise, was nonplussed.

On September 27, on behalf of the Catholic League, I called for a national boycott, announcing its commencement on *Fox and Friends.* The Catholic League then contacted more than 200 Catholic, Protestant, Jewish, Muslim, Buddhist, and Hindu organizations to join with us. The next day we mailed photos of previous Folsom Street Fair events to the 11 members of Miller's Executive Committee; it showed the sickest behavior imaginable. On October 1, the *San Francisco Chronicle*, which adores events like these, reported that at the street fair "couples led each other up and down the street with dog collars and leashes, men in thong underwear played Twister." There was also a man who was flogged to such an extent that "red lash marks covered his back." Other gay men decided to "walk around naked" in front of women and children. In addition to the Sisters, a stripper was hoisted in a cage above a Catholic church on a Sunday (there was also a man dressed as Jesus in a cage). And still, Miller stood by the event.

We then sent pictures of the S&M event to Milwaukee Archbishop Timothy Dolan (now the Archbishop of New York) and to the 211 Catholic parishes in the archdiocese. The next week we hit all 166 Protestant churches in Milwaukee. Then we hit the Jewish synagogues and the Muslim mosques. By this time, the boycott had caught up to the anti-Miller PR campaign: Mike Setto, a Chaldean Catholic who owns a beer and wine store in Lake Orion, Michigan, got the ball rolling by organizing his fellow Chaldean Catholics to join him in refusing to stock Miller beer.

Meanwhile, we sent the incriminating photos to scores of civic organizations in Milwaukee, showing them that this is the kind of event that Miller likes to sponsor. What we wanted was a statement from Miller acknowledging that it objected to three incidents (in addition to the poster ad that featured its logo). We cited the selling of religious symbols as sex toys; the hoisting of a stripper and a man dressed as Jesus in cages above a Catholic church on a Sunday; and the public mocking of nuns. Finally, Miller said that "we are aware of other disrespectful activities, objects and groups associated with or present at the fair which, like the promotional poster, violate our marketing policies. We extend our original apology to include these unfortunate events and items as well." Accordingly, we called off the PR campaign and the boycott.[63]

The Folsom Street Fair in 2008 was just as perverse—naked men having sex in the street—but there was no Miller sponsorship.

Gay Protests Turn Ugly

It is not just gay parades and street fairs that are offensive, it is gay activism in the wake of a losing effort. Consider what happened after California voters supported a resolution that effectively denied the right to gay marriage. Proposition 8, which affirmed marriage between a man and a woman, passed over the objections of gay activists. So what did many of them do? React like barbarians.

Protesters in many California cities took to the streets, snarling traffic and endangering public safety. Houses and cars were vandalized. Rioting protesters shouted "Separation of Church and Hate." Supporters of traditional marriage were called Nazis. African Americans, who more than any group oppose gay marriage, were called the *N* word. Latinos carrying pro-marriage signs were assaulted. But the biggest attack was visited on people of faith.

Mormons generally have not been major players in the culture wars. But Proposition 8 got them going: they spent a lot of time and money seeking to support it. The reaction on the part of some gays was amazing. Mormons who removed offensive signs from their property were beaten; "Mormon scum" was shouted at worshippers; the Book of Mormon was set on fire in a Mormon chapel. Other religious groups were also targeted. An elderly woman was roughed up by an angry crowd and the cross she was carrying was smashed to the ground. "Bigots Live Here" was scrawled on a Christian church; Catholic churches were trashed and swastikas were placed on their lawns; a white substance resembling anthrax was sent to a Knights of Columbus printing plant and to Mormon temples.[64]

Radical gays opposed to gay marriage—they oppose it because they don't want to be like heterosexuals—were even worse. A group called Bash Back! stormed an evangelical church in Lansing, Michigan. Protesters outside the church were beating on buckets, screaming "Jesus was a homo" on a megaphone and carrying an upside-down pink cross. Inside the church, well-dressed protesters set off fire alarms, charged the pulpit, and unfurled a huge rainbow-colored flag with the inscription IT'S OKAY TO BE GAY! BASH BACK! The church was vandalized, obscenities were shouted, and worshippers were confronted.[65] This was not the work of some unhappy campers, it was the work of gay fascists.

Bash Back! offers further evidence of the nihilistic nature of today's secular radicals. They may be on the opposite side of gay activists who want same-sex marriage, but they have one thing in common with them: they hate Christianity with a passion and will do everything they can to slaughter it.

Everyone thought that gays who objected to Proposition 8 would give up their protest once the election was over. Not only did it continue for weeks, a church was vandalized in 2009 over this issue. Most Holy Redeemer Catholic Church, a gay-friendly church in San Francisco's Castro District, had swastikas painted on its facade; the names Ratzinger (Pope Benedict XVI) and Niederauer (the San Francisco archbishop) were scrawled beside the Nazi symbols.[66]

Those who love to dabble in "root causes" would have to conclude that at least part of the blame goes to San Francisco Mayor Gavin Newsom and the San Francisco Board of Supervisors.

Both Newsom and the Board have shown nothing but contempt for the First Amendment rights of Catholics. When crucifixes are sold as sex toys and gays dressed as nuns invade a Catholic church during Mass—the same Holy Redeemer Church—at the annual Folsom Street Fair, they say nothing. Indeed, the cops are told not to arrest men who mutilate themselves and perform oral sex on each other in public. But the Board was quite vocal about showing its profound hostility to the Catholic Church in 2006, when it issued a resolution condemning the Church's opposition to gay couples adopting children; it said the Church was "meddling" in the affairs of San Francisco. When it comes to anti-Catholicism and the breakdown of civility, San Francisco has no equal in the United States.

Sexual saboteurs are never going to give up their assault on religion. That's because they are in constant rebellion against any person or institution that counsels restraint. Moreover, anyone who thinks this is a problem that can be resolved by education is living in another world. The nihilistic impulse that the sexual saboteurs embody is so thoroughly irrational that no amount of education will ever check it. Even after all the funerals they have attended, they still don't get it.

CHAPTER 4

Artistic Sabotage

Andres Serrano will forever be remembered for putting a crucifix in a jar of his own urine, declaring it to be art, and convincing sentient men and women that he isn't a fraud. Robert Mapplethorpe will forever be remembered for picturing himself with a bullwhip in his behind, declaring it to be art, and convincing sentient men and women that he isn't a fraud. Among the fooled was the United States government: the National Endowment for the Arts contributed to both of these monstrosities. Which means the taxpayers were raped.

Serrano and Mapplethorpe may be the best known of their genre, but they have not been without competition. Incapable of promoting their own vision of liberty, these depraved artists cannot resist the temptation to destroy. They are cultural nihilists of the first order, and they have nothing but contempt for the common good. "In the past two decades," writes art historian Michael J. Lewis, "artists have presented the body covered with simulated sores (Hannah Wilke), smeared with chocolate as a surrogate for excrement (Karen Finley), outfitted with grotesque and misshapen sexual prosthetics (Cindy Sherman), and in a state of rigor mortis and incipient putrefaction (Andres Serrano)."[1] In 2008, Serrano struck again, only this time his photographic display consisted of jars of animal feces; in a demonstration of his commitment to inclusion, he graciously made a contribution of his own.[2]

Obscenity often accompanies blasphemy—they are joined at the culture's hip—as many an artist can testify. Take the work of Robert Gober. He is an ex-Catholic gay man who rejects the Church's teachings on sexuality. In 1997, he was the talk of the town in Los Angeles when the Museum of Contemporary Art hosted one of his exhibitions that defiled the Mother of God.

In the promotional literature for Gober's work, it said that after sculpting Our Blessed Mother in clay and then draping her in a robe made of plaster, Gober "pierced his Virgin Mary with a phallic culvert pipe." Here's why: "The fact that the corrugated pipe's screwlike ribs penetrate the body bloodlessly evokes the Immaculate Conception by which the Virgin Mary was conceived in her mother's womb without the violent stain of original sin, as well as the miraculous conception of Christ himself. Yet, the culvert deprives the Virgin Mary of the womb from which Christ was born." Such deprivation, it is assumed, constitutes an artistic statement of some renown.[3]

The year before Gober's exhibit was shown, the Los Angeles-based Tom of the Finland Foundation awarded its grand prize for artistic expression to a drawing by Garilyn Brune: it showed a priest performing fellatio on Jesus.[4] Just as vulgar was a drawing by a Penn State female student. Done for a class assignment, she crafted a huge bloody vagina shaped in grotto-like fashion, complete with human hair, with a statue of the Virgin Mary placed inside it.[5] Similarly, in 2006, at the KFMK Gallery in New York City, an exhibit of the work of John Santerineross featured a photo of a woman with her genitals cut and bleeding; a crucifix was placed below the woman, and the blood from her mutilated genitalia was shown running into a wine glass. Just so we got the point, the photo was dubbed "The Transformation of the Madonna."[6]

These artistic assassins want to artistically assassinate Christianity, especially Catholicism. They are not artists who are simply making a statement. They are nihilists. Not to understand the difference between artists who protest Christianity's teachings on sexuality, and moral anarchists out to sabotage Christianity altogether, is not only to miss what is at stake, it does an injustice to their work.

Many of these artists have a fetish for the scatological. In 2002, at the American Center for Wine, Food & the Arts in Napa, California, an exhibition of the work of Antoni Miralda featured the display of figurines depicting the pope and nuns defecating.[7] Even sicker is the admission of "Chocolate Jesus" artist Cosimo Cavallaro who said in a radio debate he had with me that in addition to using chocolate to sculpt his creations, he also uses feces. When asked where he gets them, he said he uses his own.[8]

Not only is this stuff considered art, it is considered meritorious. In 2008, the art faculty at New York's Cooper Union for the Advancement of Science and Art voted as one of the "best" student displays a series of paintings that featured a man with his pants pulled down and with a crucifix extended from his rectum; a man with his pants down and an angel holding two Rosaries with a penis attached to each of them; and a painting of a naked man with an erection and a halo hovering over his head.[9]

No wonder such junk art has been mistaken by custodians in the United States and Britain and given the heave-ho along with the rest of the garbage. For example, in 2003, a custodian at the Boulder Public Library said there was no sign to indicate that the art was anything but what it looked like—a pile of trash. The following year, a custodian at the Tate took the artwork of Gustav Metzger and threw it in the garbage. And why not? The "art" was a clear plastic bag filled with litter.[10] None of this is new. Indeed, in 1959, *New York Times* critic John Canaday stunned the avant-garde set by suggesting that "freaks, charlatans and the misled" had passed themselves off as legitimate. "Let us admit," he wrote, "that the nature of abstract expressionism allows exceptional tolerance for incompetence and deception." He aptly concluded, "We have been had."[11]

Much of the nihilistic quality of modern art is rooted in Dada, a term that, appropriately, has no meaning. In 1916, Marcel Janco described the phenomenon that was at work when he said, "Everything had to be demolished." And by that he meant that nothing would be spared. Most especially, this meant an assault on the bourgeois "idea of art, attacking common sense, public opinion, education, institutions, museums, good taste, in short, the whole prevailing order."[12]

Sometimes the public says enough is enough. Such was the case with the uproar caused by the 1999 Sensation exhibit at the Brooklyn Museum of Art.

Sensation was a beastly British art exhibit that garnered international attention. The paintings, owned by Charles Saatchi, not only displayed dead animals and sexually mutilated bodies, they also included a painting, *The Holy Virgin Mary*, that was laced with elephant dung and spotted with pictures of vaginas and anuses. It was this "creative" display that drew fire from the Catholic League.

A reporter from the New York *Daily News* first gave me the heads-up on the exhibit. After securing a copy of the Sensation catalog, I issued a news release on September 16. Shortly thereafter New York City Mayor Rudolph Giuliani joined the Catholic League in labeling the exhibit "Catholic bashing"; he also threatened to close the museum. I called for a boycott of the museum, posting an ad asking Catholic teachers in the Brooklyn Diocese to join us in this effort. We also wrote to every member of the New York City Council requesting that the museum be defunded.

We branded the exhibit "snuff art" because it depicted mannequins of grotesquely distorted children, some with penises in place of their noses; there were two clear boxes, one filled with maggots, the other with a cow's head; there was a bisected pig in formaldehyde; and there was a 13-foot-high portrait of Myra Hindley, Britain's most famous child molester. Roger Kimball of the *New Criterion* knew what was going on: "Anyone familiar with the history of Dada and Surrealism has seen it all before: the pornography, the pathological fascination with decay and mutilation, toying with blasphemy (dressed up, occasionally, as a new religiosity)."[13] Yes, this was cultural nihilism taken to a new level.

But it was *The Holy Virgin Mary* by artist Chris Ofili that mobilized the Catholic League and that ultimately became the focus of the controversy. The position of the League, which was echoed by Mayor Giuliani, was that showing the exhibit was entirely legal. Making the public pay for it was, however, outrageous. "This has gone beyond the vulgar, the blasphemous and the scatological," I told the press.[14]

On October 2, 1999, the day the exhibit opened, the Catholic League mounted a large protest and held a press conference in front of the museum. We also did something novel. We distributed "Vomit Bags" to the first 500 attendees. The vomit bags, which had a label on them saying they were courtesy of the Catholic League, were distributed in response to the museum's warning that seeing the exhibit could make someone sick. I agreed with the museum official who made this remark, hence the vomit bags. When a TV reporter asked if it was really necessary to distribute the bags, I told her that puke not only stinks, it can be slippery as well, and we didn't want anyone to get hurt. I'm not sure she was convinced.[15]

The media, of course, loved this story. After all, it had so many permutations: there were artistic, ethical, legal, economic, religious, and political issues involved. Throughout, the position of the Catholic League was that the exhibit was entirely legal and entirely immoral. Yes, the paintings should not be censored, but no, the taxpayers should not be forced to fund it. Here's what I said on the *Today* show of September 27: "And when you throw elephant dung and have pictures of vaginas and anuses surrounding her [the Blessed Mother] in this kind of invidious fashion, my answer is go show your filth down the street. Find a fat cat bigot. There are a lot of fat cat bigots who don't like Catholics in this country—let them sponsor it. But if the government cannot sponsor my religion, and it shouldn't, it shouldn't be in the business of allowing people to bash my religion. What this is is pure unadulterated hate speech. And the government should not be involved in hate speech against my religion or anyone else's."[16]

On the day of the Catholic League rally at the museum, I was asked on National Public Radio why I objected to the art, especially given the fact that art often shocks people. "You want to shock people," I said, "why don't you take your own mother and wipe crap over her? But don't dare take our spiritual mother, the spiritual mother of people worldwide and millions of people in the New York City area, and desecrate her." At the rally, I addressed another bogus argument, the curious notion that there are multiple interpretations to this. "Only people who have been drunk on the ideas of modern art would believe this," I said. "If somebody puts a swastika on a synagogue, there's only one answer—and everyone knows what it is. When you throw elephant dung with pornographic pictures on Our Blessed Mother, there's only one meaning."[17]

One of the most commonly voiced criticisms aimed at the Catholic League was that we missed the point of the elephant dung: to Africans, so the argument went, this is seen as honorific. "That's a racist statement," I said at the rally. "I've taught in Spanish Harlem. I don't know one African-American family that when it comes to celebrating Kwanzaa, they send a pile of excrement to their friends."[18] Not only that, I will never forget a conversation I had about this issue with a man from Nigeria that I met at a Christmas party that year. I asked him if elephant dung has positive connotations in his home country. His reaction was one of anger and laughter. By the way, the offending artist, Ofili, is not African—he's a Brit; his parents were born in Nigeria. Besides, all of this misses my point. Is it also an African tradition of great honor to put clips of vaginas and anuses on pictures of revered persons?

No organization looked worse during this time than People for the American Way. The leadership not only did not condemn the art as bigoted, it defended it. It, too, took the position that the dung was a nice cultural touch. Ronald Feldman, a board member of the group, said Ofili's painting "will be understood by others as a depiction of the enduring belief in and search for holiness in the midst of a debased and debasing culture."[19] By "others" he must have meant bigots and the self-delusional, for everyone else knew what was meant by Ofili's work.

The hypocrisy in all this was too much to bear. In 1988, six months after Chicago Mayor Harold Washington died, an artist portrayed him in women's underwear and hung his painting in the Art Institute of Chicago. The Chicago City Council immediately voted to defund the museum, and a cop literally snatched the painting off the wall. Yet no one in the artistic community screamed "censorship." And what did the Chicago museum do? It took out full-page ads in two newspapers apologizing for what it did. Not only did the museum capitulate to the African American aldermen, it launched an affirmative action plan to hire more blacks.[20] All the Catholic League did was to say that the Brooklyn Museum of Art was not the right venue, and that those who wanted the exhibit should do it on their own dime. And for this we were blasted by the artistic community for simply exercising our right to freedom of speech and assembly.

There was one good thing that came out of all this—it brought principled persons together. For example, one of the persons with whom I locked horns over the museum controversy was Norman Siegel, director of the New York Civil Liberties Union. To this day, we agree on almost nothing, but we are good friends nonetheless. Norm is a tireless champion of civil liberties, and he is scrupulously honest. His interpretation of civil liberties and mine are very different, but this hasn't impeded us from joining together to denounce anti-Semitism, racism, and anti-Catholicism. We've spoken together on the streets of Harlem, outside synagogues in Queens, and at the headquarters of the New York Archdiocese.

The latter venue was the site of a press conference we had on October 4, 1999, two days after the rally at the Brooklyn Museum of Art. Norm denounced anti-Catholicism and I denounced anti-Semitism. We did this because both of us had experienced bigotry during the course of this controversy. Prior to the rally outside the museum, Norm and I had been invited to speak at a public forum debating the merits of our position. At one point, I was attacked by an anti-Catholic bigot from the audience, and Norm jumped in to defend me. At the rally, when Norm sought to speak, he was attacked by an anti-Semite, and I quickly confronted the bigot. So when we held a press conference at the headquarters of the New York Archdiocese, it was labeled by the *Daily News* as "an extraordinary joint appearance," and *Newsday* labeled it "an unlikely alliance."[21]

Perhaps not as extraordinary, but just as important, was the support that the Catholic League received from so many persons of faith. John Cardinal O'Connor and Bishop Thomas Daily of Brooklyn stood by us, as did the New York Hispanic Clergy Organization (a Pentecostal group), the Union of Orthodox Jewish Congregations of America, Agudath Israel, and the Islamic Center of Long Island.[22] The Union of Orthodox Jewish Congregations was particularly supportive. The week before the exhibit opened, it issued a press release saying, "Displaying a religious symbol splattered with dung is deeply offensive and can hardly be said to have any redeeming social or artistic value. Today, the offense is perpetrated against a Christian symbol; tomorrow, it might be a Jewish ritual item, and then of another faith." It also said, "we support those civic leaders who have questioned whether public funds should support this exhibition."[23]

As it turned out, there was more dirt to this issue than was found at the museum. The *New York Times* ran a front-page story revealing that unethical practices had colored the Sensation exhibit. The director of the museum, Arnold L. Lehman, pressed both Charles Saatchi, the owner of the art, and Christie's, the prestigious auction house, for financing. Saatchi forked over $160,000 to the museum and then tried to conceal his "philanthropy" from the public; Christie's was given perks. We called upon Lehman to be terminated for violating the public trust, but nothing was done.[24] So not only did Lehman give the green light to this offensive exhibition, he engineered a boatload of money from those who stood to personally profit from this venture.

The controversy refused to die. On December 8, the Feast of the Immaculate Conception, the Catholic League teamed with Monsignor Peter Finn, one of New York's most prominent priests, in leading hundreds of Catholics in prayer outside the Brooklyn Museum of Art. At the rally I made it clear that our efforts were not in vain. A similarly obscene and blasphemous exhibit in Detroit lasted just two days. The director who pulled the exhibit cited the trouble in Brooklyn as the reason why he stopped it; the Detroit exhibit featured a drawing of a baby Jesus in a bathtub wearing a condom. I also pointed out that the Sensation exhibition was canceled in Australia after all the rumblings in New York made international news.

Just before the exhibition closed, I sent a package to the museum's director. In it was a huge pooper-scooper and a package of ten hypoallergenic disposable latex gloves. "Just as we provided vomit bags to facilitate the process of puking when the exhibit opened," I announced, "we are now providing a pooper-scooper and surgical gloves—latex, of course—to facilitate the sanitary removal of the dung. This should put to rest the rumor that we are not eco-conscious at the Catholic League. And besides, who wants to step in barf and feces while dismantling this masterpiece?" I closed my comments by saying, "We hope Arnold Lehman appreciates our thoughtfulness and puts our New Year's gift to good use. We also hope he doesn't exploit museum workers by ordering them to clean up his filth."[25]

In February 2001, the Brooklyn Museum of Art was back in the news, and so was the Catholic League. This time the museum decided to display Renee Cox's "Yo Mama's Last Supper." It featured a color photo of Cox, a black woman, standing nude as Christ in the Last Supper. She admitted that her work was aimed at the Catholic Church, which she somehow managed to blame for slavery. When I debated her at the First Amendment Center in New York, I asked her if she would object to a portrait of white men urinating into the mouth of a black man, or an offensive portrait of Martin Luther King being displayed in a public library during Black History Month. Though I found Renee to be a nice person, I will never forget how upset she got with me for throwing these questions at her. She just didn't get it.[26]

Lots of those in the artistic community just don't get it. And some have no sense of humor. Steven C. Dubin, a professor who teaches about art and society, called me one day about the Sensation exhibit and the Catholic League's role in it. He seemed genuinely bewildered by what I had to say, and recorded his impressions in a book he wrote about controversial artistic exhibitions. Here is how he ended his book: "If you have any doubts that this [the whole controversy over Sensation] was a contrived affair, make note: when I asked whether art interests him, the Catholic League's William Donohue breezily replied, 'No. Pubs do. I go to bars, not to museums.' "[27] Come to think of it, I really wasn't joking.

Theater

The Catholic Church, rich with tradition and ritual, has been the object of artistic expression for over 2,000 years. Some of it is reverential, some pokes light fun, and some is degrading. *Sister Mary Ignatius Explains It All for You* represents the latter.

The play features a malicious nun who is confronted by four of her former students, all of whom are allegedly dysfunctional as a result of their Catholic upbringing. In the course of the play, virtually every Catholic teaching is mocked. The nuns who taught generations of schoolchildren are hatefully caricatured and stereotyped. Worst of all, the life of Christ is portrayed in the vilest way, from the Nativity through the Crucifixion; the vicious depiction of Our Blessed Mother is similarly disturbing. In the end, the nun shoots and kills two of her ex-students.

It is a sign of how much radical secularists hate Catholicism that they still perform this play at local playhouses as well as on college campuses. And it is a sign of cultural sickness that Showtime, the cable television channel, made a film version of it in 2001. The movie, which starred Diane Keaton and was directed by Marshall Brickman, was seen by Brickman as constituting just deserts. He justified the attack on Catholicism by proclaiming, "any institution that backed the Inquisition, the Crusades and the Roman position on the Holocaust deserves to be the butt of a couple of jokes."[28] It's not certain what's more galling—his torturing of history or his selective indignation.

The author of the play, another gay ex-Catholic, Christopher Durang, was still maintaining in 2008 that the Catholic League is wrong to cast his work as bigotry; it's just criticism, he said.[29] Yet, in 1983, the ADL called his play "offensive, unfair and demeaning." In 1985, the National Conference of Christians and Jews branded the play "a travesty of Catholic teaching." That's not all. In 1981, Frank Rich (not exactly a Catholic lackey) in the *New York Times* described it as a "one-act comedy [that] goes after the Catholic Church with a vengeance." In 1990, an editorial in the *Los Angeles Times* noted that the play "takes a brutal, satirical look at Catholic dogma." A theater critic for the *Dallas Morning News* said in 1998 that it was "the most virulently anti-Catholic play in American theater."[30]

There have been lots of anti-Catholic plays, but there was only one that caused thousands to take to the streets in protest—Terrence McNally's *Corpus Christi*. This play, written by yet another gay ex-Catholic, garnered an unprecedented coalition of religious conservatives.

The play is about a Christ-like character who is depicted as having sex with the apostles. It opened in New York City in October 1998, but only after it had been previously withdrawn by the play's producer, the Manhattan Theatre Club; pressure from the artistic community to put the play back on the drawing board proved irresistible. For example, when it was initially announced that the play was to be canceled, 30 major playwrights signed a letter demanding that the Manhattan Theatre Club stick to its guns. It was signed by such notables as Tony Kushner, Arthur Miller, Christopher Durang, A. R. Gurney, Stephen Sondheim, and Wendy Wasserstein.[31] When this was made public, I told New York 1, the New York City all-news cable channel, that I would debate any one of them. The station agreed to air the debate, but there were no takers. So much for their passion for free speech.

The Catholic League learned of the "gay Jesus" play in the spring of 1998. We immediately started building a coalition of Catholic, Protestant, Jewish, and Muslim groups; others later came on board. The early support from Orthodox Jews was particularly outstanding. But it didn't take long before the *New York Times*, ever the friend of the artistic community, jumped into the fray. In its editorial of May 28, "Censoring Terrence McNally," it took a veiled shot at the Catholic League: "That there is a native strain of bigotry, violence and contempt for artistic expression in this country is not news."[32] I struck back with an op-ed page ad in the *New York Times* on June 15 that set the tone for the rest of the debate.

The ad was titled " 'Shylock and Sambo' Hits Broadway." It alleged, quite falsely, that such a play was going to hit Broadway in the fall. "An advance copy of the script says that it features gay Jewish slavemasters who sodomize their obsequious black slaves. Though the play is often vulgar, it is nonetheless a major work of art. The theater company that is producing it receives federal, state and local funding." After commenting how gay, Jewish, and black groups were protesting, I threw the *New York Times* editorial back at them, attributing the comment to the *Times*: "That there is a native strain of bigotry, violence and contempt for artistic expression in this country is not news." I could not resist saying that "noted playwrights have rushed to defend the play, citing freedom of speech and respect for the arts."[33]

I then bared the truth, saying this was "fairy land," and that "The artistic community would never dream of offending gays, Jews and blacks, and the *New York Times* would never write such nonsense about them." I also took on the question of censorship. "Gays tried to shut down the movie 'Cruising,' Jews sought to stop the publication of 'A Nation on Trial,' feminists blasted 'Smack My Bitch Up,' Puerto Ricans rallied against 'Seinfeld,' etc." But none was denounced for censorship. The Catholic League, and its coalition, never called upon the government to cancel *Corpus Christi*. Our request was aimed at the producers.[34] All of which raises the question, Why is it that when Christian groups have concerns over the content of a play or book or movie it's called censorship, but when gays or feminists or just about any other group speak up they are exercising free speech?

Our ad hit a nerve with the ADL. Abe Foxman, ADL's national director, wrote to the Catholic League on July 7 expressing the

ADL's displeasure. It was the ad—not the play—that he was referring to. "We would hope that in the future you will find a way to express your legitimate concerns about matters offensive to Catholics in a manner which itself does not reflect insensitivity to other groups."[35] In other words, the fictional analogue of *Shylock and Sambo*—which was designed to shock—was troubling. But apparently a play depicting Jesus sodomizing the apostles was not. The ADL had come a long way from its pre-Foxman days when it condemned *Sister Mary Ignatius*.

The Catholic League spent the summer of 1998 trying to get the playwright or the producer to release a copy of the script; we also spent time mobilizing religious conservatives. The *New York Times* got ahold of the script, and what it had to say about the play was alarming. It said that "from the beginning to the end [the script] retells the Biblical story of a Jesus-like figure—from his birth in a Texas flea-bag hotel with people having profane, violent sex in the room next door to his crucifixion as 'king of the queers.'" It added, for good measure, that the Christ-like character, Joshua, "has a long-running affair with Judas and sexual relations with the other apostles." The Jesus-figure also has sex on the stage, albeit in a nonexplicit way, with an HIV-positive street hustler. The script ends by saying, "If we have offended, so be it. He belongs to us as well as to you."[36] This just goes to show how utterly arrogant, and shameless, McNally really is.

My view of the play, which I got to see a few days before opening night, was slightly different. The basic message was this: Jesus was no more divine than the rest of us and the reason He was crucified was because He approved of homosexuality. That is why He was branded King of the Queers.

The play, interestingly, was replete with gay stereotypes, ranging from the sexual to the scatological. There was crotch grabbing and a clear obsession with the male sex organ. The Christ-like figure pretended to urinate in front of the audience, and he was joined by three of the apostles, complete with sounds of urination piped into the theater. No doubt this was considered creative.

When Joshua (Jesus) turned to the apostles and proclaimed them all to be divine, he invoked a vile obscenity three times, referring to "your father," "your mother," and "God." Joshua, of course, had sex with Judas at a high school prom and then had another romp with Philip. At one point, Philip said to Joshua, "I hope you have rubbers." He then asked him to perform oral sex on him.

The key scene in the play came near the end. This was when Joshua condemned a priest for condemning homosexuality. After hearing the priest recite biblical teachings on homosexuality, Joshua charged that "you have perverted my Father's words." Joshua said he knows Scripture as well as anyone and that no one should take any of it literally. The Bible, he said, was about love. Joshua then presided over a "wedding" between James and Bartholomew. Not finished damning the priest, Joshua said, "I despise you," and then proceeded to hit him several times. Not surprisingly, the all-white audience responded favorably to the violence.[37]

While the play can be seen as anti-Christian, it was Catholics McNally really wanted to get. That's why he included recitations of the Hail Mary and references to priests, nuns, and Boys Town. In any event, by the time the play was ready to open, the Catholic League had persuaded a coalition of 49 organizations, representing some of the most prestigious religious organizations in the nation, to sign a formal letter of protest.[38] But it was what happened on opening night that really shook McNally and his supporters.

On October 13, the night of the gala opening of *Corpus Christi*, there were two protest demonstrations outside the Manhattan Theatre Club, a publicly funded entity. There was a rally organized by the Catholic League, which included Catholics, Protestants, Jews, Muslims, and Buddhists, and there was a protest of our protest led by People for the American Way. The *New York Times* reported that our demonstration numbered over 2,000; only 300 joined the counterdemonstration. "The protest began with a fiery speech from William A. Donohue, the president of the Catholic League for Religious and Civil Rights," the *Times* said. That this occurred on a rainy night made our protest all the more gratifying. "Holding a bullhorn inside an area barricaded by the police," the news story said, "Mr. Donohue shouted criticisms at the opposition. 'You are the real authoritarians at heart,' he said. 'We're the ones that believe in tolerance, not you phonies.' "[39]

The play turned out to be a bomb. Fintan O'Toole of the New York *Daily News* called it "utterly devoid of moral seriousness or artistic integrity." In the *New York Post*, Clive Barnes called it "dull," and David Lyons of the *Wall Street Journal* rebuked it for its "fatheadedness." The *Washington Post* got it right when it said that "Self-pitying artists (Oscar Wilde, John Lennon, et al.) have long had the habit of comparing themselves to Jesus, but this play plummets to a whole new level of grandiosity." And Ben Brantley of the *New York Times*, who was expected by many to like it, said the writing was "lazy" and in the end "flat and simpleminded."[40] It was not lost on religious conservatives that none of the reviewers slammed the play for its Christian-bashing elements.

The most satisfying aspect of the entire controversy was the fact that religious conservatives came together in a way that really made a statement. The *New York Times* correctly said that our rally "dwarfed" the counterdemonstration.[41] What it didn't say was that the other side not only lost, they looked foolish. Billed as "A Quiet Walk for the First Amendment by People for the American Way," their protest turned out to be nothing of the kind. Neither the Catholic League, nor any of the religious groups, ever called for government censorship. So what exactly were they protesting? Our right to protest? The sight of them holding their little balloons chanting quietly was price-less. Joining in this farce was the National Campaign for Free-dom of Expression, the National Coalition Against Censorship, PEN American Center, and Volunteer Lawyers for the Arts.[42] The ACLU was smart enough to beg off.

Perhaps the most troubling aspect of the entire controversy was the extent to which the Catholic League was lied about by the secularists. No matter how many times I said that we would rather endure the indignity of this play before ever calling on the government to ban it, the accusation of censorship was thrown at us. A new ad hoc group, the Catholic, Protestant, and Jewish Alliance for Freedom and First Amendment Rights, emerged to smear the Catholic League. We were not only accused of cen-sorship, it was implied that we were behind threats of violence aimed at the Manhattan Theatre Club. We were branded a "neo-Nazi" group, and our patriotism was impugned with the old anti-Catholic canard, "Is it pro-Rome or anti-American?"[43]

The charge about violence proved never-ending. According to the Manhattan Theatre Club, they received a bomb threat. And because I had said that the Catholic League was declaring "war" on the play, commentators and news stories blamed me for it. My use of the term "war," I said, was standard rhetoric voiced by all sides in the culture war. There was a "war on pov-erty," a "war on drugs," etc. James Carville, I had pointed out, had just said that the Democrats were declaring "war" on special prosecutor Ken Starr. Did anyone accuse Carville of violence? And if Starr's office had received a bomb threat, would Carville have been blamed? The charge was preposterous. Moreover, the many death threats that I received proved to be of no interest to the media, though I made mention of them several times on radio and television. In the end, I did succeed in getting newspa-pers to correct stories that falsely accused the Catholic League of violence; we chased down such stories for years.

Of all the organizations that I dealt with during this ugly time, no group proved to be more reckless than People for the American Way. Just as they were to do the next year during the Brooklyn Museum of Art debacle, they never once condemned the bigotry, just those who protested it. The most vocal spokesperson proved to be Barbara Handman, vice president of the organization. Like so many others, she tried to blame the Catholic League for violence, even when it was made crystal clear to her that we had nothing to do with it. Worse, she not only defended the play's contents, she even went so far as to say on TV that Serrano's *Piss Christ* was "glorious." What was so glorious about the crucifix submerged in urine was its message: Handman told me that it was a "reverential" statement about how "the current Catholic community was destroying the teachings of Christ."[44] When I later asked Handman, who is Jewish, if she would be offended if someone put a Star of David in a bowl of feces, she expressed horror at the mere suggestion. Different strokes for different folks?

We met again when Bill O'Reilly did two back-to-back segments on the controversy, just one day after the play opened. O'Reilly called me before the show to ask if I would confine my remarks to a description of the play; he would then take on Handman in the next segment. Though I wanted to debate her again, I agreed to his request. When I got to the green room, I met Handman and a friend of hers. Handman and I quickly clashed. After I did my interview with O'Reilly, Handman joined Bill, and I returned to the waiting room. Happy that things were going so well, I told Handman's friend that the Catholic League "should use this as a fund-raiser." At that she jumped to her feet, walked right up to me, and said, "It's enough to make you hate Catholics!" She then literally stomped down the hall screaming. It was a magnificent sight.

Not one to give up, I wrote to Handman the next day describing her friend's antics, asking, "I would like to know whether you approve or disapprove of this statement?" I also said there were "three witnesses to this bigoted comment."

In closing, I cited O'Reilly's comment to her at the end of their segment: "If somebody put on a play that said that the Holocaust was a farce or it was right to kill all of the people in Europe who got killed by the Nazis, wouldn't you say . . ." After O'Reilly said this, she barked, "That's a terrible play." I ended my letter by saying, "How do you know that it would be a terrible play? After all, you said you couldn't judge *Corpus Christi* because you hadn't seen it, so why are you so judgmental? How do you know that it wouldn't be an artistic masterpiece?"[45] She never replied.

The bigotry against Catholics, as displayed in the play and in some of the comments about the Catholic League, was profound. There is no other segment of the population that can be trashed with impunity by the artistic community and still receive the plaudits of playgoers and the cultural elites. Yet they persist in the fantasy that they are the tolerant ones.

In 2008, the play made a return trip to New York City, though this time it was shown at some no-name place in Greenwich Village. Because of the venue, it wasn't worth commenting on. Until, that is, the *New York Times* twice embraced it within a one-week period.

Jason Zinoman applauded the play for its "reverent spin on the Jesus story,"[46] making any sane person wonder just how debased a play about Jesus must be before critics like him brand it for what it is. Had the play substituted Martin Luther King for Jesus, it's a sure bet Zinoman wouldn't have labeled it "reverent." Mark Blankenship took aim at those who protested the play in 1998, saying it offered "stark reminders of lingering homophobia."[47] So when anti-Catholic homosexuals like McNally feature Jesus having oral sex with the boys, and Catholics object, it's not McNally who is the bigot—it's those protesting Catholics.

When the newspaper's public editor, Clark Hoyt, got pounded with angry e-mails from Catholic League members, he did a story on the controversy. He asked Paul Baumann, editor of the

Catholic left-wing magazine *Commonweal*, what he thought of it all. Not surprisingly, he blamed me for overreacting, saying absolutely nothing negative about the play.[48] That's because Catholic journalists like him are always interested in currying favor with secular journalists, and one way to do it is to throw their religion overboard while demonstrating how open-minded they are. What they crave more than anything else is recognition, and what they get in return is neither recognition nor respect. They've been had.

Pure Nihilism

What is most astonishing about all this is the insatiable appetite that secular saboteurs have for bashing Christians. For them, it is pure fun to see Penn and Teller rip away at Christians onstage. But sometimes the duo manage to offend even their fans. Many walked out of a performance in which Teller appeared nearly naked at the World Magic Seminar in Las Vegas in 2003. Dressed as Christ on a full-size cross, Teller allowed a midget dressed as an angel to perform simulated sex on him (Penn unveiled the scene by pulling away a "Shroud of Turin" that covered the cross).[49] Nor did everyone approve of Penn Jillette's rant against Mother Teresa in 2005. At least one of those associated with the assault refused to work with Penn and Teller again. She called me saying it was too much to watch Jillette screaming about Mother Teresa in the most vulgar of terms; he also used the *C* word to refer to her order of nuns.[50]

Unlike Penn and Teller's fans, Madonna's never protest. Her musical Confessions tour was a huge success. Between political statements of the most inane kind and her oral sex jokes, she found time to don a crown of thorns, hang from a mirrored cross, and croon her ballad "Live to Tell." The Material Girl, who believes "Catholicism is a really mean religion" (it's the teachings on sex that makes it so really mean),[51] almost succeeded in getting NBC to air her entire theatrical production on Thanksgiving Eve of 2006. What stopped her was the Catholic League and Brent Bozell's Media Research Center: we wanted NBC to pull the mock Crucifixion scene. Indeed, we threatened a boycott of one of the show's sponsors if it was included (we pledged to announce which sponsor on the day after the show aired—keeping all of them wary—just in time for the Christmas season). Though Madge said she would not allow the concert to be shown if it was edited, she swallowed her pride and decided to pocket the loot in her losing cause.[52]

It would be one thing if this secular hate speech disguised as artistic liberty were confined to the margins of society. Unfortunately, it is often given a high profile, showing up in prestigious venues.

New York's Carnegie Hall decided to welcome *Jerry Springer: The Opera in Concert*, imported from England, in 2008. The musical trashed Jesus and Our Blessed Mother with abandon, to the thrill of the well-heeled crowd. One part of the show featured Jesus and Satan engaging in "conflict resolution" in Hell. Jesus was depicted as fat and effeminate, thus giving rise to the accusation that he is a homosexual. Jesus replies, "Actually, I am a bit gay." Eve, angry at being cast out of the Garden of Eden, reaches under Jesus' loincloth and fondles him. The Virgin Mary is described as "raped by an angel, raped by God," and there is a scene where Jesus uses an obscenity to warn his critics not to mess with him.[53]

All of this occurs among such story lines as a man becoming sexually aroused by dressing up in a diaper and having his girlfriend treat him like an infant, and a mother, wearing an oversize crucifix, informing her stripper daughter that she wishes the girl had died at birth. The musical's twisted moral is summed up in a speech given by the Jerry character at the end: "Energy is pure delight. Nothing is wrong and nothing is right. And everything that lives is holy."[54]

"Nothing is wrong and nothing is right." Thus does this theatrical production underscore the central point of this book: the secular sabotage of America is driven by nihilism as much as it is by hate. All of it is deliberate and all of it is intended to offend.

CHAPTER 5

Sabotaged by Hollywood

Hollywood Hates Religion

There is more than anecdotal evidence that the secular elites in the television industry have a big problem with religion. For example, in December 2004, the Parents Television Council released a study of the major television networks that detailed 2,344 treatments of religion constituting 2,385 hours of prime-time television. After examining the findings, Brent Bozell, president of the organization, concluded that "anti-Catholic bigotry" was "rampant" on network shows.[1] Two years later the organization found that prime-time shows dealt with religion "half as much as the year before." It is significant that when they did, "religion was cast in negative light more than one-third of the time."[2] And in 2007, the Media Research Center issued a devastating report, "The Media Assault on American Values," which found that "74 percent of Americans believe the nation's moral values have declined over the past twenty years, and large majorities hold the media responsible for contributing to that decline."[3]

The secular saboteurs who dominate Hollywood are not indifferent to religion—they hate it. And that's why the moguls never tire of bashing Christianity. But let a Catholic group produce a movie, and it's enough to call out the National Guard.

When *Spitfire Grill* was released in 1996 by a Catholic organization, Caryn James of the *New York Times* got nervous: "No one seemed to notice that it was financed by a conservative Mississippi company affiliated with the Roman Catholic Church and founded, as its 'mission statement' puts it, to 'present the values of the Judeo-Christian tradition.'" If that wasn't scary enough, James said that "watching it [the film] with the Sacred Heart League [the parent company of the producing studio] in mind makes all the Biblical imagery seem slightly sinister." More important, she noted the film's "multidimensional roots—Catholic backers, Protestant characters and a Jewish director—don't diminish the eerie sense that viewers are being proselytized without their knowledge."[4]

Now if what James said is to be taken seriously, is it fair to ask what kind of proselytizing has been going on in Hollywood for the past five decades? Michael Medved, who knows Hollywood as well as anyone, once said on air, "As you know, I'm not a Catholic, but it doesn't matter what your religious orientation, everybody's got to be a little bit tired of all of the Catholic bashing out of Hollywood. In one movie after another, you've got lecherous priests or pregnant nuns or corrupt cardinals, and it's never balanced by anything positive. It's really become a form of religious bigotry, it seems to me, and I don't think it's fair."[5]

Indeed, in his book *Hollywood vs. America*, Medved chronicles a history of anti-Catholic films emanating from Hollywood.[6] The Catholic League has done the same. A fine video on this subject, *Hollywood vs. Catholicism*, made by Chatham Hill Foundation's Jodie Thompson, makes the same point. More recently, former CBS executive Bernie Goldberg, speaking of media executives in general, said that "the one group you can easily offend with no fear of repercussions . . . is American Catholics."[7]

Does Hollywood hate religion? If not, why does it continue to make movies that bash it? In December 2004, I created quite a stir among secularists when I said that "Hollywood is controlled by secular Jews who hate Christianity in general and Catholicism in particular."[8]

The context of my remarks is never mentioned by my critics. Here's what happened. Rabbi Shmuley Boteach, with whom I have often agreed, had just gone ballistic mocking *The Passion of the Christ*, speaking derisively about "the guy"—Jesus—who was mercilessly beaten in what he called this "diabolical, criminal, violent mess." In the very same segment that set the rabbi off, I said, "You have got secular Jews. You have got embittered ex-Catholics, including a lot of ex-Catholic priests who hate the Catholic Church, wacko Protestants in the same group . . ." Later in the debate I said, "There are secularists from every ethnic and religious stock," but when people talk about Hollywood, they are "talking mostly about secular Jews."[9] In short, I did not single anyone out.

Hollywood is of course dominated by secular Jews, and it is demonstrably true that the movies made about Catholics over the past several decades evince an animus. It is also true that when Hollywood was dominated by an earlier generation of Jews, films about the Catholic Church were uniformly respectful. In other words, there is nothing inherently problematic about Jews in Hollywood making movies about Catholicism. Those who are not Jewish and make movies about the Catholic Church today also evince a secular bias, disrespecting Catholicism. To put it differently, there is nothing about any demographic group that impels its members to reflexively treat religion fairly or unfairly.

All this aside, it is understandable that some reasonably minded persons in the Jewish community might raise an eyebrow about my use of the verb "controlled." After all, anti-Semites have longed advanced the invidious notion that there is some kind of cabal among secular Jews plotting to undermine Christianity. That's nonsense.[10] Of course there is no conspiracy. But there is a secular mind-set—it permeates Hollywood—and it is no secret that secular Jews are disproportionately represented in Hollywood studios. Just as we know that Harlem is associated with African Americans and Chinatown is associated with Chinese, we know Hollywood is associated with Jews. To be specific, secular Jews. It was not for nothing that the *New York Times*, writing about the Mel Gibson film, said that the movie industry "tends to be liberal and secular in outlook, as well as disproportionately Jewish."[11]

There is more than a little hypocrisy here. Why is it considered okay to cite the role that Catholics have played in pushing Hollywood to adopt decency codes, but it is not okay to mention the role that Jews have played in making movies? And as long as those who chronicle the Jewish success story in the United States note the Jewish role in Hollywood, why is it not okay for others to mention their more recent role in a critical fashion? Surely there is a difference between being descriptive and promoting bigotry. Even if it is true, and it is, that bigots will use descriptive statements of a controversial nature to further their own cause, the answer to this kind of ignorance is not denial. Oftentimes, the only way to judge whether a person is being provocative or bigoted is to measure his words against what he has said and done previously regarding said group. In this regard, I am grateful to all those Jewish friends of mine who quickly rushed to my defense during this controversy.

The day after I debated Rabbi Boteach, he was kind enough to have me on his radio show to discuss the matter further. During the conversation, I admitted there was a segment of the Catholic community that is anti-Semitic. I then asked him if he would agree that there is a segment of the secular Jewish community that is anti-Catholic, and to my astonishment he said no. He denied it without equivocation.[12] That's also nonsense.

What really angered Rabbi Boteach was the fact that prominent Jews disagreed with his criticism of me. Here is what he said: "When my debate with Donohue exploded into the newspapers, I was invited on to the radio shows of fellow Jewish conservatives Dennis Prager and Michael Medved. Both are devout Jews and outstanding ethical lights, with Dennis in particular serving as one of America's most gifted exponents of morality. Yet, I was astonished when both Prager and Medved defended and agreed with Donohue's statement that it was secular Jews who oppose Christianity who were primarily responsible for the sleaze coming out of Hollywood." He said this was "chicken feed" compared to what Rabbi Daniel Lapin, "another friend and colleague," wrote about this issue. Lapin said, "You'd have to be a recent immigrant from Outer Mongolia not to know of the role that people with Jewish names play in the coarsening of our culture. Almost every American knows this. It is just that most gentiles are too polite to mention it."[13]

The *Forward*, a Jewish weekly, published an editorial in 2004 saying it was merely a "sociological observation" to note that "Jews run Hollywood." The newspaper quite rightly said that to say "the Jews run Hollywood" is an entirely different matter, one that smacks of anti-Semitism. So it concluded that "No, 'the Jews' don't run Hollywood. But Jews do, just as Koreans predominate in New York dry-cleaning and blacks rule basketball."[14] Well said.

Jews are, quite understandably, wary of any language that has been used by their enemies to ignite the passions of bigots. So when Tom O'Neil, an astute Hollywood observer, innocently referred to "Jewish Hollywood," talk-show host Keith Olbermann was quick to say, "And let's clarify so nobody puts you on that list of folks who said things. When you said Jewish Hollywood, you meant the Jewish community in Hollywood." To which O'Neil answered, "Oh, yes, exactly. Yes, absolutely."[15] The distinction that Olbermann prodded is more cosmetic than substantive. No matter, the point was to rescue O'Neil from criticism.

The same day of O'Neil's admission, the *Los Angeles Times* said, "Hollywood was largely founded by, and the studios are still chiefly run by, Jewish executives." A week later, Ruth Marcus wrote in the *Washington Post* that Hollywood "is in fact dominated by Jews."[16] These comments are neither exceptional nor anti-Semitic, and attempts to brand them that way are pernicious. Moreover, the same sentiments were voiced at that time by many listeners to Mike Gallagher's radio show, all of whom wondered, as did Mike, what all the fuss was about. Radio talk-show host Steve Malzberg was similarly kind to me, pointing out the context of my remarks and my past associations with the Jewish community.

Ironically, I have often been accused by right-wing Catholics of being too pro-Jewish! Within weeks of starting as president of the Catholic League in 1993, I received a phone call from someone claiming to represent a Catholic defense organization warning that Catholics were wary of me because of my Jewish ties. Today, I get the same treatment. For example, in the same year that Rabbi Boteach and I had it out, the question was raised, "Is Bill Donohue a neocon plant inside the Catholic right?" Cited as a concern was my oft-cited thanks to three Jewish intellectuals who helped me get my first book on the ACLU published: Irving Kristol, Aaron Wildavsky, and Irving Louis Horowitz.[17] In any event, by 2006, it was no longer an open question. I was condemned as a "lackey" for my "neocon masters," simply because I defended Harvard Law professor Alan Dershowitz against the vicious rants of Norman Finkelstein.[18]

I speak as someone who is sensitive to all of the issues surrounding this matter. I have a long history of fighting anti-Semitism, both at Jewish conferences and at street rallies, and I have been especially outspoken in my condemnation of Islamic terrorists bent on destroying Israel. But I also have no stomach for those who make false accusations. On two occasions, I hired a lawyer to threaten a lawsuit against persons who tried to rig what I said and then pass if off as if it were anti-Semitic. Patrick Foye, the Catholic League's general counsel at the time, and left-wing activist Ron Kuby both successfully represented me and had the offenders withdraw the charge. By the way, in both cases the guilty party was Catholic; one was a priest.

What follows is a selection of some of the most salient examples of Catholic bashing, Hollywood style.

Priest

In the spring of 1995, the Catholic League became the first organization in the nation to call for a boycott of Disney. What drove the decision was Disney's connection with Miramax: Bob and Harvey Weinstein, the executives in charge of Miramax, had released a movie that was arguably the most anti-Catholic film ever made (that was how Michael Medved put it); Miramax was a Disney subsidiary. The film, *Priest*, was produced by the BBC, directed by Antonia Bird, and written by Jimmy McGovern. Bird told the *Los Angeles Times* that the movie was "against a hierarchy adhering to old-fashioned rules without looking at the way the world's changed." Though she is not Catholic, she admitted that she was "seething with rage" when she learned that the pope was opposed to condoms. McGovern, another one of those angry ex-Catholics, was fond of discussing the priests of his youth, dubbing them "reactionary bastards." It was not surprising to learn, then, that their anti-Catholicism would be displayed on the screen.

If the movie had been about one lousy priest, few would have cared. It certainly wouldn't have been branded anti-Catholic: lousy priests exist and no one doubts it. The problem with *Priest*, however, was that the audience met only five priests, all of whom were positively dysfunctional. More damning, their maladies were a function of Catholicism. It was this diabolical cause and effect that made the film so hateful. And it was this combination of morally destitute priests acting on their morally destitute religion that sustains the thesis of this book: we are not dealing with Christianity's critics, we are dealing with cultural nihilists. Their goal is to tear down, not induce change.

The priests in the movie were portrayed as either living a life that directly contravenes Church teachings or they were mean, even psychotic, individuals. Two of them had affairs, one with his female housekeeper and the other with his newly acquired male friend. Another priest was a drunk, the country pastor was obviously a madman, and the bishop was simply wicked. In short, there was not a single priest who was well-adjusted and faithful to his vows.

It wasn't just religious conservatives who saw this as anti-Catholic. The *Los Angeles Times*, for instance, noted that *Priest* was "an angry piece of invective directed at the Catholic church's hierarchy." *Premiere* said that director Antonia Bird "is basking in her blasphemy." Gossip columnist Liz Smith wrote that "Miramax is obviously looking to push Catholic sensibilities—bruised already—to the breaking point." She was referring not simply to the movie's content but to the fact that it was slated to open nationwide on Good Friday.[19]

I had a chance to preview the film on March 9; it was scheduled to open March 24 in New York and on April 14, Good Friday, around the nation. As a sociologist, I was most offended by the attempt to portray the Catholic Church as the causative agent accounting for the priests' tortured existence. As a Catholic, I saw the decision to open nationwide on one of the most sacred days of the year as the final straw.

On March 23, I held a press conference at the headquarters of the New York Archdiocese. The room was jammed with reporters and television cameras. Posted all over the wall that formed a backdrop to my presentation were familiar Disney characters: Mickey Mouse, Minnie Mouse, Donald Duck, Goofy, Beauty and the Beast, Aladdin, Snow White, the Dalmatians, and various stars from *The Lion King*. On the podium was a large stuffed version of the Lion King himself.

Just before the press conference began, I was told that executives from Miramax were in the room (one of them frantically called her office noting that the room was loaded with Disney paraphernalia). That didn't bother me, but what I found offensive was the audacity that Miramax showed by telling the press that this was a joint press conference between them and the Catholic League. So after I finished my remarks, but before I opened the floor to questions, I made a statement. I told the press corps that this was not a joint press conference and that the Miramax officials were "in my house." I then instructed them to leave and if they wanted to hold a press conference they should "do it in the street." Startled, about a half-dozen men and women got up, put their coats on, and headed to the door. It didn't take long before Miramax announced that the movie would not open on Good Friday; it opened five days later.

Turning up the heat even more, I placed an ad on the op-ed page of the *New York Times* on April 10 blasting Disney. "What's Happening to Disney?" cut right to the quick: "Think of it this way. How do you think Jews would react if a movie called 'Rabbi' portrayed five rabbis in a depraved condition? Would gays tolerate a movie that showed them to be morally destitute? What about a cruel caricature of African Americans? To top it off, what if it were the cultural heritage or lifestyle of these groups that best explained their behavior? And just think what would happen if those movies had been scheduled to open on Yom Kippur, Gay Pride Day or Martin Luther King Day."[20]

The response by Catholic leaders was impressive. John Cardinal O'Connor did what he always did—spoke with clarity. Referring to Disney and Miramax, he said, "Your movie is little more than the kind of thing kids used to take delight in scrawling on the walls in men's rooms. Call it art, go into ecstasy over its sophistication, exult in exposing the 'horrors' of Catholicism, ladies and gentlemen of Disneymax, if you will, but what you have done is cheap and odorous."[21] On nationwide TV, Mother Angelica and Father Benedict Groeschel encouraged the faithful to become mobilized against Disney, netting spectacular results. But it was the response from those outside the Catholic community that meant the most.

Former New York City Mayor Ed Koch, one of the greatest friends that Catholics have ever had, labeled *Priest* an exercise in "Catholic bashing." Other Jews, such as Don Feder, Rabbi Daniel Lapin, Rabbi Abraham Hecht of the Rabbinical Alliance of America, and Rabbi Joseph Potasnik of the New York Board of Rabbis, voiced their support for the Catholic League campaign.[22] It was heartening to see so many good people denounce this vicious movie.

Dogma

The Weinstein brothers no sooner angered Catholics with *Priest* when they teamed up with writer and director Kevin Smith to make *Dogma*.

Everyone knew there would be another Catholic League showdown with Disney over *Dogma*. In December 1998, *Playboy* said, "If members of the Catholic League don't picket this one, they're comatose." What proved to be decisive was a story in *Premiere* magazine and a piece in the *New York Post*. Independent Film Channel host John Pierson was quoted as saying, "The Catholic League will have a problem." That was it. I wrote a Catholic League news release on April 5, 1999, titled "Disney/Miramax Poised to Anger Catholics Again." Two days later, Miramax faxed a letter to me saying that the Disney/Miramax label would not appear in *Dogma*. Disney CEO Michael Eisner had told the Weinsteins that he had had enough.[23] The brothers decided to personally buy the film rights to the movie.

In its Cannes review of *Dogma, Variety* described how the movie begins: "Numerous early cheap jokes, including a nun abandoning her calling in order to pursue the pleasures of the flesh and a man reading *Hustler* magazine in the church, don't bode well for what's to come." What was to come was Bethany, "a Catholic abortion clinic worker" who is a descendant of Jesus (the movie insinuates that Joseph and Mary had sex); she meets Jay "who's obscenely rude and tells Bethany he likes to hang at abortion clinics because it's a good place to meet chicks." No wonder London's *Daily Telegraph* said, "The film is punctuated with four-letter words and toilet humor." All targeted at Roman Catholics.[24]

Cheap nun jokes are not proof of cultural nihilism. But when Jesus and his mother are sexually exploited, and when those who are not offended by a Catholic-bashing movie admit that Catholicism is trashed from beginning to end, it suggests that more is going on than just critical commentary. This isn't a matter of conjecture. Consider that when Howard Stern said to Kevin Smith that the movie "has some Jesus Christ thing in it so all the religious folks are already hating it," Smith replied, "Then we must be doing something right."[25]

It is nothing short of amazing to see how unethical some in Hollywood are. They can sure dish it out, but they can't take it. For example, after actor Ben Affleck admitted that "The movie is definitely meant to push buttons," I shot back with, "The Catholic League has a few buttons of its own to push, and we won't hold back." This was a fairly innocuous remark, but then I received an Overnight Priority Federal Express letter from Dan Petrocelli, lawyer for the Weinsteins (he was the Los Angeles attorney who beat O.J. Simpson in the civil suit). His missive was meant to intimidate: "Statements like these may be interpreted to announce or imply an intention by the League to go beyond the bounds of legitimate and peaceful dissent or protest, and to stimulate, motivate, or incite danger or violence." He then promised to hold the Catholic League responsible for any violence that might occur when the film opened.[26]

Petrocelli's bullying was a monumental failure. I had only one response. I sent him a memo indicating that I had received his "threatening letter," and even took the time to tell him that our correct address (at the time) was 1011 First Avenue, not 101 First Avenue. "Please make a note of it," I instructed.[27]

I wasn't finished with Petrocelli. On September 12, in another *New York Times* op-ed page ad, I raised the question "Will the Real Censors Please Stand Up!" In it, I recounted the Petrocelli threat and included one by Kevin Smith as well. Smith had said that "If anyone . . . ANYONE . . . gets hurt in the process of their protest, we're holding Bill Donohue and the League responsible."[28] They were really looking like thugs at this point.

When the movie opened, John Podhoretz of the *New York Post* branded it "virulently, even obsessively anti-Catholic." Even John Pierson, a friend and collaborator of Smith's, said the Catholic League's attacks "are accurate on a surface level."[29] More important, the Catholic League petition requesting Disney to dump Miramax garnered 300,000 signatures. Once again, evangelical Protestants and Orthodox Jews rallied to our side.[30]

Podhoretz's comment about the film being "obsessively anti-Catholic" is more than just correct—it is the reason why movies like this are a testimony to the agenda of moral nihilists. Only in recent decades has Hollywood really turned on Catholics, but the cultural knives they are using penetrate deep. By constantly slicing and dicing, their goal of eating away at the house of Catholicism is accomplished.

Disney and Miramax have since gone their own ways, and that is a good thing. But the Weinsteins never stop bashing Catholics. Besides *Priest* and *Dogma*, they have served up such anti-Catholic fare as *Butcher Boy*, *40 Days and 40 Nights*, and *The Magdalene Sisters*. They returned on Christmas Day 2006, delivering *Black Christmas*. The only saving grace is that most of these films have flopped at the box office. The fact that they still make them, however, suggests that profit is not their exclusive motive.

The Passion of the Christ

The Passion of the Christ was one of the most powerful religious movies to come out of Hollywood in decades, bringing together Catholics and Protestants in a way that made them proud to be Christians. Unfortunately, the Hollywood establishment not only had nothing to do with the film, it did everything it could to undermine it. As for Catholics and Protestants, their pride was undercut by constant attempts to put them on the defensive: the critics wanted to know why they would rally to such a violently anti-Semitic movie.

Almost a year before the movie opened on February 25, 2004, a 3,000-word article by Christopher Noxon appeared in the *New York Times Magazine* that raised serious questions about Mel Gibson's religion, his relationship with his father, and the movie he was completing about the death of Jesus.[31] Gibson was a traditionalist, one who belonged to a pre–Vatican II church, and his father, Hutton Gibson, was known for his searing criticisms of the contemporary Catholic Church and his outright diminishing of the horrors of the Holocaust.

My involvement with Mel Gibson began following a TV debate I had with Rabbi Marvin Hier of the Simon Wiesenthal Center on the MSNBC TV show *Scarborough Country*; no one had yet seen the film, but the controversy had already started. At one point in the exchange, Hier tried to deny any Jewish involvement in Christ's death. I said that if anyone were to blame "the Jews" for the death of Christ, I would take exception to it "because that is a collective statement which can be read by anti-Semites to include current-day Jews." On the other hand, I said those who were calling for Christ's crucifixion "weren't the Aleutian Islanders. They weren't the Pacific Islanders. It wasn't the Puerto Ricans."[32]

Shortly after this show aired, Mel Gibson called me at the Catholic League and said he had seen the debate. He wanted to meet me. A few weeks later, on July 6, he came to my office and offered a private viewing of the film on VHS tape. It was without doubt the most powerful presentation of the death of Jesus ever made. Indeed, I had never seen anything quite like it. While it was obvious that this was not a movie everyone would appreciate, it was just as obvious that the Catholic League would be called upon to defend it.

From the time of Noxon's first strike against the film to the day it opened, all the trappings of a nihilistic assault were evident. What happened was more than a series of events launched by Gibson's critics: what happened was a serious campaign to destroy the man and his work. Put the following incidents together, and what emerges is not disagreement but a strategic effort to search and destroy everything and everyone associated with the movie.

- The script was stolen and given to those who could be counted on to slam it.
- Tapes of the film were stolen and distributed to those who could be relied upon to bash it.
- Mel's faith was impugned.
- Charges that violence against Jews would occur after the movie was shown were commonplace.
- Accusations of anti-Semitism were thrown around with abandon.
- Attempts to bully Gibson into changing the film were ongoing.
- Demands for a postscript were made by those who sought to put Gibson on the defensive.
- Bishops were badgered to get Mel's friends in line.

- The Vatican was lobbied to criticize the movie.
- Vatican sources were pressured into saying the pope didn't say of the film, "It is as it was."
- Accusations that the movie was being kept away from Jewish neighborhoods were made.
- Fears that the movie might damage youngsters who saw it were expressed.
- Demands that Gibson vet his script for approval by officials of the Catholic Church were constantly made.
- Attempts to discredit the film were made by those who said it wasn't authentic, including those who had no problem with the wildly inaccurate movie *The Last Temptation of Christ.*
- Critics deceitfully gained admission into screenings of the film before it opened.
- Highly personal questions about Gibson's life were raised.
- Sneering comments that the film might make a profit were voiced.
- Derisive remarks about the way the movie was marketed were made.
- Demands that the film be censored were made at public rallies (I witnessed this firsthand).
- Catholics who defended the movie were insulted by foes of the film.
- Bishops were pressured to denounce the movie as being unfaithful to Church teachings.
- Disrespect for Gibson's artistic rights was ongoing.
- Mel's elderly father was attacked even though he had nothing to do with the movie.
- Police detectives were ordered into theaters to assess whether the movie might promote violence against Jews.[33]

This is the kind of thuggery that defines the nihilistic approach to Christianity. It is the signature politics of secular saboteurs.

The principal critics of the movie were comprised of secular-leaning Catholics and Jews, as well as radical secularists. Liberal theologians, spanning the Catholic, Protestant, and Jewish communities, were particularly offended. Many felt that the ADL seriously misrepresented the position of the Catholic bishops when it said that it had joined with the Secretariat of Ecumenical and Interreligious Affairs of the United States Conference of Catholic Bishops (USCCB) to assemble Jewish and Catholic scholars to evaluate an early version of the movie's screenplay; it never admitted that the Catholic panel was unauthorized by the USCCB. Nor did it say that the USCCB had since apologized to Gibson for reviewing a movie it hadn't seen. To top it off, it was never admitted that both the ADL and the USCCB had returned the stolen screenplay to Gibson's Icon Productions![34]

The one person who had seen the movie, and who had translated it into Aramaic and Latin, was Jesuit Father William J. Fulco, a National Endowment for the Humanities professor of ancient Mediterranean studies at Loyola Marymount University. He not only said that the ADL had nothing to worry about, he argued "there is no hint of deicide." In this regard, it is important to remember that every Sunday Catholics recite the 1,700-year-old Nicene Creed, and every time they do they mention that Jesus was "crucified under Pontius Pilate." They do not say Jesus was killed by the Romans. Nor do they say He was killed by the Jews. They individualize the guilt.[35]

On November 6, the ADL convened its 90th Annual National Meeting at New York's Plaza Hotel. One of the sessions explored the controversy over the movie. Paula Fredriksen, professor of theology at Boston University, branded the movie "inflammatory," saying it was in the "toxic tradition of blaming Jews for the death of Jesus." These were strong words from someone who had not yet seen the film. But it was not unexpected: Fredriksen was already on record predicting violence. "When the violence breaks out," she wrote in the *New Republic* months earlier, "Mel Gibson will have a much higher authority than professors and bishops to answer to."[36] Notice she said *when*, not if.

Also speaking at the meeting was Sister Mary C. Boys, a theologian at a liberal Protestant enclave, the Union Theological Seminary. She went beyond an ad hominem attack when she ridiculed Gibson for saying that he believed he was guided by the Holy Spirit in making this movie. "I don't believe that [given the divisiveness] that he could claim that the Holy Spirit is behind this," she said. She also had not seen the movie. More important, it obviously never occurred to her that she and her colleagues were contributing to the very divisiveness she so loudly deplored.[37]

When Foxman spoke at the convention, he took another shot at Gibson, saying, "I think he's infected—seriously infected—with some very, very serious anti-Semitic views." What proved to be embarrassing was the reaction of Rabbi Eugene Korn, a top ADL official. Unlike the others, he had seen the film. While he did not like what he saw, he took umbrage at the overheated rhetoric of Foxman and others. So he quit the ADL.[38] His resignation came at a time when many Jewish leaders were questioning Foxman's strategy.

For example, Elan Steinberg, an official at the World Jewish Congress, openly wondered whether Jews were alienating "those who are our allies in many struggles." Gilbert Rosenthal of the Council of Synagogues also said that the ADL's approach was backfiring. Rabbi Michael Cook, a Hebrew Union professor, warned that Jews who were predicting violence following the film "risk embarrassment when it hits the theaters." Rabbi Yechiel Eckstein, president of the International Fellowship of Christians and Jews, and Rabbi Daniel Lapin of Toward Tradition also weighed in against the ADL. Michael Medved really unloaded when he commented that Foxman's campaign "is provoking far more anti-Semitism than the movie itself ever could."[39]

Critics of the movie had the wind knocked out of them when Peggy Noonan wrote a piece for the online edition of the *Wall Street Journal* saying that Pope John Paul II had seen the movie and endorsed it. "It is as it was," he reportedly said. It didn't take long before some Vatican officials were expressing doubts about the accuracy of Noonan's story, but it also didn't take long before others sought to confirm it. Alan Nierob, a spokesman for the producer, said that "I saw it [the pope's words] in writing myself." He maintained that the e-mail in which the pope's words were printed was sent to Noonan and Steve McEveety, the movie's producer.[40] When Joaquin Navarro-Valls, the Vatican's press secretary, told Noonan that he never gave her permission to use the pope's words, she and the *Wall Street Journal* were able to trace his e-mails back to the Vatican server to prove he had.[41]

McEveety reported that the pope watched the film with his private secretary, Archbishop Stanislaw Dziwisz, and that Dziwisz was the one who disseminated the pope's words, "It is as it was." This was independently confirmed by John Allen of the *National Catholic Reporter* and by the Reuters news agency. After much hullabaloo, Navarro-Valls announced that the pope had indeed viewed the film, but that he had no public statement about it. He did not say that the pope never expressed the five controversial words. Which in Vaticanese means he undoubtedly did.[42]

We know for sure that about a week after the pope saw the movie, several top Vatican officials gave their unanimous approval to the film. Members of the Vatican Secretariat of State, the Pontifical Council for Social Communications, and the Congregation for the Doctrine of the Faith (which oversees doctrinal issues) applauded Gibson for his efforts. Most vocal was Father Augustine Di Noia, undersecretary of the doctrinal congregation.

He said the guilt for Christ's death was dispersed, leaving only Mary as "really blameless." When asked point-blank whether the movie was anti-Semitic, he replied, "There is absolutely nothing anti-Semitic or anti-Jewish about Mel Gibson's film."[43]

The behavior of some Catholic theologians, including nuns and priests, was deplorable. Father John Pawlikowski labeled Gibson a "heretic," and he, along with Philip Cunningham and Sister Mary Boys, blasted the director for violating their own carefully crafted rules for governing depictions of the Passion. But if Mel was a "heretic," then what lien did they think they had on him? Was he supposed to report to them like an obedient altar boy asking permission to distribute his movie? Did they think Mel wanted to show his film in the basement of a Catholic elementary school and needed their okay? It was obvious what was going on. These ego-bruised, self-appointed guardians of the truth were angry that Mel didn't run his script by them, tailoring his film to their liking. Their audacity was mind-boggling, but not at all out of character for those who live in the academy.[44]

There were some Jewish leaders who made remarks that were so inflammatory that they worked to poison Christian-Jewish relations. Take, for example, Harold Brackman, consultant to the Simon Wiesenthal Center. "It is Christians who bear the responsibility, after 2,000 years of religious-inspired anti-Semitism," he railed, "to inhibit rather than inflame the excesses of their own haters." He managed to top this when he said, "When filmmakers with a *Christological agenda* fail to accept this responsibility, the blood that may result is indeed on their hands" [my italics]. It made me wonder—if Christian hatred of Jews is so visceral—why have there been no pogroms in the United States in over 200 years? Just as irresponsible was Ken Jacobson, associate national director of the ADL. "We have good reason to be seriously concerned about Gibson's plans to retell the Passion," he warned. "Historically, the Passion—the story of the killing of Jesus—has resulted in the death of Jews."[45]

Not being a scholar on the Passion, I sought one out. I asked James Shapiro, a professor at Columbia University and author of *Oberammergau*, two questions: when was the last time, in any country, Jews were beaten up following a Passion play, and has this ever happened in the United States? He had no evidence of any Jews ever being beaten up in the U.S. after a Passion play, and aside from one assault in Germany in the 1930s, the most recent incidents occurred in the late Middle Ages in Europe.[46] In other words, there was no real substance to the fears of people like Brackman and Jacobson. Yes, there was the monstrosity of the Holocaust, but as former New York City Mayor Ed Koch once informed, "It should never be said that Christians were responsible for the Holocaust—Nazis were. Blaming Christians would be as unjustified as holding Jews accountable for the death of Jesus. Individuals were responsible in both situations."[47]

The movie opened on February 25, Ash Wednesday. I went to see it with Father Philip Eichner, chairman of the board of directors of the Catholic League, and several prominent members of the New York Jewish community. When the film was over, the Catholic League and the New York Board of Rabbis, headed by Rabbi Joe Potasnik, held a joint press conference outside the theater. Several speakers had their say, and there was plenty of disagreement, but it was also cordial (Joe Potasnik would have it no other way).

Movie critics who hated the film got their talking points down in predictable fashion. They were aware that attempts to brand it anti-Semitic had failed miserably, and they also knew that the "too violent" tag wasn't catching either. So they decided to label it "pornographic" and "sadomasochistic," as if they really had a principled problem with, either.

Best of all was Jami Bernard of the New York *Daily News*. She had previously expressed her love for *Quills* (the film about the S&M hero the Marquis de Sade) but branded Mel's movie "a compendium of tortures that would horrify the regulars at an S&M club" (what she had against violence was also strange given that she had voted *Gladiator* movie of the year in 2000).[48] Then there was Frank Rich of the *New York Times* who called the film "pornographic." Most embarrassing for Rich was the box office tally. On August 3, 2003, he said that "it's hard to imagine the movie being anything other than a flop in America." After a couple of weeks, the film was already grossing well in excess of $200 million.[49]

Father John Pawlikowski, director of the Catholic-Jewish Studies Program at the Catholic Theological Union, also looked foolish. He wrote that "Christians who react favorably to Gibson's film are shamefully evading their religious responsibilities." Thus did he indict Pope John Paul II, several leading Vatican officials, and many bishops throughout the world, all of whom embraced it, to say nothing of the millions of Catholics and Protestants worldwide who loved it. All because he felt snubbed by Mel for not letting him vet the script.[50] No sooner had Pawlikowski gone bonkers when Joaquin Navarro-Valls spoke for the Vatican. He called the movie "a cinematographic transcription of the Gospels. If it were anti-Semitic, the Gospels would also be so." To top it off, he said that the pope would have criticized the movie if it were bigoted against Jews, but, he declared, there is "nothing anti-Semitic about it."[51]

Also looking dumb were all those critics who claimed that the film would trigger violence against Jews. Not a single act of violence against Jews took place anywhere in the world. No one looked worse than Paula "when-the-violence-breaks-out" Fredriksen. When asked to explain how she could be so wrong, she insisted she was not wrong: she decided to simply redefine violence to constitute a "hostile environment." Still spinning, she said it was Mel's supporters who have "redefined violence" to exclude anything less than "dead bodies strewn everywhere."[52] Funny thing is, there *was* violence. It was directed at Dario D'Ambrosi, who played the burly, sadistic Roman soldier who took delight in whipping Jesus: he was cursed and spat upon in real life and his daughters were heckled at school.[53] Not exactly what Professor Paula had in mind.

Nothing demonstrated the pure hypocrisy of the critics more than their passivity to the story in the *New York Post* that reported how 20 detectives of the NYPD were ordered into theaters to monitor the movie. Had they been ordered into theaters to monitor an anti-Catholic film—to see if it might provoke a backlash against Catholics—all hell would have broken loose. In this regard, no one appeared less principled than the woman from the New York Civil Liberties Union to whom I spoke. After she got my press release on the detectives going into the theaters, she called wondering why I sent her a copy. I had to explain to her that I thought the NYCLU might be concerned about the "chilling effect" this police action entailed. She was slightly amused, acknowledged that I had a point, and then said it was proper for the police to assess whether the film might promote violence![54]

Mel's blockbuster was, of course, snubbed by the Hollywood establishment when it came time for the Oscars. Many media outlets reported on Hollywood's hatred of *The Passion*. As one Oscar campaign veteran put it, "a lot of older Academy voters, who are largely Jewish, refuse to even see this movie." Tom O'Neil, one of the most prominent students of the Oscars, described what happened when the film was being considered by the experts: "At this religious movie, there was more cussing and swearing by Oscar voters than has ever been seen in an Academy screening before." That said it all.[55] Hollywood would never forgive Mel for standing behind a movie it intentionally snubbed, and this was doubly true given that it proved to be a box office home run. Thus did he incur the wrath of the secularists.

The Da Vinci Code

In all likelihood, had Dan Brown never claimed that *The Da Vinci Code* was based on historical fact, the reaction to the movie version of his book would have been muted. Brown, however, was good at playing both sides of the street. While pitching the book as a novel, he also said it was historically true. For example, on June 9, 2003, Matt Lauer of the *Today* show asked him, "How much of this [the book] is based on reality in terms of things that actually occurred?" To which Brown said, "Absolutely all of it." It was this dishonesty that motivated me to write to the movie's director, Ron Howard, asking him to put a disclaimer at the beginning of the film noting that it is a work of fiction.[56]

This genre of mixing fact with fiction is intellectually dishonest. It had been done before by people like Alex Haley, who coined the term "faction" to describe *Roots* (he said it was a blend of fact and fiction) and by Oliver Stone (*JFK*) and Steven Spielberg (*Amistad*). Bad as they were, they were nothing when compared with the extraordinary claims that Dan Brown was making. Given all this, it seemed absolutely reasonable to request a disclaimer in the film. Both Sony and Howard, it should be noted, had previously inserted disclaimers in their movies.

The debate over whether the film was anti-Catholic ended long before it opened. In August 2005, nine months before Howard's adaptation debuted, John Calley, one of the coproducers of the movie, admitted that the film was "conservatively anti-Catholic."[57] It should be obvious that there is not a single producer in all of Hollywood who would brag about his association with a racist, anti-gay, or anti-Semitic movie. But when it comes to Catholic bashing, it is perfectly legitimate to boast about it.

The Da Vinci Code was more than anti-Catholic—it was littered with lies. The biggest of them all was the one that claimed that the divinity of Jesus was made up out of whole cloth in

325 at the Council of Nicaea. It fact, there are 25 references to the divinity of Christ in the Gospels and more than 40 references in the New Testament. Not only that, the letters of Paul were written in the 40s and 50s—earlier than the Gospels. All of these writings are much closer to the time of Jesus than the so-called Gnostic Gospels, and even those books—which were excluded from the New Testament—regard Jesus to be the Son of God.

If Constantine concocted the idea that Jesus was divine in the fourth century, then how does one explain the Apostles' Creed in the second century? After all, it explicitly mentions the divinity of Jesus. Brown said Constantine decided which books to include in the New Testament when, in fact, he had nothing to do with it. Indeed, the Council of Nicaea never addressed this issue. The question was how to understand Jesus' divinity, not whether he was divine. Was Jesus the first being created by God (as erroneously assumed by a priest named Arius), or was He coeternal with God the Father? As Christians everywhere now believe, Jesus was begotten, not made.

Another fiction was the one which posited that Jesus married Mary Magdalene. There is absolutely no evidence to support this position. Brown said it would be highly unlikely for a Jewish man to be celibate, but again he was wrong. We know that Paul the Apostle was celibate, as was John the Baptist. Indeed, so were the Essenes, the Jews who produced the Dead Sea Scrolls. Speaking of which, Brown contended that the Dead Sea Scrolls imported new information about Jesus, when in fact they never mention him.

Throughout his book, Brown tells us about the evil machinations of the Vatican and how it consolidated its power base under Constantine. But there was no Vatican in the fourth century—it didn't exist until the fourteenth century. The book also claims that witch burning led to 5 million women being killed by the Catholic Church, but the number that most scholars accept is somewhere between 30 and 50 thousand. Not all were women and, more important, most were killed by civil authorities, not the Catholic Church.[58]

In other words, the movie was based on a book that was a malicious fraud. Even *60 Minutes*, hardly an arm of the Catholic Church, took the book apart just a few weeks before the film debuted. Ed Bradley put the definitive question to Bill Putnam, an author who investigated the book's thesis. Putnam was asked, "When you look at the list of hoaxes that have been perpetrated throughout history, where would you place this one?" He replied, "At the top."[59]

What places this film in the category of secular sabotage is threefold: a fable that smears Christianity is marketed as fact; the plot is a frontal assault on Christianity; and a producer admits that the film is anti-Catholic. Each aspect, standing by itself, is disturbing enough, but when they are spliced together, the outcome smacks of bigotry.

The Golden Compass

There is no debate about Philip Pullman's qualifications for entry into the Secular Sabotage Hall of Fame—he practically begs to join.

Pullman is regarded as one of England's great storytellers. He is also known as one of England's most outspoken atheists. Indeed, his real talent is pitching atheism to kids. That is what he did so successfully with his trilogy *His Dark Materials*. All of his books teach children the virtues of atheism and the evils of Christianity, especially Roman Catholicism, and in each successive volume the hostility becomes more palpable. Pullman made his biggest splash when *The Golden Compass* debuted on the big screen in 2007; it was based on the first volume of his series.

Kiera McCaffrey of the Catholic League offered a good summary of Pullman's works: "Though much of Pullman's trilogy involves kid-pleasing romps through mystical worlds with talking animals and magical witches, the underlying theme is no simple fantasy. In the fictional universe of *His Dark Materials*, there is no real God; rather there is a high angel called the Authority, who purports to be God. The Church does the bidding of the Authority, repressing physical pleasure and subverting the will and wisdom of the people."[60]

Several months before the film opened on December 7, 2007, it was evident that the movie version was being toned down so as not to anger Christians. The concern of the Catholic League was that unsuspecting parents might take their children to see *The Golden Compass* and then buy the trilogy for them, perhaps as a Christmas gift. The movie, we argued, was "bait for the book." In a nation that is overwhelmingly Christian, it was not likely that most parents would intentionally choose to introduce their kids to the wonders of atheism and the horrors of Christianity, especially at Christmas. Which is why the Catholic League published a booklet unmasking Pullman's agenda.

The duplicity of those associated with the movie easily rivaled Dan Brown's. Pullman, for example, when put on the defensive about his real goal, said "my main quarrel has always been with the literalist, fundamentalist nature of absolute power, whether it's manifested in the religious police state of Saudi Arabia or the atheist police state of Soviet Russia."[61] This is simply dishonest. Pullman did not choose the politburo as the evil empire—he deliberately chose the magisterium, the official teaching body of the Catholic Church. That is why his books are sprinkled with such Catholic terms as "pope" and "cardinal." It was not just any ideology or institution that Pullman was smearing, it was Catholicism.

Pullman's hostility is easily documented. Here are a few of his more famous chestnuts: "I'm trying to undermine the basis of Christian belief"; "Give them [the Catholic Church] half a chance and they would be burning the heretics"; "I am all for the death of God"; "My books are about killing God"; and so on.[62]

One astute critic of Pullman's books, Mark Hadley, spoke with candor when he said that the author "may prove to be to children's literature what Richard Dawkins is to science. Both of their writings express a negative opinion of Christianity and its institutions that falls little short of hatred." Another Brit, Peter Hitchens, brother and ideological nemesis of Christopher Hitchens, went further: "The atheists have driven God out of the classroom and off the TV and the radio, and done a pretty good job of expelling him from the churches as well. But one stubborn pocket of Christianity survives, in the Narnia stories of C. S. Lewis." Hitchens is right about this. "I loathe the Narnia books," Pullman has said. "I hate them with a deep and bitter passion, with their view of childhood as a golden age from which sexuality and adulthood are a falling away," he adds. In fact, Pullman considers the Narnia series "one of the most ugly and poisonous things I've ever read."[63]

But nothing could be more poisonous than trying to seduce youth into believing the worst about Christianity. At least Christopher Hitchens is honest—he loathes all religions equally and he does so unabashedly. By contrast, there is something unethical about trying to sneak atheism in the back door, as Pullman has done.

It was the deceitful stealth campaign associated with the movie that impelled the Catholic League to call for a boycott of the movie. The producers, New Line Cinema and Scholastic Entertainment (an arm of the mega-publisher of elementary and secondary school materials, Scholastic), tried to lowball the anti-Christian themes of Pullman's work, hoping to make a quick buck off the uninformed. But few were fooled in the end. Just before the film opened, Hanna Rosin wrote in the *At-*

lantic Monthly that Pullman's books were "antireligious" and "subversive."[64]

The Golden Compass was supposed to be the new *Lord of the Rings* or *Chronicles of Narnia.* But it made a mere $25.8 million its opening weekend and an even paltrier $9 million the following weekend. Contrast this with three other holiday movies in 2007: *Enchanted* made $34 million its first weekend; *I Am Legend* pulled in $77.2 million; and *Alvin and the Chipmunks* raked in $45 million. In other words, the boycott worked.[65] Even Pullman conceded that the campaign against *The Golden Compass* was a success: "I've no doubt to say it did influence a number of people not to go to see it." Indeed, Pullman admitted that the scheduled film release of *The Subtle Knife*, the second work of his trilogy, was not going to happen in 2009.[66]

One of the most embarrassing aspects of this controversy was the laudatory review the movie received from the Office for Film and Broadcasting of the bishops' conference, the USCCB. Written by the office's director, Harry Forbes, and an associate, the review completely sidestepped the anti-Catholic nature of the movie and the book upon which it was based. Forbes actually said that Pullman's use of the term "magisterium" was "a bit unfortunate," thus evincing a stunning cluelessness. There was nothing "unfortunate" about it—Pullman chose that term because he wanted to slam the Church. In any event, when American bishops were being inundated with complaints, Forbes had to pull his piece from the USCCB's Web site.[67]

Angels & Demons

Dan Brown and Ron Howard are quite a tag team. After exploiting Catholicism in *The Da Vinci Code,* they were back in

2009 with *Angels & Demons*. It proved to be more demonic than angelic.

Brown's defenders went back to their talking points, saying he was a novelist and no one should take what he says seriously. But Brown's stock in trade is to mix fact with fiction, and Howard has certainly proven to be a great student of the master. They take real-life characters, such as Copernicus and Galileo; and real-life organizations, such as the Illuminati; and real-life issues, such as science and religion, and blow them to smithereens.

Dan Brown is a master of disinformation. In other words, he knows what the historical record says, and yet he misrepresents it. Worse, he seems to do so with malice: his distortion of the truth smears the Catholic Church. His readers are left to believe that the Catholic Church sees science as the enemy, an accusation that is as baseless as it is scurrilous.

Brown begins with a "Fact" page that mentions CERN, the European Organization for Nuclear Research. He distorts the truth so badly about this organization that it was forced to put several pages on its Web site setting the record straight. More important, Brown says on the very next page that "The brotherhood of the Illuminati is also factual." And what are the Illuminati up to? In the novel it says that "the Illuminati were hunted ruthlessly by the Catholic Church." In the movie, Tom Hanks, who plays the protaganist, Harvard professor Robert Langdon, says that "The Catholic Church ordered a brutal massacre to silence them forever. They've come for their revenge."[68]

All of this is nonsense. Not a single member of the Illuminati was ever hunted, much less killed, by the Catholic Church. Exactly who the Illuminati were shows how bogus Brown's claims are.

In the novel, Brown says the Illuminati were founded in the 1500s; the movie says the same. The book also says that "Word of Galileo's brotherhood started to spread in the 1630s, and scientists from around the world made secret pilgrimages to Rome hoping to join the Illuminati." The film's director, Ron Howard, concurs: "The Illuminati were formed in the 1600s. They were artists and scientists like Galileo and Bernini, whose progressive ideas threatened the Vatican."

Brown, on his Web site, hammers this point home: "It is *a historical fact* that the Illuminati vowed vengeance against the Vatican in the 1600s. The early Illuminati—those of Galileo's day—were expelled from Rome by the Vatican and hunted mercilessly" (my italics).

This kind of libel is easy to disprove. The Illuminati were founded by a law professor, Adam Weishaupt, in Bavaria on May 1, 1776. This isn't a matter of dispute. So dragging Galileo into this fable is totally irresponsible—he died in 1642, almost a century and a half before the Illuminati were founded. Brown must know all this because on his own Web site there is a section on the Illuminati that correctly identifies the group's founding in 1776.

Brown says that the goal of the Illuminati is to create "A New World Order based on scientific enlightenment." This puts him in some choice company. No one in the twentieth century promoted this Illuminati "New World Order" thesis more than Robert Welch, founder of the John Birch Society. In recent years, it has become a favorite notion of people such as Protestant leader Tim LaHaye.

Conspiratorialists believe that the Illuminati were behind everything from the French Revolution to 9/11; they assassinated as many as a half-dozen American presidents, as well as Princess Diana; they somehow managed to give us both AIDS and Hurricane Katrina; and now Brown says they tried to blow up the Vatican. Not bad for an organization that collapsed in 1787.

Just as preposterous, but much more pernicious, is Brown's portrayal of the Catholic Church as antiscience. Nothing could be further from the truth. Just who does he think was responsible for keeping the universities afloat in Europe in the Middle Ages?

"For the last fifty years," says professor Thomas E. Woods, Jr., "virtually all historians of science . . . have concluded that the Scientific Revolution was indebted to the Church." J. L. Heilborn of the University of California at Berkeley writes that "The Roman Catholic Church gave more financial aid and social support to the study of astronomy for over six centuries, from the recovery of ancient learning during the late Middle Ages into the Enlightenment, than any other, and, probably, all other institutions."[69] The scientific achievements of the Jesuits alone reached every corner of the earth.

What was it about Catholicism that made it so science-friendly, and why did science take root in Europe and not someplace else? Baylor sociologist Rodney Stark knows why: "Because Christianity depicted God as a rational, responsive, dependable, and omnipotent being, and the universe as his personal creation. The natural world was thus understood to have a rational, lawful, stable structure, awaiting (indeed, inviting) human comprehension."[70]

But Brown will have none of it. In his mind, the Catholic Church is fearful of science and has always tried to repress it. It would be interesting to know how he would explain the fact that the first leader of the Vatican's Pontifical Academy of Sciences was none other than his favorite "martyr," Galileo Galilei.

What got Galileo into trouble was less his ideas than his arrogance: he made claims that he could not *scientifically* sustain. Copernicus, also a Catholic, never got in trouble for hypothesizing that the earth revolved around the sun. And neither did scientists like Father Roger Boscovich: he continued to explore Copernican ideas at the same time Galileo was sentenced to house arrest (the Church erred in its punitive approach, but it needs to be stressed that Galileo was never tortured or imprisoned, as many contend). The difference is that Galileo, who was initially showered with awards by two popes, refused to state his theories as mathematical propositions; even the scientists of his day knew he didn't have the kind of evidence he purported to have.

"It's certainly not anti-Catholic." That's how Brown characterizes his book. So was the Vatican wrong to bar the film crew from shooting on its grounds? The Vatican took that step because it properly regarded Brown's other movie, *The Da Vinci Code*, to be a patently unfair presentation of Catholicism.

Recall that before *The Da Vinci Code* was released, coproducer John Calley admitted to the *New York Times* that the movie was "conservatively anti-Catholic." How telling it was, then, that the *New York Times* reported that coproducer Brian Grazer said he wanted the movie version of *Angels & Demons* "to be less reverential than 'The Da Vinci Code.'" That about seals it. The final nail in the coffin was unwittingly offered by the movie crew of *Angels & Demons*.

Father Bernard O'Connor is a Canadian priest and an official with the Vatican's Congregation for Eastern Churches. In 2008 he was in Rome while director Ron Howard was shooting the movie. O'Connor had two encounters with the film crew, informal discussions with about 20 of them. He was dressed casually so no one knew he was a priest. They spoke openly, thinking he was just "an amiable tourist." He wrote an article about his experiences for the monthly magazine *Inside the Vatican*.

One self-described "production official" opined, "The wretched Church is against us yet again and is making problems." Then, speaking of his friend Dan Brown, he offered, "Like most of us, he often says that he would do anything to demolish that detestable institution, the Catholic Church. And we will triumph. You will see." When Father O'Connor asked him to clarify his remarks, the production official said, "Within a generation there will be no more Catholic Church, at least not in

Western Europe. And really the media deserves to take much of the credit for its demise."

This should put to rest all reservations about the real intent of at least some in the media—their goal is to weaken, if not totally disable, the Catholic Church. They do not point their guns at Islam or Judaism. It's the Catholic Church they want to sunder. It also makes nonsensical any attempt by apologists for Brown and Howard not to dub them secular saboteurs of the first order.

"The public is finally getting our message," boasted the movie official. The message was clearly defined: "The Catholic Church must be weakened and eventually it must disappear from the earth. It is humanity's chief enemy. This has always been the case." He credited "radio, television, Hollywood, the music and video industries, along with just about every newspaper which exists, all saying the same thing." He also cited the role that colleges and universities have played in undermining Catholicism.

After Father O'Connor's article was published, I contacted him about a few issues. I wanted to know how he approached the crew, who they were, and how he could verify his comments.

"I wanted frankness from a variety of people," he told me. "Technicians, film crew, extras, anyone who came by the coffee bars(s) adjacent to Via della Conciliazione." He said he "sort of 'hung out' there" for a couple of afternoons. All but one of those to whom he spoke were male, and "the ages varied between early thirties and late fifties." He said the comments he heard were "almost entirely negative." As soon as he got back to his apartment, he started jotting down what he heard.[71]

Hollywood would never make a movie about the *Protocols of the Elders of Zion*, and it wouldn't matter a whit if it was made on the grounds that it was nothing but fiction. What would matter is that a film version of this slanderous anti-Jewish tract might promote intolerance.

The secular sabotage of American society that Hollywood has contributed to is motivated by a deep-seated hostility to the nation's Judeo-Christian ethos. Those who think it can all be explained by profit are mistaken. Surely there is a market for movies that bash blacks, Jews, and gays, but don't look for Hollywood to start churning them out. The protests would be far too loud. Money matters, but often it is ideology, not cash, that proves controlling in the end.

CHAPTER 6

Sabotaged by Lawyers

Perverting the First Amendment

The secular assault on Christianity carried out by activist groups and sympathetic judges represents nothing short of a bastardization of the intent of the Framers: just as the secular left likes to play fast and loose with Scripture, they also like to play fast and loose with the Constitution. Fidelity to the original text means nothing to ideologues bent on winning at all costs. Their goal is a wholesale reordering of the First Amendment, the purpose of which is to weaken the public role that Christianity has historically played.

How did we arrive at the point where it is taken for granted—mistakenly so—that the First Amendment can be invoked to stop a schoolchild from singing "Silent Night" at a "holiday" concert? Similarly, how did we get to the point where a Bible study and prayer meeting for New York City residents who lost loved ones on 9/11 was banned because the rented room was in a public housing development? Examples like these—and there is an endless list of them—convinced David Limbaugh to conclude that we have reached "new heights of absurdity."[1]

Absurd though these examples are, their roots lie in bigotry and the agenda of the secular saboteurs. Philip Hamburger's

Separation of Church and State is already a classic in constitutional jurisprudence, and it is his conclusion that "the separation of church and state became popular mostly as an anti-Catholic and more broadly antiecclesiastical conception of religious liberty."[2] But according to the gospel of the secularists, it was Thomas Jefferson who gave us this concept. They cite, among other things, Jefferson's refusal to honor the tradition of Washington and Adams of issuing a proclamation for days of "fasting and thanksgiving."

In 1808, Jefferson wrote a letter to a Presbyterian minister and Princeton professor explaining why he resisted this tradition. He maintained that when he served in state offices—as a Virginia legislator and as governor—he supported state laws allowing for public fasts and thanksgiving. But as president of the United States, he did not think it appropriate to use the powers of the federal government in this manner. In other words, he was expressing his republican convictions.

Secularists who say that Jefferson was somehow hostile, or even indifferent, to religion's role in society are pitching pure propaganda. Literally two days after he penned his "separation of church and state" metaphor (contained in a letter to Danbury Baptists in 1802), he attended church services in a government building, the Capitol, for the first time as president. This was no accident: he was intentionally making a public statement rebutting the accusation that he was some sort of heretic. And if Jefferson were the secularist that today's saboteurs try to make him out to be, then how do they explain the fact that he provided federal funds for the building of a Catholic church for the Kaskaskias Indians?[3] Today, Catholics who send their kids to parochial schools can't get money for maps, never mind funds to build a church.

Hamburger's contention about the anti-Catholic roots of church-state separation is verified by examining how Jefferson's metaphor became law. It wasn't until after World War

II, in the 1947 *Everson v. Indiana* decision, that this concept took hold. Justice Hugo Black, writing for the majority, declared that what had been understood from the time of the Founders was wrong: it was wrong to dispense federal funds even when there was no government favoritism, not simply in cases of preferential treatment. It was Black who said there was an impregnable "wall" between church and state, one that even barred government from supporting all religions equally. So where's the anti-Catholic bias? It's not in the wording—it's in Black's motivation.

During the 1920s, Black was a member of the Ku Klux Klan in Birmingham, Alabama. Unlike those Klansmen who primarily hated African Americans, Black's hatred was directed toward Catholics. In his first Alabama Senate race, his campaign manager bragged that "Hugo could make the best anti-Catholic speech you ever heard." No wonder he was active in drumming up anti-Catholic sentiment against Al Smith when the Catholic New Yorker ran for president in 1928.[4] Even Black's son admits to his bigotry: "The Ku Klux Klan and Daddy, so far as I can tell, only had one thing in common. He suspected the Catholic Church. He used to read all of Paul Blanshard's books exposing abuse in the Catholic Church."[5] The "abuse" he was referring to was the tax-exempt status of the Catholic Church—the same legally granted right exercised by Protestant churches. And like the notorious anti-Catholic bigot Blanshard, Hugo Black was obsessed with the alleged power of the pope to affect public policy decisions in the United States.

Black's influence on the *Everson* decision, and Blanshard's influence on him, were rendered at the same time that anti-Catholicism was considered sport. "In the late 1940s—when the U.S. Supreme Court would eventually establish separation as a First Amendment freedom," writes Hamburger, "many Protestants were participating in yet another surge of anti-Catholicism."[6] Indeed, it was a time when Blanshard's hate-filled book *Ameri-*

can Freedom and Catholic Power became a best seller; it went through six printings and sold 250,000 copies.

Blanshard's book was actually a series of articles he wrote for the *Nation*, a left-wing magazine that was as anti-American as it was anti-Catholic (it still is). In the book, he trotted out the old canard about "dual loyalties," i.e., unsubstantiated charges that American Catholics owed their primary loyalty to the pope. What made Blanshard's work so different from the nativistic publications of the nineteenth century was its polished appearance: it was anti-Catholicism made respectable for the literati.

John Dewey loved Blanshard's work—it didn't make him feel like a bigot. As Hamburger says, "Blanshard gave old fears a thoroughly modern cast by exploring the growing worries of political liberals that Catholicism impeded modern social policy."[7] Indeed, he told the public about the "Catholic Plan for America," a scheme that included "seizing the government, repealing the First Amendment, outlawing divorce and making the pope the president's official superior."[8] Only left-wing intellectuals and the institutionalized have an imagination so fertile as to believe such rubbish.

Once Black prevailed in his "wall of separation" opinion, it led the courts to become increasingly hostile to religious liberty. This hostility was given a new shot in the arm in the high court's 1971 *Lemon v. Kurtzman* ruling. This decision held that for a statute governing religious liberty to pass constitutional muster, it must have a secular purpose, must not advance or inhibit religion, and must not foster "excessive government entanglement with religion." As Robert Bork sees it, "So few statutes or governmental practices that brush anywhere near religion can pass all of those tests that, were they uniformly applied, they would erase all traces of religion in governmental affairs." Bork makes the point that the only reason this hasn't happened is because "there are too many entrenched traditions around for *Lemon* to be applied consistently."[9]

Like its predecessor *Everson*, the *Lemon* decision was rooted in bigotry. As Notre Dame's John McGreevey notes, "Justice William O. Douglas broke new ground in his concurring opinion with a favorable citation to a 1962 anti-Catholic tract, Loraine Boettner's *Roman Catholicism*"; the book made the familiar argument that Catholic kids were so "indoctrinated" that they could not think independently.[10]

What made the *Lemon* ruling so invidious was what happened three years earlier. In *Flast v. Cohen*, the high court made an exception to orthodox jurisprudence regarding "standing." This doctrine maintains that before someone can sue he must show how he was directly burdened. The exception made by the Supreme Court applied only to so-called establishment cases: in these instances just being a taxpayer was now declared sufficient grounds to sue. The result has been destructive to religious liberty. Every provision in the Constitution, as Bork has written, "is immune from taxpayer or citizen enforcement—except one. Only under the establishment clause is an ideological interest in expunging religion sufficient to confer standing."[11] So when the *Lemon* decision was made, it was a home run for those out to scrub society free from religious expression.

Lemon made it exceedingly difficult for cases involving the public expression of religion to pass constitutional muster. In the wake of raising the bar so high, towns were told they could not have a nativity scene displayed on public property without a reindeer. Similarly, the parents of children who had been receiving remedial education from public school teachers in a parochial school—for two decades without a single complaint—were suddenly informed that this practice violated the Constitution. Even candy canes with religious messages had to be confiscated lest some secular saboteur object.

To make matters worse, not only have the courts chopped the religious liberty clause in two, assigning a subordinate position to the free exercise provision, they have assigned a subordinate position to religious speech vis-à-vis secular speech. For example, the courts typically grant constitutional protection to obscene speech—including obscenities that target religion—but they quickly become censorial when it comes to religious speech. So absurd has this condition become that the student who spews vulgarities in a high school commencement address has a much better chance of proceeding with impunity than the student who invokes the name of Jesus. Indeed, a student who curses Jesus has a better chance of escaping the wrath of school officials than the student who quotes Jesus.

When secularists find that history gives little or no support to their agenda, they do not seek to ignore it as much as they attempt to reconstruct it. Few are better at this game than Susan Jacoby, author of *Freethinkers: A History of American Secularism*. Influenced by her hero, the nineteenth-century agnostic Robert Ingersoll, Jacoby would have us believe that the Founders were more interested in separation of church and state than they were in religious liberty. In making her case, she entertains the fiction (one that is now taken as truth by the nation's most influential constitutional law professors) that there are two clauses in the First Amendment: a religious liberty clause and its alleged opposite, the establishment clause.

John Noonan is one constitutional scholar who hasn't accepted this nonsense. His dissection of the First Amendment is impeccable: "There are no clauses in the constitutional provision. Clauses have a subject and a predicate. This provision has a single subject, a single verb, and two prepositional phrases."[12] Therefore, no calculated disharmony between religious liberty and the establishment of religion was ever contemplated. Regarding the establishment provision, we know from the author of the First Amendment, James Madison, that it was his intent to prohibit the Congress from establishing a national church and to prohibit the federal government from showing favoritism of one religion over another; what the states decided was their business. Furthermore, the reference to the "free exercise" of religion was clearly meant by Madison to insulate religion from the state. Neither he nor any of the Founders sought to insulate society from religion; just the opposite.

University of South Dakota law professor Patrick M. Garry sees through this muddle. Under the current view, Garry instructs, "the exercise and establishment clauses [are] seen as being 'at war with each other,' with the exercise clause conferring benefits on religion and the establishment clause imposing burdens."[13] He wryly notes that "It was as if the Framers had intended two clauses to cancel each other out, producing a kind of zero-sum result with regard to religion." He adds that "such an approach makes no textual sense, because the exercise clause is essentially being nullified by the establishment clause."[14] In other words, such reasoning has resulted in a form of judicial jujitsu.[15]

Garry is correct to say that "there is no constitutional basis for interpreting the establishment clause as contradictory to the exercise clause," and that is why he sees them forming "a single, unified religion clause that seeks exclusively to protect religious liberty." He aptly quotes Michael Paulson to the effect that the establishment clause "prohibits the use of the coercive power of the state to *prescribe* religious exercise, while the exercise clause prohibits the use of government compulsion to *proscribe* religious exercise."[16]

"Textually," says Patrick Garry, "the Constitution provides greater protection for religious practices than for any secular-belief-related activities."[17] In fact, he contends, not only is religious speech afforded protection via the free exercise provision, it receives further immunity via the free speech clause of the First Amendment. It is precisely because Garry is so right about this that it is positively maddening to read court decisions that allow the establishment provision to trump religious speech. Such revisionism has created more than a legal nightmare. Its tentacles stretch to the nucleus of our culture: the public expression of religion has atrophied under the weight of judicial activism.

Activists Declare War on Religion

When the Constitution was written, crèches were permitted on public property and blasphemy was punishable by death. Now we've banned the crèches and provided public funding for blasphemy (e.g., the National Endowment for the Arts supported Serrano's *Piss Christ*). This inversion has much to do with a profound shift in the tastes of the cultural elite and the tenor of contemporary legal arguments. No organization has had more to do with facilitating this change than the American Civil Liberties Union.

Founded in 1920, the ACLU has from the very beginning been hostile to religious expression. Indeed, in its first annual report, it listed its defense of every First Amendment freedom—speech, press, and assembly—except for freedom of religion. Fixated on church-state issues, the ACLU has had much to say about paring back religion's role in society, but precious little about its free exercise. That's because the ACLU actually fears religion. This is a strong statement, but it can easily be backed up by simply considering an exchange I had with the founder of the ACLU, Roger Baldwin.

In 1978, I interviewed Baldwin in his home in New York City. One of the questions I asked was why the ACLU is opposed to a moment of silence in the classroom. If a child voluntarily prays, I asked, whose rights are being infringed upon? I then asked, "Are you afraid they are going to proselytize the rest of the class?" To which he responded, "Well, they tried to get around it. They've tried to get around it even further than you by calling it meditation." I couldn't help but question, "What's wrong with that?" His answer was unnerving: "You don't say anything about God or religion or anything. I suppose you can get by with that but it's a subterfuge, *because the implication is that you're meditating about the hereafter or God or something,*"[18] (my emphasis). It makes me wonder what Baldwin and his ilk would do if they had the technological means to monitor thought.

The ACLU can protest all it wants that it is not anti-Christian or antireligion, but its record suggests otherwise. Consider what it regards as unconstitutional: the right of churches, synagogues, and all houses of worship to be tax-exempt; prayer, including voluntary prayer, in the schools; release time, the practice whereby public school children are released early so that they may attend religious instruction; shared time, the practice whereby parochial school children in need of remedial instruction (most are poor and nonwhite) are afforded remedial work by public school teachers in the parochial schools; religious invocation at graduation ceremonies; the right of religious foster-care institutions that receive municipal funding to select and teach the children according to their own precepts; the right of religious day-care institutions to receive federal funding even when the institutions agree neither to teach about religion or to display any religious symbol; and the right of Congress to maintain its chaplains.[19]

Some of what the ACLU objects to borders on the insane. For example, it objects to all of the following: public school performances of the play *Jesus Christ Superstar*; the distribution of Gideon Bibles on public school grounds; the inscription "In God We Trust" on coins; the words "under God" in the Pledge of Allegiance; the right of a nun to wear a habit while teaching in a public school (even if she is teaching math); the right of students to sing "Silent Night" at a school concert; the right of city employees to have a Christmas event at a local zoo; and the existence of a nine-foot statute of Jesus Christ located three miles off the coast of Key Largo.[20] When it comes to Muslims, however, the ACLU thinks it is okay for Muslim women to leave their veil on when getting photographed for their driver's license.[21] In other words, anything that disables American society sits well with the ACLU.

Why is the ACLU so nervous about religion? It is impossible to answer this question without referencing its impoverished vision of liberty. To the ACLU, individual rights equal freedom. It further believes that rights emanate from the state, not from God. Add to this the conviction that religion is an obstacle to the reach of government (which it is), and it becomes clear that religion is a problem. To civil libertarians, freedom is measured, at least in part, by the extent to which society represses the public expression of religion. In any event, when the "guardians of liberty" find the time and passion to protest a statue of Jesus on the ocean floor, it is clear that Christianity scares the hell out of them.

If the ACLU has been beating up on Christianity longer than any other organization, no group has been more single-minded about doing so than Americans United for Separation of Church and State. Just as radical as the ACLU, Americans United has the luxury of spending all of its financial and human resources on squashing the public expression of religion. It really loathes Christianity, and its current fixation on evangelicals has replaced Catholicism as its favorite whipping boy.

It was right at the time of the *Everson* decision in 1947, and Blanshard's best-selling screed against Catholicism, that the bigots were mobilized to do something about the Catholic menace. The result was the founding of Protestants and Other Americans United for Separation of Church and State (POAU), an organization that Blanshard sank his teeth into from the beginning. Its first executive director, Dr. Glenn L. Archer, took command in 1948; he held this post until he retired in 1976. When he died in 2002, Barry Lynn, the current director, heralded Archer as "a strong defender of religious liberty through separation of church and state."[22] Notice that Lynn was unable to say that it was Archer's staunch defense of the free exercise of religion that made him so great. That is why Lynn opted for the clumsy construction about defending religious liberty "through" church and state separation.

Lynn conveniently chose not to mention that it was under Archer's tutelage that the Roman Catholic hierarchy was dubbed "more dangerous and clever than communism."[23] This is a rather strange construction itself given that POAU, as Charles Morris put it, "tended to take an extremely benign view of the Soviet Union."[24] What makes Archer's remark really revolting is the fact that he said this after Stalin had murdered tens of millions of his own people, starving the Ukrainians to death in the world's first man-made famine. Furthermore, it was Archer who petitioned the Federal Communications Committee to deny TV licenses to Jesuits, claiming they were an "alien organization." Archer also demanded that Catholic cardinals have their citizenship revoked. And it was Archer who asked the House Un-American Activities Committee to investigate "the intentions, scope and achievements of Vatican espionage here," charging that the Catholic clergy had learned "American secrets hardly anyone except the president knows."[25]

Americans United tries hard to put a shiny gloss on its bigoted roots, but it fails miserably. For example, when George Washington University law professor Jeffrey Rosen wrote a searing article in the *New York Times Magazine* about religion in public life, he set off the alarms at Lynn's organization by referencing the ignoble beginnings of POAU.[26] Americans United immediately responded by issuing a lengthy rebuttal, accusing Rosen of taking "a cheap shot." The cheap shot, it said, was "implying that the group was anti-Catholic because it opposed the political goals of the Roman Catholic Church in the 1940s and '50s." Showcasing its ability to spin, it said, "Americans United did strongly oppose some of the political activities of the Catholic Church during this period, but its opposition was to the church's *political* efforts, not the church itself, its members or its theology"[27] (its italics). Is that why POAU circulated a bogus Knights of Columbus Oath, a revision of a nineteenth-century anti-Jesuit forgery, blaming lay Catholics for committing atrocities against Protestants?[28]

Americans United entertains an extremist interpretation of

the First Amendment. The Framers never expected religion to be privatized, nor did they seek to curb religion's role in shaping morality. Yet over the Fourth of July weekend in 2008, Americans United downplayed religious liberty by flagging on the home page of its Web site "Celebrate Separation of Church and State." It also ran an incredible video featuring actress Catherine Dent. She explained why she couldn't share her religious beliefs with the public: "You see, it is not because I don't want you to know anything about me, but is because I don't know anything about you. I can't see your history. I can't see your beliefs. And what matters deeply to me could be an *intrusion* on what matters most to you"[29] (my emphasis). How thoughtful of her. This is more than spin—it is a revealing look at the mentality behind the secular assault on religion.

To accomplish its goal of attacking the public role of Christianity, Americans United has embarked on a secular mission that includes filing suit to ban prayers before evening meals at Virginia Military Institute;[30] blocking a bill authorizing federal funds to be spent in the restoration of Spanish missions in California (even though the bill was supported by liberals such as California Senator Barbara Boxer);[31] stopping the city of Las Cruces (Spanish for "the crosses") from using three Christian crosses in its logos;[32] and banning a portrait of Christ that had been in a West Virginia school for 37 years (a portrait of Buddha in the same school was found acceptable).[33]

Lynn, who is an amiable and capable debater, even objects to secular symbols associated with Christianity. He complains that Christmas trees are "a sign of religion," and that they may make a non-Christian "feel like a second-class citizen." Though no evidence is offered to support this preposterous assertion, Lynn opts for censorship and wants the trees banned from public property.[34]

So concerned is Reverend Lynn about the right of non-Christians that he sued the U.S. Department of Veteran Affairs for refusing to include Wiccan symbols on its list of officially recognized emblems for government headstones and markers.[35] So it's the witches who get the minister's attention, not Christians. What also gets his attention is singing "God Bless America" in a public building. Americans United, along with a team from Yale Divinity School, alleged in 2005 that the Air Force Academy was creating an oppressive atmosphere for non-Christians when it allowed the singing of "God Bless America."[36] Hope they take my advice and stay away from New York Yankee games: Kate Smith's "God Bless America" is played during the seventh-inning stretch at every game, and the new Yankee Stadium was built partially with tax-exempt bonds.

In 2009, Americans United showed its true colors when it refused to condemn a proposed takeover of the Catholic Church's financial affairs by the state of Connecticut. After Catholics rallied and forced the withdrawal of a bill that would have done just that, the best Americans United could say was that the legislation was "misguided." In fact, communications associate Sandhya Bathija took the opportunity to lecture the Church about its alleged hypocrisy, noting the Church's opposition to gay marriage.[37] But had a bill been proposed granting the bishops the authority to police the state budget, Americans United, for positively good reasons, would have gone mad. In short, its alleged concern about separation of church and state really cuts one way.

It is for reasons like this that Morgan Bergman, a researcher who did an in-depth report on Americans United, concluded: "By trampling on the constitutional rights of Americans to practice their faith, Lynn and his merry band of zealots weaken the American traditions of tolerance and free expression they claim to profess."[38]

Secularists Unmasked

None of the antireligious organizations will admit that their real agenda is to drive religion from the public square and to weaken it in general. They prefer to hide behind a professed loyalty to the First Amendment. But their real motives are not hard to discern.

If fidelity to the First Amendment is what counts, how does one explain why the ACLU, the ADL, and American Atheists have a huge problem with a nativity scene on public property but not a menorah?[39] When questioned about the disparate treatment, ACLU attorney Deborah Lieberman spun the issue by saying the menorah was small in size and located in an inconspicuous spot.[40] It's a sure bet, however, that the ACLU would object to a miniature nativity scene placed behind a tree. Americans United is just as slippery.

In 2000, a pornographic homosexual film festival, Reel Affirmations X, was held in Washington, D.C. Among the sponsors was Americans United. When asked what this had to do with its mission, Lynn said, "We oftentimes lend support to organizations which have a constituency sympathetic to our goals and objectives."[41] In other words, those who promote gay porn are seen as sympathetic to the goals and objectives of Americans United. How telling. None of this is by happenstance: before Lynn took over at Americans United, he directed the Washington office of the ACLU, and one of his pet projects was to push for the legalization of pornography. Reverend Lynn even went so far as to defend the sale and distribution of child pornography, along with the rights of masochists.[42] Given this pedigree, it is hardly surprising to learn that Americans United is a big fan of gay marriage (not exactly a church and state issue, at least not yet).

The First Amendment does not apply to the private workplace, yet that didn't stop Americans United from blasting the Catholic League when it called for a boycott of Wal-Mart in

2005. The dispute was over the department store's neutering of Christmas that year and had absolutely nothing to do with separation of church and state. Hence, it should have been of no interest to Americans United. Yet a year after the short-lived boycott was triggered, Lynn was still burning mad: he said that when places like Wal-Mart "cave into these demands, they are really making a statement that non-Christians should probably go elsewhere this holiday season."[43] Evidently, it is simply not possible for Christians to celebrate anything without angering non-Christians. Either that, or the underlying assumption—that all non-Christians are bigots—is a contrived and phony excuse to assault Christianity.

Another giveaway is when the secular saboteurs get angry with groups like the Catholic League for exercising their First Amendment right to free speech. That is why People for the American Way was upset with the Catholic League's protest of *Corpus Christi*. Its rally in defense of the First Amendment was positively absurd. What exactly did it think the Catholic League's demonstration was all about?[44] A year later, the same group teamed up with American Atheists to condemn the Catholic League for protesting the Brooklyn Museum of Art exhibition that defiled Our Blessed Mother; American Atheists "lauded" the exhibition, blaming the Catholic League for being intrusive and acting as a "Vatican operative."[45] Not surprisingly, when *The Golden Compass* opened, American Atheists loved it.[46] They also loved it when Kathy Griffin shouted "Suck it, Jesus" at the Emmys.[47] In all of these cases, it is not the Catholic bashing that upsets the radical secularists, it's the fact that Catholics respond.

Even voluntary expressions of religion bother the saboteurs. When an elective Bible study course was offered in Odessa, Texas, in 2007, the ACLU and People for the American Way filed suit. The infraction? Religious indoctrination.[48] Similarly, when Florida Governor Jeb Bush launched a contest encouraging students to read the C. S. Lewis Christian allegory *The Lion, the Witch and the Wardrobe*, Americans United objected (*The Golden Compass* would have been fine).[49] If ailing veterans elect to access religious services, count on the Freedom From Religion Foundation to sue,[50] and bank on the same group to protest state government invocations, even when they are nondenominational, nonsectarian, and nonproselytizing.[51] Not only do school vouchers bother the ACLU, the ADL, Americans United, and People for the American Way, they object to the right of the voters to decide whether they want them; these groups filed suit trying to block a Florida referendum on this issue in 2008.[52]

What really gets the goat of these zealots is when a prominent politician references God or religion in public. So when George W. Bush said in his 2000 presidential campaign that Jesus was his favorite philosopher, People for the American Way demanded that he "explain why he picked [Jesus]."[53] The same group, and others, went after Senator Joseph Lieberman in 2000 when all the Democratic vice presidential candidate did was say that "there must be a place for faith in America's public life."[54] Following the logic of these secular extremists, the Founders were un-American.

When Bush mentioned God and religion in his second inaugural address, Barry Lynn accused the president of sending a message that "in order to be truly American, you must also be religious."[55] As a matter of fact, the weekend before Bush gave his address, the ACLU, Americans United, People for the American Way, Freedom From Religion Foundation, and many other radical secular groups held an "emergency meeting" in anticipation of Bush's remarks; the umbrella group that organized the strategy session was the American Humanist Association.[56]

There are occasions when the efforts of secularists to sabotage the United States become so indefensible that they actually serve to undermine their mission. Consider what happened after 9/11. After the House voted 404-0 urging public schools to display "God Bless America" posters, Lynn chastised the congressmen: "I think they have their priorities out of line."[57] What really drove the secular nihilists mad was the sight of steel beams in the shape of a Christian Cross that was left standing amid the World Trade Center rubble. When government officials decided to include the Cross as a permanent memorial at Ground Zero, American Atheists issued a news release calling it "insulting" to nonbelievers and pledged to fight the issue in court.[58] These people are obviously incapable of being shamed.

The actions of some secular activists are so depraved as to be beyond any reasonable defense. Any woman who would write a book titled *Abortion Is a Blessing* has disqualified herself from national discourse on this issue. The author, Anne Nicol Gaylor, founder of the Freedom From Religion Foundation, published her screed just two years after the *Roe v. Wade* decision. She was applauded by Gloria Steinem, Betty Friedan, and NARAL.[59] Her atheist organization has become increasingly aggressive in recent years, posting its antireligion message on billboards across America and displaying similar signs next to nativity scenes on state grounds.

Of all the persons involved in the secular sabotage of America, none is more infamous than Madalyn Murray O'Hair, the queen of American Atheists and another sexual libertine. Known mostly for getting prayer kicked out of the public schools, she ripped off her own members by absconding with more than $600,000 in the 1990s. The FBI revealed in 2001 that it had found the bones of her mutilated body.[60]

O'Hair's belief that "Religion is the most monstrous idea in the world"[61] was something she came to quite early in life: when she was about 12 or 13, she read the Bible "from cover to cover" in one weekend. That was it—she just knew it was a lie. It certainly had a profound effect on her own morality: "I will defecate and urinate when I damn well please and as the spirit—and the physical necessity—moves me." Even dogs know better. She also said, "I will engage in sexual activity with a consenting male any time and any place I damn well please."[62] The refrain "not in my backyard" never sounded more persuasive. In any event, when she is remembered by secularists like Alan Wolfe as being "dictatorial, irresponsible, racist, overbearing, corrupt, anti-Semitic, homophobic, anti-Catholic and at times criminal,"[63] then there really isn't much more that can be said to salvage her reputation.

Battle Over the Courts

The secularists have used and abused the law to get what they want, and much of their success is due to left-leaning judges who delight in writing the law, not interpreting it. But religious conservatives have struck back, alarming those who seek to use the courts as their favorite forum in the culture war. This issue spiked in 2005 when Tony Perkins, president of the Family Research Council, brought Catholics and Protestants together in Louisville for what was billed as "Justice Sunday." It was an event designed to mobilize Christians in an effort to secure fair treatment for traditional Catholics and evangelicals being considered for the federal bench. Speakers included Dr. James Dobson, Dr. Al Mohler, Bishop Harry R. Jackson, Charles Colson, and myself.

The secular left was predictably apoplectic. Reverend Jim Wallis led a protest of the event accusing the participants of instigating "a religious war."[64] Reverend Barry Lynn spoke with his usual restraint when he declared, "This is the closest thing to a civil war within the religious community that I've seen in the past 25 years."[65] Before a single speaker made his remarks, Frank Rich of the *New York Times* called the forum a "judge-bashing rally."[66]

We had such a good time in Louisville that Perkins called another "judge-bashing rally" in Nashville. I was particularly pleased that the *New York Times* ran an editorial denouncing my suggestion that the Supreme Court should be able to overturn a congressional enactment only by a unanimous vote. Actually, the idea (which the *Times* said was "terrible")[67] was first floated by Supreme Court Justice John Marshall in the early nineteenth century and was later advanced in the 1960s by New York University professor Sidney Hook (under whom I studied as an undergraduate).

The secular saboteurs are deathly afraid of losing the courts. Indeed, they will stop at nothing, including reaching into their portfolio of bigoted tricks. Consider what happened within 24 hours of the nomination of John Roberts to the Supreme Court by President Bush. Adele M. Stan of *The American Prospect* ran a piece in its online edition charging Bush with "Playing the Catholic Card." She had the audacity to say that Bush was "betting he's bought himself some insulation—any opposition to Roberts, particularly because of his anti-abortion record, will likely be countered with accusations of anti-Catholicism." She went even further than this on her blog when she said that "Rome must be smiling" at Bush's choice.[68]

Mario Cuomo was so bold that he said on *Meet the Press* that Roberts should be asked, "Are you going to impose a religious test on the Constitution? Are you going to say that because the pope says this or the Church says that, you will do it no matter what?" John MacArthur of *Harper's* put his elitist mind to work by dragging Roberts's wife into the matter: "The Roberts couple seem to be very well-educated; I wonder whether in their high-minded socializing with Clarence and Virginia Thomas (at the College of Holy Cross) and Robert and Mary Ellen Bork (at the lay Catholic John Carroll Society), they find time for informal book chat." Dahlia Lithwick, legal analyst for *Slate*, looked into her crystal ball: "And I wouldn't underestimate the influence of his religion, that Scalia and Thomas, one of the very reasons they may not have drifted leftward has a lot to do with very, very strong religious views that pull them to the right. And I think that probably John Roberts will fall into that camp in that sense."[69]

Catholic liberal E. J. Dionne said "it would be helpful if Roberts gave an account of how (and whether) his religious convictions would affect his decisions as a justice." Imagine Dionne asking a secularist whether his agnostic convictions would affect his decisions—it would never happen. Christopher Hitchens, my sparring buddy, proved once again his fondness for Catholics, at least orthodox ones: "If Roberts is confirmed there will be quite a bloc of Catholics on the court. Scalia, Kennedy, and Thomas are strong in the faith. Is it kosher to mention these things?" NPR's Nina Totenberg opined, "Don't forget his wife was an officer, a high officer of a pro-life organization." She then went in for the kill: "He's got adopted children. I mean, he's a conservative Catholic."[70] Adopted kids? That's a sure sign he doesn't like abortion. Probably believes in God, too. How Roberts survived all this is still unexplained.

The courts matter so much to radical secularists, of course, because they know the people are not prone to validate their extremist views via their lawmakers. *Power to the People*, as Laura Ingraham demonstrated in an influential book by that title, is the one power this gang really abhors.

Secular zealots have always professed a love of the masses in the abstract—it's just people they hate. That's why they loathe the legislature and love the courts: lawmakers answer to the people, judges do not. "Democracy by the people, for the people and of the people" may roll off the lips of schoolboys, but to radical secularists it is the refrain of chumps. They always think they know better, and that is why they smirk at the idea of government by consent. As far as they are concerned, the masses would be lucky to have them occupy the command posts. Which explains why consulting the people is the last thing they would ever do.

CHAPTER 7

Democratic Sabotage

Secularists Capture the Democratic Party

The role that Catholics have played in shaping the Democratic Party is legendary, but those who were born a few decades ago would never know this from their own experience. When at one time the Irish cop was the prototypical Democrat, today it is the gay activist. This is surely one of the most dramatic sociopolitical stories of our time.

Beginning with the presidential election of 1972, a trend has been evident: religious conservatives have chosen the Republican Party as home base and secularists have taken command of the Democratic Party. According to Geoffrey Layman of Columbia University, "the religious differences between the activist bases and electoral coalitions of the Democratic and Republican parties are growing."[1] After examining the data, Layman concludes that "There was a clear growth in Democratic secularism between 1976 and 1992, but it took place in fits and starts."[2] It has continued ever since, notwithstanding Barack Obama's attempt to reverse course. Though Obama tried to bridge the "God gap," it did not help his campaign when he spoke about those folks (the white working class) who like to "cling to guns or religion." Nor did it help that his religious mentor was Reverend Jeremiah "God damn America" Wright.

A whole array of issues emerged in the 1960s and 1970s that saw the strength of secularists within the Democratic Party; in the 1970s and 1980s religious conservatives mobilized against them. But there is more to this than just choosing up sides—there is a tremendous amount of hostility between the two groups. For example, two political scientists from Baruch College, Louis Bolce and Gerald De Maio, analyzed the results of the 2004 American National Election Studies and found that "Two-thirds of white secularist Democrats registered negative feelings toward the Catholic Church and of this group of anti-Catholic Democrats, 86% also expressed antagonistic feelings toward fundamentalists."[3]

Arthur C. Brooks, former professor at Syracuse University, looked at the data from the same source and found that "liberals in 2002 were less sympathetic than conservatives to Catholics, the Catholic Church, Protestants, and, especially, fundamentalist Protestants."[4] Thus, the culture war is reflected in the political war, with religious conservatives and secularists going at it in a way never before seen in American history. Brooks, who is now president of the American Enterprise Institute, notes how quickly this occurred. "The transformation of the Democratic Party into the party of secularism came about in a relatively short time," he writes.[5] He is referring to the Democratic Party of JFK in the early 1960s and its radically altered status only a decade later. No one doubts the change was for real.

"The cultural liberalism of George McGovern and the secularism of his Democratic supporters in 1972 seems to have appealed to secular voters to a much greater extent than any other religious group," writes Layman.[6] Indeed, as Jeane Kirkpatrick first pointed out, 21 percent of all delegates and 24 percent of first-time delegates to the 1972 Democratic National Convention were secularists.[7] "Secularists first appeared as a political force within a major party at the 1972 Democratic National Convention," note Bolce and De Maio. "Prior to then," they say, "neither party contained many secularists nor showed many signs of moral or cultural progressivism."[8] The secularists may have found a home in 1972, but they also got clobbered: McGovern was so radical that he carried only one state, Massachusetts, and was even rejected by the voters in his home state, South Dakota.

McGovern lost in 1972, but McGovernism—the secularization of the Democratic Party—won. It won because the McGovern Commission (formerly called the Commission on Party Structure and Delegate Selection) was established during the 1968 presidential campaign to effectively alter the way presidential candidates were chosen. Mark Stricherz correctly notes that the New Deal coalition that included "white Southerners, Catholics, union members, blacks, and intellectuals" gave way to a party run by "secular liberals."[9] One of the reasons this happened, Stricherz says, was what happened to Catholics: "Catholics had made up about one in four Humphrey votes in 1968, yet they received only one in fourteen slots on the commission in 1969."[10] Four decades later Michael Gerson observed that not only do secular Americans prefer the Democrats over Republicans by a margin of 3 to 1, they harbor a strong animus against religious conservatives as well.[11]

Driving the secularists have been cultural issues, foremost among them being matters of sexuality and lifestyle choices. Though the 1972 Democratic Party platform did not mention abortion, women's issues, or homosexuality by name, they were implied in the adopted language. Terms like "The Right to Be Different," "Rights of Women," and "Family Planning" are codes for gay rights and abortion, and everyone knew it.[12] These were not issues attractive to rank-and-file Catholic voters, and they certainly had no appeal to blue-collar workers, the mainstay of the Democratic Party. Coupled with the libertine lifestyle of acid-head hippies and their notoriously antipatriotic stand, the flower children of the late '60s and early '70s were alienating religious conservatives from coast to coast. And to the extent these young nihilists were identified with the Democratic Party, it only served to push Catholics to reconsider their political allegiance.

Catholic author David Carlin understands what was happening. There had long been "FDR liberals" in the Democratic Party, men and women who identified with the interests of labor unions and the working class in general. "Civil rights liberals" were another important strand, activists and their supporters who stood for racial equality. As Carlin sees it, the years between 1968 and 1972 witnessed the arrival of a third group, the "moral/cultural liberals." They pushed the boundaries of sexual freedom to an extent no one ever dreamed of, exercising a radical individualism that touched everything from abortion to homosexuality. Unlike the other segments of the party, the sexual free-spirits alienated many veteran members of the Democratic Party. Count Carlin among them.[13]

In other words, the cultural nihilists who make up the third prong of the Democratic Party today have little in common with the "FDR liberals" and the "civil rights liberals." The key to Democratic victory rests, in part, in keeping this destructive segment in its place. And the key to Democratic governance rests heavily in not acceding to their agenda.

As Layman points out, the proportion of secularists among Democratic delegates "increased noticeably between 1980 and 1984." The issues that were central to this secular shift were women's rights, abortion, homosexual rights, and church and state issues.[14] It was clear that both parties were moving in opposite directions, the net losers being the Democrats.

It is now generally assumed that regular churchgoers are much more likely to vote Republican. By contrast, those who rarely, or never, attend church services are much more likely to vote for Democrats. But as William Galston has shown, this was not always the case. Indeed, he found that in every presidential election between 1952 and 1988, whether one regularly attended church services was not particularly helpful in predicting how one voted. "But starting in 1992," he says, "you have an unbroken string of double-digit differences." Indeed, he offers, "Something very dramatic happened starting in 1992." So much so that he now declares that "If you look at the relationship between church attendance—frequency of church attendance, and not party identification but ideological identification—you will see an unbroken linear relationship." Churchgoers are more likely to be conservatives and liberals are more likely to be secularists.[15]

Noting what happened in 1992, Layman observes that "The Democratic Party now appears to be a party whose core of support comes from secularists, Jews, and the less committed members of the major religious traditions."[16] According to Bolce and De Maio, "60 percent of first-time white delegates at the [1992] Democratic convention in New York City either claimed no attachment to religion or displayed the minimal attachment by attending worship services 'a few times a year' or less." Moreover, "About 5 percent of first-time delegates at the Republican convention in Houston that year identified themselves as secularists."[17] What is particularly significant about this split is the extent to which it has disfigured the Democratic Party.

Why is the voice of secularists drowning out the voice of the faithful in the Democratic Party? Mike McCurry, former press secretary to Bill Clinton, explained it this way: "Because we want to be politically correct, in particular being sensitive to Jews, that's taken the party to a direction where faith language is soft and opaque."[18] It was not as though some Democrats working for John Kerry hadn't tried to give religious issues more attention. "Every time something with religious language got sent up a flagpole, it got sent back down, stripped of religious language," said one Democratic operative.[19] Kenneth Wald, a political scientist and director of the Center for Jewish Studies at the University of Florida, was just as blunt as McCurry: "There is a very strong tendency within the Jewish community to be worried about the people who are supporting Bush and Bush's tendency to promote Christian values from the bully pulpit."[20]

It is also true that money talks. As one Democratic operative told Zev Chafets, "You can replace Jewish votes, which might be four percent nationally, but you can't replace Jewish money. Big-donor lists begin at twenty-five thousand dollars, and at that level of national politics, forty to fifty percent are Jews. The higher the bracket, the higher the percentage."[21] Thus, any movement on the part of Democrats to reach out to churchgoers is likely to be met with some resistance on the part of wealthy Jewish contributors.

Marc Stern of the American Jewish Congress is surely correct to say that "Most Jews are much more liberal than the rest of the population. On abortion, on homosexual marriage, on premarital sex, Jews are fundamentally different than everyone else except the most secular." He is also right to say that "There's nothing the Democrats can do to appeal to people who are religious without alienating that part of their base."[22] What's stoking the problem is understood by the Jewish *Forward*: "Most Jews continue to view Christian majoritarianism as a threat to their interests. The calculus hasn't changed much since Jefferson's day."[23] But it is also true, as Nathan Diament points out, that "religious American Christians and Jews may share many faith-informed views on specific public policy issues." He cites gay marriage, school vouchers, and a "disgust [with] the popular culture" as examples.[24]

Perhaps as important as anything, a Pew survey in August 2006 showed that only 26 percent of the public thought the Democrats were "friendly to religion" (the figure for Republicans was 47 percent). As Bolce and De Maio observed, the numbers for the Democrats were "down significantly from just three years earlier. They also found that more than four in ten respondents said that "non-religious liberals have too much control over the Democratic party."[25]

When astute political scientists like Bolce and De Maio can declare, after looking at the data, that 53 percent of secularists have a negative attitude toward the Catholic Church, and that the same percentage identifies themselves as liberals, something profound has happened.[26] In many cases, this shift has had a deep personal effect on long-time Democrats. David Carlin is typical. For him (and for many others), being a Democrat was as natural as being an Irish Catholic—they were one and the same. And his love for both was eternal. Until he felt betrayed, that is. Carlin now refers to the Democrats as the "Anti-Christian Party."[27]

Carlin's observation may seem unduly harsh to some, but to religious conservatives who have tracked the affinity of left-wing activist groups and their role in the Democratic Party, it rings true. Consider what happened in 1988 when Democratic candidate Michael Dukakis boasted of his ACLU membership. This certainly did more to unite Catholic, Protestant, and Jewish conservatives than any other issue.

To religious conservatives, the ACLU embodied the worst of what American culture had become. At the time, I was a Bradley fellow at the Heritage Foundation, writing a book on contemporary social problems. What attracted Heritage to me was the publication of my 1985 book on the ACLU. It was not surprising, then, that when Dukakis made an issue of his ACLU status, the Bush presidential campaign would turn to me for advice and evidence of the ACLU's positions. I gladly did what I could to help them. Garry Wills, no friend of conservatives, wasn't happy. Referring to fights over the meaning of the First Amendment, Wills wrote that "The Bush campaign was able to exacerbate this struggle, calling on the advice of William A. Donohue, the sociologist who wrote the right wing's favorite book on the subject, *The Politics of the American Civil Liberties Union*. Donohue, for instance, gave the campaign the useful political charge that the ACLU would keep 'kiddie porn' legal."[28]

The left went after Bush with a vengeance for calling Dukakis "a card-carrying member of the ACLU." I. F. Stone, no stranger to communist circles, said Bush "injected into the campaign a pale whiff of the witch-hunting McCarthyite 50's." Similarly, the *New York Times* editorialized that Bush was guilty of a McCarthyite "smear" by mentioning Dukakis's "card-carrying" membership in the ACLU. Samuel Walker, ACLU official and house author, also said that Bush "introduced the ACLU into the 1988 presidential campaign."[29] As I demonstrated in my second book on the ACLU, all of them were wrong. It was Dukakis, not Bush, who initially sought to make the ACLU a campaign issue. In May 1987 in Los Angeles, and again in August 1987 in Spencer, Iowa, Dukakis explicitly boasted, "I'm a card-carrying member of the American Civil Liberties Union."[30] That those words came back to haunt him is hardly Bush's fault.

"It sometimes seems as though the election is more about the ACLU than anything else," said Tom Brokaw of *NBC News*. It sure seemed that way. Peter Jennings at ABC was on the same page with Brokaw on this issue. Indeed, he asked Bush during the first debate why he continued to bring up the Dukakis-ACLU affiliation. Bush replied that he didn't like most of the positions of the ACLU and offered four examples: opposition to the voluntary movie ratings system; a legal challenge to the tax-exempt status of the Catholic Church; a defense of child pornography; and a desire to gut "In God We Trust" from our coins. Though the ACLU and the *New York Times* protested that Bush had misrepresented the Union's positions, they were wrong: I supplied the Bush campaign with all of these positions, and they were taken right out of the ACLU's Policy Guide.[31]

If churchgoers were soured after the 1988 presidential campaign, they were infuriated after the next one. Layman found that the Democratic Party's platform of 1992 was "the most polarized" ever on cultural and moral issues. In addition to its unyielding support for abortion rights, "The 1992 platform was the first in which the Democrats specifically mentioned gays and lesbians."[32] So radical had the Democratic Party become that it even sought to punish one of their own because of his pro-life views. In 1992, Pennsylvania Governor Robert Casey, a strong pro-life Catholic Democrat, was blocked from speaking at the party's national convention. Some of the Catholic-hating delegates even wore buttons denouncing Casey as a papist.

The Clinton Years

Clinton's appointment of Dr. Joycelyn Elders as Surgeon General was one of the president's early blunders with the faithful. Even before she drew the ire of the Catholic League, she made headlines. A longtime advocate of condom distribution in the schools, Elders saw teenage pregnancy rates increase during her tenure as director of the Arkansas Health Department; rates had actually decreased in the period prior to her appointment. However, it was her cavalier attitude toward condoms that was most interesting. "I tell every girl that when she goes out on a date—put a condom in her purse," she said. Known for keeping a "condom plant" on her desk, Elders also offered these words of wisdom: "We have had driver's ed for kids. We've taught them what to do in the front seat of the car, but not what to do in the back seat of the car."[33] It was the job of the government, she reasoned, to do just that.

It was on the subject of abortion that Dr. Elders got into big trouble. She was on record saying that those who oppose abortion were "non-Christians with slave-master mentalities." Besides speaking derisively, she got downright insulting when she said that those who were pro-life "love little babies so long as they are in someone else's uterus." In fact, she even went so far as to say that pro-lifers should get over their "love affair with the fetus."[34] Bad as these remarks were, they were no match for what she had to say about Catholics.

Elders was a secular saboteur par excellence. On January 18, 1992, she gave an address to the Arkansas Coalition for Choice wherein she accused the Catholic Church of being "silent" and doing "nothing" about such issues as slavery, the treatment of Native Americans, the Holocaust, and the disenfranchisement of women. Moreover, at a 1992 pro-abortion rally, she said, "Look at who's fighting the pro-choice movement—a celibate, male-dominated church."[35] The Catholic League quickly charged that what Elders said "smacked of ignorance or malice," a conclusion that was supported by the *Washington Post*; it ran an editorial saying, "The League was right."[36] Elders proved to be a liability to the administration and was eventually fired, but not because she offended Catholics or had loopy ideas about sex. She was simply deemed incompetent.

The United Nations International Conference on Population and Development in Cairo made relations between the Clinton administration and Catholics even worse. It was expected that the issue of abortion would separate the Holy See and the Clinton administration, but what made matters ugly was the prevalence of anti-Catholicism at both the Cairo conference and the preparatory session that preceded it at the U.N.

Since nearly all of the Catholic bashing came from the nongovernmental organizations (NGOs), and since the Clinton administration worked closely with the offending NGOs, it was clear that at least some of the Clintonites were involved. From the hoots and howls that greeted representatives of the Holy See to the anti-Catholic buttons and literature that were distributed at the conferences, it was obvious that Catholics were not welcome. Indeed, the anti-Catholic group, Catholics for a

Free Choice, was accorded more respect than delegates from the Vatican.

It was left to State Department spokeswoman Faith Mitchell to deliver the most telling low blow. She charged that the Vatican's disagreement over the Cairo conference "has more to do with the fact that the conference is really calling for a new role for women, calling for girls' education and improving the status of women."[37] The statement so outraged Harvard Law professor Mary Ann Glendon that she wrote an open letter to the president registering her concerns; it was signed by the leaders of organizations representing hundreds of thousands of Catholic women and was published in the *New York Times* under the sponsorship of the Catholic League.[38]

About a month after the Cairo conference ended, I received a phone call from Jim Castelli of the Office of Public Liaison in the White House. He was disturbed to see that the Catholic League monthly journal, *Catalyst*, featured a story titled "League Assails Clinton Administration for Bigotry." This, coming on the heels of the *New York Times* open letter, was found to be troubling. Castelli began by stating that he could cite "chapter and verse" why the Clinton administration was not anti-Catholic. I accepted the challenge and began citing chapter and verse why it was. Castelli, who had previously written patently unfair columns about Cardinal O'Connor and who had contributed to the *National Catholic Reporter*, identified himself as a "fellow traveler in Catholic circles." That was the most revealing comment he made. It also sheds light on why Castelli's office was the venue for a host of dissident Catholic organizations in July 1993.[39]

If there was one Catholic official in the administration who was not a phony, it was former Boston Mayor Ray Flynn. In his July 6, 1994, letter to the president, Flynn, the Ambassador to the Vatican, blasted the Clinton administration for being anti-Catholic. He said he was "embarrassed" about the "ugly anti-

Catholic bias that is shown by prominent members of Congress and the administration."[40]

DNC v. Catholic League

Journalist Mark Shields is a moderate Catholic Democrat. It was not surprising, then, that when the Democratic National Committee (DNC) established an association with Catholics for a Free Choice (CFFC), he would protest. Instead of engaging in religious outreach, the DNC was reaching out to anti-Catholic bigots. The whole thing read like a suicide pact.

It was in late July 2002 that Shields blasted the DNC for providing a link on its Web site to Frances Kissling's anti-Catholic front group. "I have written to DNC chairman Terry McAuliffe imploring him to 'act quickly and decisively by removing Catholics for a Free Choice from the DNC's links of interest organizations,'" Shields said. On July 31, the Catholic League followed suit. What was particularly galling was the fact that at the time, CFFC was the *only* Catholic group listed on its Web site.[41]

On August 6, the Catholic League warned that "the Democrats are playing with fire" and pledged "to spend considerable resources informing the public of what the DNC considers its Catholic base." This was not an idle threat. In the September 15–21 edition of the *National Catholic Register*, the Catholic League launched the first in a series of ads that would be run in Catholic and secular newspapers targeting the DNC. Two Democratic congressmen, Tom Lantos and Tim Roemer, wrote to me expressing their concerns over the damage the DNC was doing; Lantos, who has since passed away, was Jewish and Roemer is Catholic. But most Democrats did nothing. No matter, the DNC was pounded throughout the fall with angry phone calls, faxes, and e-mails, the listings of which were provided by the Catholic League.

Not getting a response from the DNC, the Catholic League ran ads in two other Catholic weeklies, *Our Sunday Visitor* and the *Wanderer.* The secular audience was not overlooked, either: an ad was placed in *Roll Call*, a prominent newspaper in the nation's capital. Every member of the House and Senate was contacted by mail, as were all of the nation's bishops. The campaign was starting to have an effect: the DNC was deluged with calls and letters of protest. At the request of the Most Reverend Wilton D. Gregory, president of the United States Conference of Catholic Bishops, Reverend Monsignor William P. Fay, general counsel to the bishops' conference, wrote a letter to McAuliffe registering his objections. Fay stressed that the bishops' conference has publicly maintained on two occasions that CFFC is not a Catholic organization and that indeed it works to undermine Catholicism. He requested that the DNC remove its link to Kissling's group. McAuliffe's only response was to pad the "Catholic" section of its Web site with two other Catholic organizations, Call to Action and NETWORK; both are dissident groups, sister organizations to CFFC.[42]

It was impossible for McAuliffe not to know that Kissling was not simply pro-abortion—she was decidedly anti-Catholic. That's because I contacted him prior to Kissling's interview on October 12 on PBS radio, alerting him to her true status. Kissling did not disappoint. On the show she explicitly said that it was her goal "to neutralize the political power of the Church" and "to defrock the Catholic Church of its massive power."[43] But even at this, McAuliffe was unmoved. The Democrats had gotten into bed with the Catholic bashers. Worse, most were positively clueless as to why practicing Catholics were abandoning the Democratic Party.

If the DNC had reached out to a dissident Catholic organization, one that was in the abortion-rights camp, that would have been bad enough. But CFFC is not a dissident Catholic group—it is an explicitly anti-Catholic entity founded to sabotage the

Catholic Church. It does not work from within the Church, but it does work externally to foment disorder within it. Without doubt, it is the most nihilistic enemy of the Catholic Church in the nation. And this is the group that the DNC was embracing.

October 28, 2002, turned out to be quite a day in the DNC's relationship with Catholics. When I left work on Friday, October 25, the link with CFFC was still on the DNC's Web site. But when I returned to work on Monday, October 28, it was gone. The links section had been rearranged over the weekend; a new category, "Religious Affiliated," listed some legitimate Catholic and Jewish organizations and publications, but nowhere to be seen was CFFC. I immediately put out a news release stating that the Catholic League had led a three-month protest about this issue, spending thousands of dollars on ads in Catholic magazines and secular newspapers. "Finally," I wrote, "we have won."[44] As it turned out, I was wrong.

It didn't take long before someone alerted the DNC to my statement. CFFC was quickly added to the "Religious Affiliated" section, prompting me to say the following: "Someone at the DNC isn't too bright. Now they've really created a hornet's nest for themselves. First they delete Frances Kissling's Catholics for a Free Choice from their website and now they put her back up. There's obviously a fight going on at the DNC over this and for now the Kissling forces have won. But they won't win in the long run."[45] Little did I know when I wrote this that I would issue another news release on the DNC's second blunder of the day. The release was titled "Democratic National Committee Sponsors Hard-Core Teen Porn."

In the links section of the DNC's Web site, there was a category called "Hispanic." On the day that I visited the Web site by clicking on the second-to-last link, a hard-core teen porn site appeared, with pictures of four young women depicted in full frontal nudity with the inscription "FREE, Live Amateur, Teen, Anal, Hardcore Picture SEX site." In my news release, I said that "The DNC is spinning out of control. Its support for anti-Catholic bigotry is now matched by its support for hard-core pornography. Whoever is operating its Web site should be fired immediately." I added that "The DNC may have violated federal law by sponsoring a Web site with arguably under-age girls." I concluded by imploring the DNC to dump both the porn site and CFFC.[46]

News of the Catholic League statement hit more than the Internet—it reached the desk of Joseph M. Birkenstock, the DNC's chief counsel. "This letter is to put you on notice that your press release dated October 28, 2002," he wrote, "entitled 'DEMOCRATIC NATIONAL COMMITTEE SPONSORS HARD-CORE TEEN PORN' is false and defamatory." His letter, written on October 28 and faxed to me the same day, denied that the DNC would ever sponsor porn of any kind. Indeed, he strongly defended the DNC, and blasted my statement. His concluding paragraph was precious:

> <u>You are hereby advised not to destroy or alter any documents that in any way refer or relate to the creation or publication of this press release, and to notify the officers and directors of the Catholic League for Religious and Civil Rights, as well as anyone involved in the creation or publication of this press release of their potential liability in this matter.</u>[47]

Birkenstock's fatal mistake was his use of the word "potential." That gave away the store. Either he was going to sue or he wasn't. He obviously wasn't and that's because he had no grounds to do so. After all, it was undeniable that the teen porn link was on the DNC Web site. He called me that same day and we got into a shouting match, resolving nothing. The next day I wrote him a three-sentence response: "Your attempt to intimidate the Catholic League has failed. We will continue our protest against the DNC's alliance with an anti-Catholic organization,

Catholics for a Free Choice. Moreover, we will not be distracted by your inflammatory phone calls."[48]

That was the last I heard from him. I closed this chapter by releasing a comment to the press stating that "It may be that the porn Web site was inadvertently linked to the DNC." However, I also let the DNC know that the Catholic League was not going away. The next sentence read, "But there is nothing resembling human error regarding the conscious decision of the DNC to provide a link with an anti-Catholic organization."[49]

We did not let up. The Catholic League built a coalition to work against Kissling. We succeeded in getting Father Frank Pavone's Priest for Life, Deal Hudson's *Crisis* magazine, Reverend Thomas Euteneuer's Human Life International, Ave Maria Law School (headed by Bernard Dobranski), Ken Connor's Family Research Council, Merlyn Scroggins and the Catholic Defense League of Minnesota, Bud McFarland's Mary Foundation, Reverend Louis Sheldon's Traditional Family Values, and many others to work with us. We also wrote to every member of the United Nations Committee on the Rights of the Child contesting Kissling's attempt to get that body to institute sanctions against the Vatican for allegedly violating a U.N. treaty protecting children. Word was fast getting out that the DNC's darling was anything but. After Reverend Michael C. McFarland, president of Holy Cross, revoked an invitation by women's studies professors to have Kissling speak there, she went nuts, saying, "I'm tired of speaking off-campus and in Unitarian churches about issues that are important in my church."[50]

We didn't give up. On September 16, 2003, I wrote an ad that was published on the op-ed page of the *New York Times* titled "Why Are the Democrats Insulting Catholics?" It made the same appeal—the DNC should drop its association with CFFC. Finally, on April 13, 2004, just as the presidential campaign was heating up, the DNC did what I always thought it would do: it quietly redid its Web site, dropping the links page altogether. By sleight of hand, then, the DNC-CFFC link was broken. My parting words were: "The DNC deserves no credit for this action. It brazenly offended Catholics for years by embracing a Catholic-bashing organization. But now that its leader, Senator John Kerry, is in trouble with Catholics for a whole host of reasons, prudence dictates that the DNC distance itself from anti-Catholic bigotry."[51]

Kerry's Idea of Religious Outreach

Secular nihilists are so consumed with power that they find their way into federal, state, and local politics; they have a particular interest in penetrating presidential politics, and they often don't even bother to conceal their real intentions. One might think that offices which specialize in religious outreach might be off-limits to them, but this is simply not the case. They manage to worm their way into everything.

John Kerry sold himself as a "devout Catholic" during the 2004 presidential campaign, but it was a hard sell given his support for abortion on demand and embryonic stem cell research, as well as his opposition to school vouchers. His public image was that of a secularist, not a "devout Catholic." Thus it was greeted by many with a sigh of relief when his campaign announced the hiring of a Director of Religious Outreach.

As soon as the Catholic League learned that Mara Vanderslice had been chosen for the post, we sought to find out more about her. What we learned was disturbing. So much so that we shared it with the press, as well as with Protestant and Jewish conservatives.

Vanderslice was raised without any faith and didn't become an evangelical Christian until she attended Earlham College, a Quaker school known for its adherence to pacifism. When in college, she was active in the Earlham Socialist Alliance, a group that supports the convicted cop killer Mumia Abu-Jamal and openly embraces Marxism-Leninism. After graduating, she spoke at rallies held by ACT-UP, the anti-Catholic group that disrupted Mass at St. Patrick's Cathedral in 1989. In 2000, she practiced civil disobedience when she took to the streets of Seattle in a protest against the World Trade Organization. In 2002, she tried to shut down Washington, D.C., in a protest against the International Monetary Fund and the World Bank. As I said at the time, "Her résumé is that of a person looking for a job working for Fidel Castro, not John Kerry. Just wait until Catholics and Protestants learn who this lady really is."[52]

At first, John Kerry was considered too moderate for Vanderslice, which is why she became Howard Dean's Religious Outreach Director. She admitted that she was a freak in the Dean campaign: her colleagues dubbed her the "church lady," informing her that Dean was liked precisely because he didn't talk about religion. "How in the world did you get hired?" is how one staffer put it. Her experience was not unique. When Democratic activist Eric McFadden volunteered to reach out to Catholics, he was told by his boss, "We don't *do* white churches."[53] All this from the party of inclusion. It is a sure bet that gay activists were never treated as outsiders in either the Dean or Kerry campaigns.

Only four days after I notified Catholics, Protestants, and Jews about Vanderslice's résumé, Julia Duin of the *Washington Times* detailed how the Kerry camp reacted to my news release. Vanderslice was silenced—she was no longer allowed to talk to the press. Which raised the question, Why bother to have a director of religious outreach if she is forbidden from reaching out to the religious? As Duin reported, the Kerry campaign was in a "panic mode" over Vanderslice's role. It didn't take long before Kerry operatives were blaming me for causing the uproar. "The Kerry campaign hires a 29-year-old ultra-leftist who consorts with anti-Catholic bigots and the Catholic League is supposed to take this lying down," I responded. "And if Vanderslice is so innocent," I asked, "why have they gagged her?"[54]

Next up at bat was Reverend Brenda Bartella Peterson. On July 23, DNC Chairman Terry McAuliffe announced that this ordained minister in the Christian Church (Disciples of Christ) was appointed the DNC's Senior Advisor for Religious Outreach. Again, the Catholic League did some scratching around to find out more about her, and as with Vanderslice, we were struck by what we found.

As it turned out, Reverend Peterson was one of 32 clergy members to file an amicus brief on behalf of Michael Newdow's attempt to excise the words "under God" from the Pledge of Allegiance. The brief made it clear that Peterson was infinitely more concerned about the sensibilities of atheists like Newdow than she was for the 90 percent of Americans who believe in God. The questions I posed were made public in a news release: "And this is the person the Democrats want to dispatch to meet the heads of religious organizations? Are they out of their minds? Would they hire a gay basher to reach out to homosexuals?"[55]

The next day, August 3, I delivered another news release on Reverend Peterson. This time I disclosed how she was chosen as the first executive director of a new group, the Clergy Leadership Network (CLN). Its stated mission was to fight the Religious Right and "get a national leadership change." The group seemed more at home with politics than religion. For example, when Peterson was asked whether Christians and Muslims worship the same God, she breezily answered, "I would rather you not quote theology." CLN, we discovered, also took no position on abortion. Not surprisingly, CLN's office was right across the street from the DNC's headquarters. Just as unsurprising was the revelation that Peterson believed that "paying taxes is a way of loving thy neighbor."[56]

Keeping the pressure on, the next day I sent out another news release. The CLN's Web site said a great deal about separation of church and state but virtually nothing about religious liberty (e.g., it was against faith-based initiatives). It also had a love affair with taxes: "Taxes provide a way to look out for our neighbors. . . . Slashing taxes denies that!" Indeed, it said that slashing taxes is "inevitably an appeal to our greed, not to our generosity or compassion." In other words, the greedy want to keep the money they've earned; those who want to take it from them are the altruists. No wonder Peterson said, "The federal budget is a moral document."[57] This became a mantra throughout the campaign and was picked up by the Obama campaign in 2008.

Regarding gay marriage, while the CLN Web site said nothing about it, its CEO, Albert Pennybacker, was on record favoring it. William Sloan Coffin, who at one time was among America's most famous radical men of the cloth, chimed in by saying that most of the other CLN officials "view marriage as a human right, not a reward for being heterosexual." Incredibly, the CLN Web site also had links to an anti-Catholic site, Chuck Currie's blog, which featured a piece titled "When Catholic Girls Go Wild," and to MoveOn.org, a left-wing group that has nothing to do with religion.[58]

After being pounded for three days, Reverend Peterson decided to hang it up. She told Religion News Service that "it was no longer possible for me to do my job effectively." The *Washington Post* added that her decision was made "after the New York-based Catholic League issued three blistering news releases attacking her positions."[59]

Edwards Hires Bigots

During the 2008 presidential campaign, Democratic candidate John Edwards managed to make the Kerry and DNC appointments look good by comparison. Edwards also brought religious conservatives together, one more time.

On February 6, 2007, the Catholic League demanded that Edwards fire Amanda Marcotte as blogmaster and Melissa McEwan as netroots coordinator. He chose to fire them, then rehire them, thus imploding his credibility with Democrats as a man who could be trusted to make tough decisions. They were then pressured to resign. It was their writings penned before they went to work for Edwards that finished them.

On December 26, 2006, Marcotte had written on the Pandagon blog site that "the Catholic church is not about to let something like compassion for girls get in the way of using the state as an instrument to force women to bear more tithing Catholics." On October 9, 2006, she said that "the Pope's gotta tell women who give birth to stillborns that their babies are cast into Satan's maw." On the same day, she wrote that "it's going to be bad PR for the church, so you can sort of see why the Pope is dragging ass." And on June 14, 2006, Marcotte offered the following Q&A: "What if Mary had taken Plan B after the Lord filled her with his hot, white, sticky Holy Spirit?" To which she offered the reply, "You'd have to justify your misogyny with another ancient mythology."[60]

On November 21, 2006, McEwan wrote on the Web site AlterNet that "some of Christianity's most prominent leaders— including the Pope—regularly speak out against gay tolerance." On November 1, 2006, on her blog Shakespeare's Sister, she referred to President Bush's "wingnut Christofascist base" when lashing out against religious conservatives. On February 21, 2006, she attacked religious conservatives again, only this time she unloaded with a string of expletives.[61] She even described herself in terms so vulgar that no mainstream media outlet could print or repeat them over the airwaves.[62]

My first response to these outrageous comments was to say, "John Edwards is a decent man who has had his campaign tarnished by two anti-Catholic vulgar trash-talking bigots. He has no choice but to fire them immediately." Edwards not only stood by them, he had the audacity to say that "We're beginning a great debate about the future of our country, and we can't let it be hijacked." The implication, of course, was that the Catholic League was not responding in a responsible fashion. According to him, we were out to hijack his campaign. That did it. "We will launch a nationwide public relations blitz that will be conducted in the pages of the *New York Times*," I said, "as well as in Catholic newspapers and periodicals. It will be on-going, breaking like a wave, starting next week and continuing through 2007." I promised to enlist my allies in the Catholic, Protestant, Jewish, Muslim, and Buddhist communities.[63]

Edwards made his pledge to stand by Marcotte and McEwan on February 8, and three days later Marcotte lashed out at Christians in general by saying, "The Christian version of the virgin birth is generally interpreted as super-patriarchal where god is viewed as so powerful he can impregnate without befouling himself by touching a woman, and women are nothing but vessels."[64] Marcotte quit right after that, blaming me for her problems. She said she had to resign because "I can't do the job I was hired to do because Bill Donohue doesn't have anything better to do with his time than harass me."[65] McEwan folded the next day.

The Catholic League was delighted with the news, but we quickly had to cancel our plans. President's Day was coming and we had reserved a spot on the op-ed page of the *New York Times* to make our case against Edwards. What made this whole episode so surreal was being turned down originally by the lawyers for the *New York Times* because they said our proposed ad for February 16, which I wrote, violated the newspaper's policy on indecency. They cited Marcotte's remark about the "hot, white, sticky Holy Spirit" and McEwan's comment about religious conservatives. This played right into my hands.

I rewrote the beginning of the ad: "This ad was to begin with two vile anti-Christian quotes penned by two women on the payroll of John Edwards. Though neither contained obscene words spelled in full, the *New York Times* said it violated their policy and therefore rejected them. The first quote was a reference to the Virgin Mary being injected with semen by the Lord. The second used a patently vulgar term to describe religious conservatives. The first part of the word is 'mother.' To read what was actually said, please see the Catholic League Web site."[66]

We didn't have to wait long before the lawyers said we could go with the original version. They no doubt reasoned, as I knew they would, that the *Times* would look rather prudish next to the Catholic League if the revised version were printed. In any event, the bloggers folded, making the ad moot; it never ran.

Demonizing Christians

In the buildup to the 2004 election, radical secularists went on a tear, issuing blistering attacks on Christians. They went even crazier when they lost. Some of the comments were so off-the-wall that it made one wonder whether these crackpots would ever recover. And there weren't just a few of them who crashed.

George Soros's MoveOn.org was so upset with a Gallup poll showing Bush with a 14-point lead in September that it took out a full-page ad in the *New York Times* referring to George Gallup, Jr., as a "devout evangelical Christian" who could not be trusted to be fair.[67] As the election neared, Robert Wright, visiting professor at Princeton, said Bush's "divine-feeling feelings" were part of today's "problem, not the solution." A *New York Times* editorial said that if Bush won again, he would appoint judges who would allow states to become "mini-theocracies." David Domke, a University of Washington professor, remarked that "one is hard pressed" to distinguish between Osama bin Laden's religious views and Bush's. New York University professor Mark Crispin Miller said Bush wanted a "theocracy." University of Southern

California professor Neal Gabler commented that Bush's ideas were "the stuff of a theocracy—the president as pope or mullah." Yale emeritus professor Harold Bloom feared that if Bush was reelected, "we could be faced with theocracy, an eventual tyranny of the twice-born." Robert Kuttner of the *American Prospect* said Bush "seems to want to move the United States toward a theocracy." Journalist James Ridgeway wrote that "Bush's goal is to blur the lines between separating church and state and turn the U.S. toward theocracy."[68]

Once Bush won, the secularists really lost it. Writing in the *Wichita Eagle*, Mitch Albom of the *Detroit Free Press* wondered if Bush understood that "he was not chosen god, bishop, rabbi or high priest." The publisher of *Harper's* magazine, John R. MacArthur, showed his incredible narcissism when he blasted Bush *and* Kerry for advertising "their subservience to Jesus Christ and the Christian god, without the least concern about whether it might offend me." Ex-seminarian Garry Wills demonstrated his usual arrogance in the *New York Times*: "Can a people that believes more fervently in the Virgin Birth than in evolution still be called an Enlightened nation?" He ended his piece by saying that "moral zealots" will scare moderate Republicans with their "jihads."[69]

New York Times columnist Maureen Dowd accused Bush of running "a jihad in America so he can fight one in Iraq." Dowd's colleague, Thomas Friedman, said Bush's base wanted "to extend the boundaries of religion" and promote "intolerance." Without providing a single example, Margaret Carlson opined in the *Los Angeles Times* that Catholic bishops "demonized" Kerry's supporters by warning them "they could go to hell just for voting for him." Sheryl McCarthy of *Newsday* accused Bush of "pandering to people's fears, petty interests and prejudices" against gays and others. Sidney Blumenthal, writing in Salon.com, nervously observed that the new Senate majority was "more theocratic than Republican." In the same spot, Sean Wilentz must have embarrassed his colleagues at Princeton when he said that "religious fanaticism" had "seized control of the federal government."[70]

A week after the election, the secularists were still steaming. Onetime presidential hopeful Gary Hart proclaimed in the *New York Times*, "There is a disturbing tendency to insert theocratic principles into the vision of America's role in the world." DeWayne Wickham of *USA Today* fretted, "Putting God in the public square runs the risk of turning our democracy into a theocracy." *Miami Herald* writer Leonard Pitts, Jr., warned that social conservatives were "the soldiers of the new American theocracy." Ellen Goodman of the *Boston Globe* said that people like her "don't want their country racked by the fundamentalist religious wars we see across the world." Similarly, Barbara Ehrenreich argued that we were polarized because of "Christian fundamentalism." Syndicated columnist Byron Williams warned that we were moving "closer to a theocracy." And playwright Tony Kushner believed we now had "a kind of unholy alliance between theocracy and plutocracy."[71]

These are not the words of rational people. The theocracy they envisioned has not taken place. But religious conservatives have learned a lesson: many of their adversaries are not simply without faith—they harbor a hatred against them that is so visceral as to make them mad.

Some Democrats have also learned a lesson. Obama, for instance, is not embraced by religious conservatives, but he has shown a deftness in handling the issue of religion that his predecessors have lacked. His presidential campaign had a religious outreach program that was professional, and it paid off: 54 percent of voters saw Obama as "friendly" to religion, a 16-point improvement over his party's numbers. While John McCain was seen as "friendly" to religion by 58 percent of voters, it was Obama who made the largest gain.[72] Nonetheless, as Pew researcher John Green said, the overall numbers did not produce a religious "realignment," and that's because economic issues trumped cultural ones in 2008.[73]

Obama may be good at "God-talk," but that didn't stop him from moving quickly to satisfy his secular base. For example, his stimulus package barred colleges from using federal funds to build or repair buildings used for religious services. Worse, he moved with lightning speed to strip healthcare workers of their right not to perform services they find morally repugnant.[74] The fact is that radical secularists, not the faithful, were emboldened by his victory. And it is they who are a threat to democracy—not religious conservatives. If they had things their way, they would silence the faithful and drive them underground. They are a menace to liberty.

CHAPTER 8

Self-Sabotage: Catholicism

If Only He Would Die

They couldn't wait for him to die. Although Pope John Paul II was held in higher regard by evangelicals than anyone in their own community, including Jerry Falwell and Pat Robertson,[1] Catholics seeking to sabotage the Church's teachings had actually been praying for him to drop dead for years. Before a packed house of dissident Catholics at the annual Call to Action convention in November 1997, Sister Maureen Fiedler proclaimed that "a lot of people in this Church are waiting for a person in this Church to pass away."[2] Everyone knew whom she meant.

When their death wish came true in 2005, they started bashing "John Paul the Great" as soon as they heard the news. John Carroll left the priesthood a long time ago, but he has never been able to overcome his anger. "John Paul II has faithfully tried to preserve this medieval, absolutist notion of pope-centered Catholicism with everything going out from the Vatican," he opined.[3] Father Andrew Greeley said the pope was a "brave, holy man," but quickly added that he had an "authoritarian style" on sexual issues that "polarized the Church."[4] A radical dissident group, We Are Church, said the pope deserved to be criticized because he strengthened "authoritarian structures within the Church itself."[5] Thomas Cahill was featured in the *New York Times* predicting that John Paul "may, in time to come, be credited with destroying his church."[6] And St. Louis University theologian Ronald Modras condemned the pope because he once chastised Anthony Kosnik for writing "a dull book on human sexuality."[7] What he failed to mention was that the "dull book" spoke nonjudgmentally about sex between man and beast, among other perversions, and was required reading in some of the wild seminaries a generation ago.

In the two-week period following the death of John Paul II and preceding the election of his successor, the saboteurs laid down the gauntlet. New Ways Ministry, a group that rejects the Church's teachings on homosexuality, admonished the Church not to oppose gay marriage initiatives "being enacted in secular governments." Dignity, an organization of Catholic gay dissidents, implored the Catholic hierarchy "to learn how God is speaking through GLBT [Gay, Lesbian, Bisexual, Transgender] people to spread the gospel." Feminists such as Sheila Durkin Dierks boasted that "Groups of women are gathering in their homes [to] celebrate the liturgy without an ordained presider." Call to Action said it hoped "the new pope recognizes the necessity of lifting the mandatory celibacy ban," and made another pitch for women priests. They were joined in this chorus by Women-Church Convergence, We Are Church, Catholics Speak Out, and the National Coalition of American Nuns, all of which are pro-abortion;[8] the latter group urged Catholics to vote for pro-abortion and pro-gay marriage candidates in 2006.[9]

During this period, I had another one of my run-ins with Christopher Hitchens, someone I love to debate. Three days after the pope died, I was asked to debate Hitchens on the MSNBC show *Scarborough Country*. The show, which was taped, never aired.

Hitchens started bashing the pope, blaming him for the sexual abuse scandal, obstruction of justice, etc. As he often does, he provided no evidence for his ridiculous charges. When asked by Joe Scarborough whether I agreed, I replied that only a madman or a bigot would do so. At that, Hitchens started screaming bloody murder and stormed off the set (he was in Washington and I was in New York). I continued with my comments, as did Pat Buchanan. But Chris Matthews, who was also on the show, was uneasy. The pope had not yet been buried and already the fireworks had begun. Matthews persuaded his colleagues that the show should not air (it was bad timing), and though this was the right call, I only wish the viewers could have seen Christopher flip out.

With the pope dead, the dissidents thought their day had come. Finally, they stood to get a pope who would deliver on all the reforms they so craved. Little did they know that their worst nightmare was about to come true.

If there was one cardinal the malcontents hated, it was Joseph Cardinal Ratzinger, John Paul II's right-hand man. So when Ratzinger addressed his fellow cardinals the day before the new pope would be named, his detractors paid close attention. He spoke forcefully about a "dictatorship of relativism" that had gripped the West, and of libertinism, the descent of liberty into license. This was music to the ears of conservatives, but to Catholics like E. J. Dionne they were "fighting words."[10] Interestingly, Reverend Richard P. McBrien of Notre Dame took some consolation in Ratzinger's address: "I think this homily shows he realizes he's not going to be elected. He's too much of a polarizing figure. If he were elected, thousands upon thousands of Catholics in Europe and the United States would roll their eyes and retreat to the margins of the Church."[11] Both Dionne's and McBrien's comments appeared in the *Washington Post* on April 19, 2005, literally hours before the newspaper's Web site posted the news that Cardinal Ratzinger was named the new pope.

Deborah Caldwell of Beliefnet accurately summed up what was going on: "For a couple of decades now, liberals taking shots

at the Vatican would telegraph their disgust with one word—
Ratzinger. That sour puss German Inquisition meister. Prince
of the New Dark Ages. Torquemada of the 21st century. God's
Rottweiler."[12] Father Robert Drinan, a former congressman from
Massachusetts, said he was "pretty depressed," and Sister Fiedler
confessed that "I was standing in St. Peter's Square when I heard
the news [of the election] and my heart sank."[13]

Dissidents as Nihilists

What would make them happy? It's not clear even the dissidents know at this point. That is why they have become nihilists: they reckon that if they can't get their way, neither should
the rank and file get what they want. Indeed, they'd rather be
a nuisance than bolt. They could join another religion, but that
wouldn't be as much fun. Besides, they have too much invested
at this point—in many ways—to cut and run.

They're also dishonest. For example, they complain endlessly
about papal power but if they ever had a pope who accepted
their views on women and sexuality, they would insist on blind
obedience. This isn't a matter of conjecture. For example, dissidents never put capital punishment on the table for dialogue,
and that's because they like the way Pope John Paul II spoke
against it in most instances. So when the left wins one, they take
a "shut up and get in line" position. Which explains why they
still want to dialogue about abortion—they haven't gotten their
way on that one. Nor will they.

Similarly, the dissidents were bent out of shape in 2004
when some bishops threatened to withhold Communion from
pro-abortion politicians. Tom Fox, publisher of the *National
Catholic Reporter*, said at the time that "some Catholic bishops
and conservatives now fail to distinguish moral from civil law,
the ideal from the real."[14] When exactly this occurred, he did

not say, but it's a sure bet that this alleged blurring of the lines wasn't operative in the 1960s when New Orleans Archbishop Joseph Rummel was busy excommunicating prominent local Catholic politicians for their pro-segregation politics. Outside the Church, the secularists took the same position. The same *New York Times* that was aghast over bishops who threatened sanctions against pro-abortion officials congratulated Archbishop Rummel for his "unwavering courage" and for "setting an example founded on religious principle."[15]

Much of the anger directed at the Church begins and ends with sex. Quite frankly, the dissidents don't ascribe to the Church's ideal of sexual restraint. Here's a perfect example. In 2002, I debated Tom Roberts, a colleague of Tom Fox's at the *National Catholic Reporter*, on MSNBC's *Hardball*. At one point, I said, "Now guys like Roberts, the *National Catholic Reporter*, they don't believe in anything the Catholic Church says on sexuality anyhow, so of course he doesn't want to talk about homosexuality." Mike Barnicle, sitting in for Chris Matthews, interrupted me: "Wait, Bill, please. Tom, take it up. I mean, you just got whacked across the face. Take it up." To which Roberts replied, "I'm not going to take that up."[16] How could he?

The issue of women's ordination continues to fire dissidents. Some of the dissidents are masochists who park themselves where they're not wanted. If masochism isn't at work, then only self-delusion could explain why eight adult women would board a sailing ship and go through a make-believe three-hour ceremony "ordaining" themselves as priests in a religion whose teachings and traditions they loathe. Their little stunt, which the media loved, got them excommunicated, but the riverboat queens were nonplussed. Six of the eight worked for the Catholic Church in one capacity or another.[17] Similarly, it came as no surprise that when Jean Marie Marchant resigned her position in 2006 as director of health-care services for the Archdiocese of Boston—after revealing that she had participated in a secret "ordination" ceremony a year earlier—she admitted that it was her goal "to stay within the church and to push the boundaries." Just as unsurprising was the fact that her husband is an ex-priest.[18]

The *National Catholic Reporter* is the *New York Times* of Catholic dissidents. In an editorial on the subject of women "ordaining" themselves priests, the weekly said the rebels "aren't discussing whether women should be ordained; they aren't asking for permission to be ordained; they are just doing what, as they see it, a church crying 'priest shortage' needs them to do." They also managed to get themselves excommunicated. The editorial then got downright silly when it said, "The hierarchy is rightly nervous about women declaring themselves ordained, however illegally, because these ceremonies carry a strong implicit message."[19] It is doubtful that any bishop ever lost a single night's sleep fretting over elderly women playing priest.

Father Greeley, who alternates between writing sex novels and offering sociological insights, likes gay marriage. In fact, he calls those who are opposed to it—which would be most Americans—bigots. Consider what happened in 1996 when President Clinton signed the Defense of Marriage Act, a bill that protects states from being forced to recognize gay marriages performed elsewhere (only 14 senators voted against it).

Greeley called the legislation the "Gay-Bashing Bill," wondering aloud why "the gay-bashers just don't leave gays alone." He added, "Nor do I understand the profoundly un-Christian hatred for them,"[20] making clear that anyone who supports the traditional understanding of marriage as being between a man and a woman (this would include the Catholic Church) was a gay-bashing SOB. Greeley is so committed to the radical gay agenda that he thinks men who abuse boys are not "necessarily gay." So what would they be? "They might just be the kind of people who enjoy variety in their sexual partners."[21] Either that or child rapists.

Gay marriage is not only something Catholic dissidents

rally to defend, they seek to sabotage Catholic theology. Father James F. Keenan is a Jesuit theologian who is convinced that homosexuality is not an unnatural orientation, it is a manifestation of human love.[22] His interest in reworking the Bible makes it easier to understand why he testified before a committee of the Massachusetts State Legislature in opposition to a bill that would prevent for gay unions legal benefits that are identical to those afforded married couples. "I cannot see how anyone could use the Roman Catholic tradition to support [the bill]," he testified in 2003. "On the contrary," he explained, "the Catholic theological tradition stands against the active and unjust discrimination against the basic social rights of gay and lesbian persons."[23] True enough, but what he failed to say was that the Catholic Church does not consider it "unjust discrimination" to deny identical rights to gay men that are afforded married men and women.

Father Keenan was not alone in misrepresenting Catholic teaching on the subject. Two other priests, Thomas J. Carroll and Richard P. Lewandowski, also testified before the Joint Committee on the Judiciary; they, too, left the impression that gay marriage was okay. What they said deviated so badly from what the Catholic Church pronounces that the Massachusetts Catholic Conference was required to issue a public memorandum titled "Erroneous Testimony on Catholic Teaching." The memo said that "all three [priests] mischaracterized the teaching of the Catholic Church, while two mischaracterized the position of the Catholic Bishops specifically." In conclusion, the priests were indicted for communicating "their personal opinions to the committee under the false guise of authority to the detriment of the integrity of the public hearing process."[24] This is a serious charge, and it is entirely warranted.

Deconstructing Catholic teaching is not only a favorite tactic of pro-gay Catholics, it is a popular strategy with pro-abortion Catholics as well. Beginning in 1984, pro-abortion

Catholics such as Catholics Speak Out started taking out full-page ads in the *New York Times* declaring there was a plurality of legitimate Catholic positions on abortion. The person who was most responsible for advancing this dishonest idea was Mario Cuomo, the three-term governor of New York. In 1984, he gave his infamous Notre Dame speech where he floated the "I'm personally opposed but" position on abortion. It was not Biology 101 that informed us that human life begins at conception, he argued, but religion. Picking up on this view was vice-presidential candidate Geraldine Ferraro, the result of which was an ensuing public battle between her and New York's Cardinal O'Connor. She maintained, without any evidence, that there was more than one Catholic view on abortion that was legitimate. House Speaker Nancy Pelosi and Obama's VP pick, Joe Biden, spouted the same nonsense in 2008.

Worse than Ferraro was Father Robert F. Drinan. He actually defended President Clinton's veto of a bill that would have banned the killing of innocent human children who are 80 percent born. Astonishingly, he said that he agreed with Vatican II when it said that "abortion is virtually infanticide," but he then went on to conclude that a bill banning "so-called" partial-birth abortions "would not reduce the number of abortions." He never explained why. But he was very sure that such a bill "would allow Federal power to intrude into the practice of medicine in an unprecedented way."[25] It was left to Cardinal O'Connor (again) to put Drinan in his place: the New York Archbishop blasted the former lawmaker in *Catholic New York*, the weekly newspaper of the archdiocese. Drinan was smart enough to drop the issue once and for all.[26]

Catholics for Choice

Most people are aware that the Catholic Church does not have multiple positions on abortion any more than it has several teachings on genocide, but this hasn't stopped anti-Catholic members of the establishment from trying to sell this invidious notion to the public. To be specific, the Ford Foundation, George Soros's Open Society Institute, the Buffett Foundation (named after the money tycoon), the MacArthur Foundation, the Hewlett Foundation, the Packard Foundation, and an array of others fund a phony Catholic group, Catholics For Choice (CFC—formerly Catholics for a Free Choice).[27] Unlike the Catholic League, which is a true membership organization, the CFC is a foundation-supported entity. Indeed, it is nothing more than a well-greased letterhead led for decades by Frances Kissling, and now by Jon O'Brien. If the fat cats who fund CFC were to fund Jews for Jesus, they would be branded anti-Semitic. However, the charge of anti-Catholicism doesn't have the same sting, thus allowing them to stick their secular noses into the affairs of the Catholic Church.

The truth is that to many—and count me among them—the CFC is really just an anti-Catholic front group that promotes abortion on demand all over the world. Consider what Kissling once admitted: "I spent twenty years looking for a government that I could overthrow without being in jail. I finally found one in the Catholic Church."[28]

CFC was founded in 1973, setting up shop in the headquarters of New York's Planned Parenthood. Once abortion was legalized, CFC joined with the Religious Coalition for Abortion Rights, moving decisively to counter efforts for a Human Rights Amendment. Its first president, Father Joseph O'Rourke, was expelled from the Jesuits in 1974, but that didn't stop him from serving as president until 1979. Kissling took over in 1982.

The following statement is typical of the way CFC distorts

Catholic teaching: "The bishops won't tell you, but CFC will: There is an authentic prochoice Catholic position." It was due to disinformation like this—there is no pro-abortion position that is authentically Catholic—that on November 4, 1993, the United States Catholic bishops released a statement reading, "many people, including Catholics, may be led to believe that it [CFC] is an authentic Catholic organization. It is not. It has no affiliation, formal or otherwise, with the Catholic Church." They added that CFC "is associated with the pro-abortion lobby in Washington, D.C." and "attracts public attention by its denunciations of basic principles of Catholic morality and teaching." In May 2000, Bishop Joseph Fiorenza, the head of the bishops' conference, denounced CFC again for rejecting and distorting Catholic teachings on life issues.[29]

Perhaps the most severe blow to the reputation of CFC came on April 21, 1995. That was the day the *National Catholic Reporter* printed a letter by Marjorie Reiley Maguire blasting CFC. Maguire, an attorney who was once married to the ex-Jesuit and Marquette University professor Dan Maguire, was once a prominent member of CFC. Indeed, she and her radical husband were once the CFC's poster couple. But like many others who came of age in the 1960s, Marjorie began to have second thoughts. Included in her intellectual migration were second thoughts about CFC and Catholicism.

In her letter, Maguire branded CFC as "an anti-woman organization" whose agenda was "the promotion of abortion, the defense of every abortion decision as a good, moral choice and the related agenda of persuading society to cast off any moral constraints about sexual behavior." She further explained that it was not the Catholic Church that is "hung up on sex." Questioning the right of CFC to call itself Catholic, Maguire said, "When I was involved with [CFC], I was never aware that any of its leaders attended Mass. Furthermore, various conversations and experiences convinced me they did not."[30]

The only reason why this shell of an organization exists is because it serves the interests of secular saboteurs out to gut the Catholic Church. In 2008, it published a lengthy "investigative report" on me (for which it received funding from the Robert Sterling Clark Foundation). Alas, there was no new dirt, just some recycled stuff. I graciously corrected some typos and returned it to them requesting a correction.

Homegrown Dissidents

The secular left that funds CFC may be responsible for Kissling's agenda, but it has nothing to do with homegrown dissidents within the ranks of priests and religious. Take nuns. In 1978, Sister Mary Theresa Glynn testified before the Florida State Senate Rules and Calendar Committee in opposition to a proposed constitutional convention on a human life amendment to the state constitution. "I am here to say that the Catholic position on abortion is not so cohesive," said the Sister of Mary nun, "not so monolithic as is often presented."[31]

How is it possible to be a pro-abortion nun? Realistically, it makes no sense, but in the minds of some of those associated with the social justice wing of the Catholic Church, it is not hard to fathom. To be sure, it's not as though left-wing Catholics are actually in favor of abortion, it's just that they don't agree with the Church that it is "intrinsically evil." Take, for example, the Catholic organization NETWORK.

NETWORK was founded in the early 1970s by radical nuns professing a strong belief in social justice but no interest whatsoever in abortion. It is so radical and unrepresentative of American Catholics that it has butted heads several times with the Church hierarchy in the United States, as well as in Rome. In 1983, it took the side of a dissident nun who refused to denounce publicly funded abortions. When the Sisters of Mercy nun refused, the Vatican stepped in to force her to leave her order. NETWORK responded with boilerplate, saying it "deeply regrets the authoritarian exercise of administrative power on the part of Vatican officials."[32] The very next year, Sister Marjorie Tuite, a founder of NETWORK, was herself threatened with expulsion from her order for signing an ad calling for the Catholic Church to reconsider its opposition to abortion. When she died two years later, she was remembered for accusing the Church of treating women unjustly.[33]

In 1988, the National Coalition of American Nuns joined with CFC and others filing an amicus brief in support of abortion rights. In 1996, the same group of nuns joined the usual suspects in warning Catholic bishops "to refrain from the single-issue partisan campaign against abortion that has characterized your activity in this election season." The following year, the abortion-happy nuns wrote President Clinton protesting the lack of federal funds for poor women seeking an abortion.[34]

It is because so many of the women religious have thrown Catholic doctrine overboard that few young women are drawn to them. After all, why give up the joy of starting a family if the lifestyle of a nun is almost indistinguishable from that of a social worker? Not only have the more "progressive" orders of nuns exchanged their habits for polyester suits, they no longer live and pray together in a community. So it is hardly surprising to learn that, with the important exception of orthodox nuns like the Sisters of Life, the convents have long been emptying. At the end of Vatican II in the mid-1960s, there were 180,000 sisters in the United States. Today there are 65,000, with an average age of 70.[35]

Dominican Sister Laurie Brink, who teaches at the Catholic Theological Union in Chicago, addressed 750 leaders of women's religious communities in Kansas City, Missouri, in 2007. Admitting that dissident nuns have failed to accomplish their mission, she advised that some congregations could "rightly and valiantly" choose death; thus did she suggest that it was defensible to shut down altogether rather than continue and thereby give tacit assent to the status quo. Another method for dealing with reality was "reconciliation." As she put it, "Reconciliation first with our hierarchical church from which we have experienced abuse, oppression, neglect and domination."[36] Why she simply didn't want to blow it up she did not say. But she did admit that "we may not avail ourselves of the sacraments," adding that some sisters have "moved beyond Jesus."[37]

It would be unfair to say that Sister Brink speaks for all nuns. Legions of nuns have led a life of dedication to the Catholic Church, asking little in return. Indeed, many are happy with the Church the way it is and resent the fact that Sister Brink appears to be speaking for them. Nonetheless, as *Our Sunday Visitor*'s Ann Carey observes, "Women Religious are among the most public Catholics ignoring or challenging Church teaching and authority." As examples, she cites Catholic hospitals sponsored by women religious that permit sterilizations, pro–gay marriage nuns, sisters who have worked with Catholics for Choice trying to get the Holy See kicked out of the United Nations, pro-abortion nuns, and women religious who attend pagan events such as Earth Spirit Rising.[38] In other words, they are out to sabotage the Catholic Church. Most Catholics, never mind others, would be shocked to learn just how out of control some of these nun activists have become.

Just as mind-boggling is the fact that the ranks of lay dissidents are full of ex-priests and ex-nuns, as well as those who studied to become priests or religious and dropped out. The average Catholic has no idea that these disaffected Catholics have taught religion or have worked in some capacity for the Church for several decades. They are disproportionately represented in the bureaucracy of the bishops' conference as well as in chancery offices and have found their way into teaching CCD to Catholic students who attend public schools. Overwhelmingly left of center in their politics, they assert the primacy of conscience over the directives of the magisterium (the official teaching body of the Catholic Church, i.e., the pope in communion with the bishops).

Take Catholic Charities, for example. Tied to the welfare establishment (it would collapse absent federal funding), it turned so far to the left in the 1960s that it literally lost its bearings. Brian C. Anderson captured what was happening at the time. "Catholic Charities first announced its politicization in a wild-eyed manifesto that invokes such radical sixties icons as Malcolm X, Gloria Steinem, Herbert Marcuse, and—above all—the Marxist-inspired liberation theology movement that (to put it crudely) equates Jesus with Che Guevara."[39] Anderson is not given to hyperbole. Unfortunately, much of the good work that Catholic Charities does has been tarnished by those who harbor a political agenda.

Accepting the teachings of the Catholic Church on important moral issues is not a condition of employment at Catholic Charities. This is especially true of abortion and gay rights. Here are two unassailable examples. In 2008, four employees of Catholic Charities in Richmond, Virginia, were arrested for helping a 16-year-old Guatemalan girl get an abortion; it is against the law in Virginia for a social worker to sign a parental consent form for an abortion.[40] As a result of this fiasco, all Catholic Charities employees in the diocese were required to learn what the Catholic Church teaches on various moral issues. Why it wasn't done earlier is a disgrace.

In the same year, San Francisco's Catholic Charities held a fund-raiser for HIV/AIDS programs. That was fine, but what was sickening was the sight of professed enemies of the Catholic Church attending the party in their capacity as event organizers. For instance, San Francisco mayor Gavin Newsom has a long history of publicly condemning the Catholic Church over its teachings on sexuality, yet he was chosen to be an honorary committee member of the event. So, too, was Bevan Dufty, a member of San Francisco's Board of Supervisors. The board is so imbued with hatred of all things Catholic that it was sued in 2006 by the Thomas More Law Center, representing the Catholic League, for unconstitutionally promoting hostility to the Catholic Church; the board had passed a unanimous resolution that year condemning the Vatican for "meddling" in the city's customs and traditions. The Vatican's crime? Its opposition to gay adoptions.[41]

Sociologist Joseph Varacalli rightly credits Monsignor Michael Wrenn and Kenneth Whitehead for substantiating "the reality that large parts of a liberal 'catechetical establishment' have refused to teach the official Church line on homosexuality and on a host of other hot-button issues."[42] Catholic higher education is worse still.

Theologian Michael Novak sees two kinds of dissent at Catholic colleges and universities. The first is represented by faculty who entertain a secular mind-set, one that is preparing them "for the Church of the future." The other kind of dissent, he says, "is that of faculty who are openly anti-Catholic, and who abhor a great deal of what the Church teaches."[43] Another astute student of the Church, Father Joseph Fessio, estimates that about 90 percent of theologians on Catholic campuses do not accept Catholic teaching on sexuality and the priesthood.[44] Whatever the correct figure might be, as sociologist Anne Hendershott has detailed, it is beyond dispute that the secularization of Catholic higher education did not happen by accident: it happened because Catholic dissidents worked hard to make it happen.[45]

Catholic colleges have declined so much that a lay organization has been established to call them back to their moorings: the Cardinal Newman Society blows the whistle on Catholic institutions that have lost their way. It has its work cut out for itself. I worked at a Catholic college where the president was a feminist nun who favored Protestant women candidates to succeed her over a competing monsignor; he was deemed unworthy simply because he was a priest. The same college used to hire nothing but Protestant chaplains. None of this, of course, has anything to do with being ecumenical—it has to do with a calculated attempt to sabotage Catholicism from within.

The saboteurs have also engaged in campaigns of religious cleansing at Catholic schools. When a student at Boston College wanted to start a Holy Name Society he was denied on the grounds that it was an all-male organization. At the same school, it was left to Jews and Muslims to protest the removal of crucifixes from the classroom: they wisely accused school officials of assuming they were anti-Catholic bigots who might be offended by the Christian symbol.[46] Stung with criticism, Boston College officials decided to study the issue of increasing the presence of religious symbols on the campus.

Eight years later, in 2009, the crucifixes were put back up in the classrooms. But it didn't please Maxim D. Shrayer, chairman of the department of Slavic and Eastern languages and literatures. "I believe the display of religious signs and symbols, such as the crucifix, in the classroom is contrary to the letter and spirit of open intellectual discourse that makes education worthwhile and distinguishes first-rate universities from mediocre and provincial ones," he said.[47] So typical. The secularists at Catholic institutions are always scared to death that their colleagues at secular institutions will think less of them for teaching at one of those Catholic schools. If they had any integrity, they'd pack up and leave.

When Georgetown announced that it was going to remove crucifixes from its classrooms in 2004, the most vocal critic was Yahya Hendi, the school's Muslim chaplain.[48] Georgetown is also home to a pro-abortion group, Hoyas for Choice, and is so far gone that when an African cardinal spoke at a graduation ceremony in 2003 saying that an anti-life mentality exists in many parts of the world, angry professors left the stage where he spoke and 70 faculty members signed a letter of protest. His offense? He said such a mind-set is "mocked by homosexuality," among other things. That was it.[49]

Ends and Means

Ask an anti-American in the United States why he hates America and the likely answer is that the U.S. is great for what it stands for, but not for what it has become. The same is true of Catholic saboteurs: they profess an allegiance to a Church that doesn't exist. Meantime, they do everything they can to undermine the only one that does.

Most of the dissidents are dreamers. And of all the dreams they ever had, none was more exciting than the vision of the Church they witnessed on the ABC TV show *Nothing Sacred*. Until the Catholic League killed their dream, that is. At least 37 sponsors, and as many as 50 plus, withdrew their ads as a direct result of a boycott. Indeed, the Catholic League was credited as the first advocacy organization in the nation to successfully use its Web site to launch a boycott. The show, which aired during the 1997–98 season, also bombed in the ratings: after the first 11 episodes, it was tied for 107th place.

It would be an understatement to say that disaffected Catholics liked the show. No, they worshipped it. Like little boys and girls, they literally cried their eyes out when it aired, rearranging their life to keep pace with the show's ever-changing schedule (there isn't a big market for shows that appeal only to alienated Catholics, so ABC constantly had to experiment with new days and times). When the show died of natural causes—with more than a little help from the Catholic League—a Brooklyn nun literally held a vigil for her friends. Yes, it was just that sad.

What they liked most about the show was Father Ray. He looked scruffy, came from a dysfunctional family, thought of his vocation as merely a job, openly admitted he wasn't sure about the existence of God, violated his duty as a confessor, and rejected the Church's teachings on sexuality. But he loved the homeless. We knew this because he gave them a cup of coffee. By contrast, those Catholics who were loyal sons and daughters of the Church were portrayed as coldhearted, tyrannical, and bigoted.

The show's pilot had Father Ray telling his parishioners from the pulpit that it was time to "call a moratorium on the sins of the flesh." There is nothing sweeter to the ear of dissidents than this. He also told the faithful that the Church's teachings on homosexuality, promiscuity, abortion, and contraception could be ignored because the Bible says little or nothing about them. He boasted that he was not a "sexual traffic cop," and advised the faithful that if that was what they wanted, they had better shop around for another priest.

It wasn't just Father Ray who was a loser priest. One of his colleagues, Father Leo, was shown dutifully apologizing to Rachel: she had had an abortion and Leo was guilty of being "judgmental." Then there was Father Eric, the boob who was shown being utterly unable to explain basic theology to his high school kids. But at least he didn't have strange spots on his hands like Father Philip. Like all the other priests, poor Phil was depressed; he was also an alcoholic. To show balance, the show introduced Sister Mo, a nun who pretended she was saying Mass (inmates in the asylum have been known to do the same), all the while drifting between Catholicism and Buddhism.

The most telling commentary came from cardinals, bishops, priests, brothers, and nuns who either praised the show or attacked the Catholic League for protesting it. The Los Angeles archdiocesan newspaper, *The Tidings*, hailed the show as worthy of a "Lenten reflection." Four bishops took out an ad criticizing the Catholic League's campaign. Writers such as Father Greeley went ballistic. Best of all was Brother Michael Breault, a Jesuit writer for the show. He admitted that the show was based on his experiences at St. Francis Xavier in New York City. Until recently, he confessed, women preached after the Gospel, the church was run by parishioners (many of whom he identified as gay), liturgies were invented, etc.[50] No wonder Father Ray was his alter ego.

If *Nothing Sacred* symbolizes the ends, the means is revisionism. The left has always been good at discrediting the past as a way of discrediting the present. So when Garry Wills, John Cornwell, and James Carroll write books smearing the Catholic Church's response to the Holocaust, they seem to be less interested in the purported subject than they are in weakening the prestige of the Church today. It's a game they play, and many Catholics and Jews have fallen for it. But not Rabbi David Dalin, author of *The Myth of Hitler's Pope.*

"The anti-papal polemics of ex-seminarians like Garry Wills and John Cornwell, and of ex-priests like James Carroll, and of other lapsed and angry liberal Catholics," writes Dalin, "exploit the tragedy of the Jewish people during the Holocaust to foster their own political agenda of forcing changes on the Catholic Church today." He cites their opposition to "issues relating to sexuality, abortion, contraception, priestly celibacy and the role of women in the Church" as the basis of their agenda.[51] Dalin is exactly right.

Take Wills. In his book *Papal Sin: Structures of Deceit*, he assigns collective guilt to the entire Catholic Church for any actions taken by any Catholics during the Holocaust that were sinful. But this is nothing more than a ruse. Wills not only wants the Catholic Church to change its teachings on women and sexuality, he wants the Church to junk its theology. "In the course of the book," writes Catholic author Robert Lockwood, "he rejects the teaching authority of the Church if exercised without lay involvement and agreement, the concept of papal infallibility and any possible divine guidance to papal teaching, the ordained priesthood, the doctrine of the Real Presence in the Eucharist and that the priest has sacramental powers alone to consecrate the Eucharist. Apostolic succession, the Immaculate Conception and Assumption, and Church teaching on homosexuality are dismissed as well."[52] That just about covers it.

The Englishman John Cornwell made quite a splash when he promoted the utterly baseless charge that Pius XII was "Hitler's Pope" (he later recanted this accusation, though it got little play in the media). What was most striking about his book was the way he used the Holocaust as a foil for his politics. How do we know? How else does one explain why a book on the Catholic Church and the Holocaust would end with a chapter attacking Pope John Paul II for reaffirming Church teachings on celibacy, women priests, artificial contraception, and abortion? What does any of this have to do with Nazi Germany? Nothing. But casting aspersions on Pius XII serves to weaken the moral base of his successors.

Bob Lockwood nailed James Carroll for playing the same game. *Constantine's Sword* was allegedly about its subtitle, *The Church and the Jews*. But as with Cornwell, the last section of his book has nothing to do with his professed subject: he closes with a clarion call for Vatican III. As summarized by Lockwood, Carroll says, "The Church must abandon claims to universal and objective truth, realize the Gospels are anti-Semitic, abandon theology of the atonement of Christ for the sins of mankind, reject papal infallibility, ordain women, elect bishops, dismantle the 'medieval clerical caste' [and] forget the belief that Jesus is the only means to salvation." Lockwood properly labels Carroll's solution a call for Unitarianism.[53]

Now, if Wills, Cornwell, and Carroll were to have their way, then the *Nothing Sacred* Catholic Church they so pine for would materialize. Then the saboteurs wouldn't have to talk about the Holocaust ever again. Unfortunately for them, there is still something called Rome.

Dissidents Are a Dying Breed

Buoyed by "the spirit of Vatican II" and encouraged by Pope Paul VI's 1971 appeal to Catholics that they "address a fresh and insistent call to action," a group of bishops, priests, religious, and laypeople assembled in Detroit in 1976 to form Call to Action. The delegates ranged from those who wanted the Church to adopt the social policy of secular leftists to those who wanted radical doctrinal changes. Russell Kirk said the delegates were quite candid in their aspiration to remake the Catholic Church in the image and likeness of "the extreme left-wing of the Democratic Party."[54] John Cardinal Dearden of Detroit chaired the conference, calling it "a new way of doing the work of the church in America."[55] No one could disagree.

Guess who was there? According to Call to Action's own words, those in attendance "represented the church's 'middle management'; 64 percent were church employees."[56] Those were the good years. By 2000 they were ready for assisted living. Colleen Carroll described what went on at the annual conference, held in Milwaukee: "The conference spilled over with gray-haired radicals, priests wielding canes, and nuns dressing as defiantly as septuagenarians can." To make matters worse, in order to fill a room of "the next generation," conference organizers "defined young adults as anyone between the ages of eighteen and forty-two—a move that provoked snickers among the college-aged students in attendance."[57]

Call to Action has flipped out so much over the years that Bishop Fabian Bruskewitz of Lincoln, Nebraska, announced in 1996 that any Catholic who joined the group would be excommunicated. In 2006, Bruskewitz celebrated the 10-year anniversary (he excommunicated dissidents on the right who also rejected Vatican II) by branding Call to Action "an anti-Catholic sect composed mainly of aging fallen-away Catholics, including ex-priests and ex-nuns."[58] The dissidents took their final hit in 2007 when the Vatican's highest court ruled against them: Call to Action wanted the Vatican to overturn Bishop Bruskewitz's decision to oust them, but the jurists in Rome contended they had no right to do so.[59]

In 2008, the codirectors of Call to Action announced their retirement. Dan and Sheila Daley had done their best to sow dissent among the faithful, and now it was time to move to Florida. Like other embittered ex-priests and ex-nuns, the Daleys were unable to move on with their lives without fighting yesterday's battles time and again. What they left behind was in such shambles that Tom Roberts, one of their fans, questioned whether the organization had a future, especially given the fact that it is "old and graying."[60]

Call to Action got some competition in 2002 when Voice of the Faithful (VOTF) was founded in Boston. Unlike Call to Action, VOTF sells itself as a reformist movement, brandishing its motto "Keep the Faith, Change the Church." But it has been obvious from the beginning that the lay group, formed in response to the scandal in the Church (Boston was the epicenter), had a lot more in common with Call to Action than it was prepared to admit. Indeed, only months after VOTF started, Call to Action welcomed them with open arms. Commenting on the inaugural convention in Boston, Call to Action director Dan Daley boasted, "It is a wonderful coming of age of another strong lay voice in the reform movement."[61]

The inaugural convention was quite a display of dissidents, as well as those whose hostility to Catholic values was palpable. Non-Catholics like Debra Haffner, who works tirelessly against the Church's teachings on sexuality, were invited to speak. Haffner was once president of the Sexuality Information and Education Council of the United States, an organization that is pro-gay marriage and pro-abortion. Paul Lakeland, a Catholic professor from Fairfield University, thrilled the crowd by informing them that they were "suffocating from structural oppression" (as opposed to random oppression), and imagined a future Church that might resemble the United Church of Christ.[62] This is not exactly encouraging news given that the United Church of Christ is collapsing.

The following year, VOTF held its conference at Fordham University, this time inviting Eugene Kennedy to give the keynote address. Kennedy is another ex-priest dissident, and his big interest is sex. In his address, "The Unhealed Wound: The Church and Human Sexuality," he blasted the Church's teachings on sexuality, blaming them for causing so much "grief, guilt and self-hatred in its members down through the centuries."[63] Makes one wonder how Catholics managed to have such big families.

Self-hatred might be the proper term to describe angry ex-priests, and someone who might know is Richard Sipe. Sipe is a former Benedictine monk who specializes in writing about sexual abuse, but only if committed by priests. Married to a former Maryknoll nun, he dazzled the crowd with his dissident views. Anthony Massimini was there as well. His contribution was to alert everyone to "the psychological and spiritual damage being done to the Church" by priestly celibacy; he said the damage was "immense."[64] Oh yes, Massimini is another ex-priest.

Things had gotten so out of hand with VOTF that by 2006 journalists were openly questioning the fidelity of the organization to the Catholic Church. Why, for example, does VOTF, which claims to "keep the faith," constantly feature in its newsletter people like Valerie Schultz, a pro–gay marriage Catholic religion teacher, and Daniel Maguire, a man who positively loathes the Church's teachings on a wide range of subjects?[65] And why is it that when the Catholic League fights bills in states that would end the priest-penitent privilege, which is analogous to exemptions afforded psychologists and others, it winds up fighting with a VOTF member who pushed for the legislation in the first place?[66]

Almost all Catholics who hear bad news about the Church are disappointed, saddened, or angry, but not the dissidents: they love it. As they see it, it's another reform opportunity to seize. What they don't like is good news. To wit, when the Catholic League ran an op-ed page ad in the *New York Times* in 2006 citing data that showed how priestly sexual abuse had practically come to a halt, it was criticized the next day by VOTF for being too optimistic.[67] The *National Catholic Reporter* ran a lengthy editorial also criticizing our statement,[68] though they were fair enough to allow me a lengthy reply.[69]

A profile of Catholics who belong to VOTF shows they have more in common with Call to Action than just ideology. "With their gray hair and their overwhelming preference for decaffeinated drinks," wrote the *San Francisco Chronicle* in 2005, "the nearly 100 members of the lay Catholic group Voice of the Faithful who gathered inside St. Matthew's Catholic Church gym in San Mateo on Sunday didn't look too intimidating."[70] Then they did what they always do—they burst into singing and broke into small groups for discussion. They love that.

On the east coast, John Marshall Lee, who owns an insurance company, went to a VOTF meeting in Connecticut in 2003 "and the first thing that surprised him was the age of the people." As he told a reporter, "I met a group of people who were alert, probably average of 70 to 75."[71] This is the kind of comment one might expect from someone visiting a nursing home, not a meeting on how to revamp the Catholic Church.

Even Paul Lakeland is forced to admit that the typical person who attends Call to Action and VOTF meetings is over the hill. "While the statistics may not be available," he writes, "it would be a fair wager that many if not most spent some time in the seminary or the convent, even if the majority of them did not proceed to ordination or solemn profession in their religious congregations. A good sprinkling are ex-nuns and resigned priests." A realist, Lakeland says, "Today they continue to fight for a more progressive future for the Catholic Church, though as they look around them for younger faces at their meetings, they must wonder if it's a losing battle."[72] Peter Feuerherd of the *National Catholic Reporter* agrees with this assessment, estimating that many of those who graduated from the Pastoral Formation Institute during the tenure of Rockville Centre

Bishop John McGann, 1976 to 2000, "are now active in Voice of the Faithful."[73]

A month after Lakeland wrote that statistics weren't available on VOTF, the numbers were in. Two researchers from Catholic University of America, William V. D'Antonio and Father Anthony Pogorelc, published their findings on the group. "One of the most distinctive characteristics among members is their high level of education, with 87 percent holding college degrees and six out of 10 also earning a master's or professional degree," they said. In fact, "Almost a quarter of Voice members hold degrees in theology, canon law or scriptural studies, and almost as many said they participated in diocesan- or parish-sponsored courses in theology." They are overwhelmingly Irish (64 percent), senior citizens (41 percent are 65 or older), and wealthy (the majority earn in excess of $100,000 annually).[74] Though they are rich, they are also stingy: only 25 percent donate money to VOTF.[75]

By 2007, it was evident that VOTF was spent. The same organization that lectured the Catholic Church on financial accountability was running a deficit of $100,000 with no end in sight. To top it off, only 1 to 5 percent of its members even bothered to provide input on proposals when asked to do so in 2007.[76] The old-timers gave it their best shot and failed. Indeed, in VOTF's "Strategic Plan for 2008–2010," they confessed to "general apathy and discontent among leadership, which continues to hinder our fundraising ability."[77] Yes, it isn't easy to raise funds when the leaders are in a state of depression.

Once the Church made necessary reforms, VOTF became increasingly irrelevant. So it was left with two choices: either pack up and go home or go off the deep end. It did the latter. In 2008, it sponsored a dissident Australian bishop, Geoffrey Robinson, in a tour of the United States. Robinson was censured by his own bishops for calling into question "Catholic teaching on, among other things, the nature of tradition, the inspiration of the holy scripture, the infallibility of the councils and the pope, the authority of the creed, the nature of the ministerial priesthood and central elements of the church's moral teaching."[78] For good measure, he also questioned the teachings on adultery and homosexuality. His views were so far off the charts that Los Angeles Archbishop Roger Mahony told him he wasn't welcome to speak in his archdiocese.[79] But he was right at home with VOTF—their beliefs were one and the same. In the fall of 2008, VOTF formally broke from its mission of fostering "structural change": it issued a statement calling for an end to priestly celibacy.[80]

Church dissidents, with the same profile, showed up in Philadelphia in July 2008 to attend a meeting convened by Catholics in Alliance for the Common Good and NETWORK. They were there to support Obama for president, though they billed the event as nonpartisan. According to one of the attendees, "Almost everyone was over 60; out of 700 only about 30 were any younger." Another observer opined, "In looking over the registration list, I would estimate that 25% or more of the attendees were sisters. If many of the older women there were religious, you would not have known it by their dress."[81] So fitting.

In 2009, it looked like the old timers at VOTF had won: two Connecticut lawmakers angry at the Catholic Church's opposition to gay marriage introduced legislation authorizing the state to reorganize the Catholic Church. Under the bill, all priests and bishops would lose their administrative and fiscal power: Parishioners would be granted that right. And we know which kind of parishioners they would be—they most certainly would not be Catholic League types. We know this because the legislation was right out of the VOTF playbook. Moreover, Tom Gallagher, who proposed the legislation, was also a contributor (not surprisingly) to the *National Catholic Reporter.*

As it turned out, all of them were caught off-guard. Connecticut bishops, led by Bridgeport Bishop William Lori, the Connecticut Catholic Conference, the Catholic League (which called for the legislators to be expelled), and thousands of Catholics across the state, erupted in protest. The fascist power grab died quickly and the bill was withdrawn.[82] But that didn't stop 5,000 Catholics from showing up the next day to voice their outrage.[83] The results were conclusive: the Catholic left went down in defeat.

After their loss, one of VOTF's champions, Paul Lakeland, said the bill was justified because the bishops, while stripped of their right to run their dioceses, still had control over doctrinal matters. His defense of the failed coup underscores the thesis of this book: he is chairman of the Catholic studies department at Fairfield University, a Jesuit institution.[84]

Rebels Cry Uncle

It is one of the great myths of our day that the Catholic Church is an oppressive institution that brooks no dissent. Quite frankly, there are few institutions that tolerate more of it. For several decades, rebellious nuns and priests have carried on in a way that would have gotten them fired had they worked for any major newspaper in the nation. Without doubt, there is more tolerance for contrarian views in the Catholic Church than exists on the typical college campus, and this is doubly true of the elite institutions. But reality doesn't count for Catholic dissidents— they are convinced that the Church is the great oppressor. One of the more recent examples they cite is the fate of Father Roger Haight, a Jesuit whom the Vatican has prohibited from teaching theology, at least temporarily.

Father Haight is not just a priest. He has spent years teaching seminarians and instructing the faithful through his writings. In the name of teaching what the Catholic Church believes, he taught what he believes, and what he believes is not what the Catholic Church believes. At issue is not something like priestly celibacy, a discipline the Church requires but is not part of Church dogma. Haight's problem with the Catholic Church is much deeper: he rejects, among other teachings, the divinity of Jesus, the Holy Trinity, the saving value of Jesus' death, and the Resurrection.[85]

Now, if a geography teacher were to teach that the earth is flat, or a math teacher were to insist that two plus two equals five, he would be terminated. Moreover, no one would rise to his defense, not even the teachers' unions, and cries of oppression would be laughed at universally. But Father Haight was not bounced out of the priesthood. All he was told to do was stop teaching theology. If he ever comes around to accepting the Church's teachings, he can return to the classroom. This sanction, which is typical of the way the Vatican treats theologians who entertain heretical views, was not imposed until a five-year investigation was completed. In the meantime, Haight, who had been suspended by the Jesuit-run Weston School of Theology, continued to teach theology at the Union Theological Seminary in New York, home to radical Protestants.

Not surprisingly, his ideological friends at the Catholic Theological Society of America, an organization with a long track record of dissent, raced to his side. Ten members of the board of directors, all professors, issued a statement expressing their "profound distress" at the Vatican's decision.[86] They issued no statement of regret regarding Haight's insubordination or his corrupting effect on the faithful.

In 2009, the Vatican asked Father Haight not to teach Christology at any university. And how was this slap on the wrist accepted by the Jesuits? As a slap in the face. Father Giuseppe Bellucci, spokesman for the Jesuits, quickly pronounced Haight to be "an excellent Jesuit" and said that the decision by the Congregation for the Doctrine of the Faith was not "definitive"; he added that a committee of Jesuits would "study" Haight's positions.[87] What exactly there was to study—did Haight really mean that Jesus wasn't divine when he said He wasn't?—he did not say.

When not complaining about oppression, the dissidents complain that they are the true representatives of the laity and should therefore be treated as their spokesmen. They point to public opinion polls that appear to show that a large segment of the Catholic laity would have no problem with either married priests or women priests and are prepared to accept some changes in Church teachings on human sexuality. Call to Action, for example, which is a small organization, says it represents 70 percent of American Catholics.[88] The evidence shows, however, that such projections are not simply wrong, they are delusional.

On Ash Wednesday, 1990, Call to Action ran a *New York Times* ad calling for reform in the Catholic Church. It was signed by more than 4,500 dissidents, and a pledge was made to garner 100,000. A half-year later, James Carroll, the angry ex-priest, predicted, "I'll be surprised if they don't make it."[89] Over a year later, and after more than a year and a half of collecting signatures, the final tally was in: 21,000. At that time, Call to Action had 9,000 members, and considering that they started with 4,500 signatures and could only get an additional 16,500, it suggests that they were living in a cocoon.[90] They still are.

Sister Maureen Fiedler thinks most Catholics agree with her. In April 1996, she launched a petition drive aimed at getting one million Catholics to sign a statement calling for radical changes in the Church's teachings on women and sexuality. The campaign was dubbed We Are Church and was richly funded by the establishment: the Ford Foundation laundered millions to Sister Maureen by way of Kissling's Catholics for Choice. "We were blessed with substantial grants," she said. "We had organizing kits, we had grass-roots [efforts]; we did full-page ads [in newspapers]; we had massive mailings; we did public collections in front of cathedrals, like St. Patrick's in New York," she added. She forgot to mention that she even bribed kids by giving them a dollar for every signature they snatched.[91]

After a year was up, the results were so disappointing that Sister Maureen was generous enough to give her group an extension of six months. The final tally: 37,000. Which means she was off by over 96 percent. She actually did worse than this given that one-third of the signatures came from non-Catholics. The good sister addressed her utter failure at a Call to Action meeting in Detroit in 1997, blowing up at lay Catholics: she agreed with one conference coordinator who said that progressives "overestimated Catholic theological maturity, and underestimated the pietism of the Catholic laity."[92] In other words, the rank-and-file simpletons just didn't get it. That's what the Marxists have always said about the proletariat's refusal to rebel—they haven't matured enough to understand their own oppression.

The 1960s

Sociologically, it made sense that Vatican II would occur in the 1960s. If the reins were too tight in the 1950s, it made sense that Vatican II would be the corrective. But when institutions change, they need to be careful that an easy stride doesn't turn into a raging gallop. This is what happened to the Catholic Church.

Pope John XXIII is famous for saying that the Catholic Church needed "to open its windows to the modern world." But as George Weigel has observed, the Church "opened its windows just as the modern, western world was barreling into a dark tunnel full of poisonous fumes." Indeed, "By the time the Church got its windows open in the mid-1960s, there were all sorts of toxins in the air."[93] Those toxins included radical individualism and a celebration of narcissism. Critical distinctions between authoritativeness and authoritarianism were lost, undermining the rights and responsibilities of parents, teachers, coaches, policemen, priests, ministers, rabbis, and others. Some in the Catholic Church, like the Sisters of Immaculate Heart of Mary (IHM) in Los Angeles, welcomed these assaults on hierarchy and discipline and openly participated in a revolt against them.

In 1965, humanistic psychologist Carl Rogers sought to apply his ideas of self-actualization—each person is the arbiter of his own truth, and only by acting on our feelings can we truly be human—to any institution that sought to challenge authority. Interest was expressed by the IHM and soon Rogers was at work, assisted by William Coulson, in a two-year experiment designed to free them from their "artificially induced psychological shackles." It didn't take long before every aspect of their life was put under a microscope and found wanting. By participating in encounter groups, the sisters liberated themselves from all the norms they had committed themselves to and proclaimed themselves emancipated. In actual fact, they collapsed: the result of this grand "opening up" was the destruction of the IHM community. Some of the nuns began to experiment sexually—many became lesbians—and most left the order. The only good news is that Bill Coulson saw the truth, dropped his Rogerian connections, and went on to become a distinguished Catholic psychologist. But not before more damage was done.[94]

When priests from St. Anthony's Franciscan Seminary in Santa Barbara approached Rogers to employ his madness, they also paid a big price: a quarter century after being liberated—seminarians were told they could visit friars' rooms whenever they wanted to—the priestly order was making headlines around the world for its notorious pedophilia ring.

Liberals, of course, would have us believe that those nuns, seminarians, and priests who became sexually reckless did so because of the Church's "repressive" ideas about sexuality. Thus do they buy into the very Rogerian view that gave rise to the problem in the first place. In fact, it was the wholesale rejection of restraint, and the total celebration of hedonism, that created the problem of predatory priests. Had the priests acted on their vows, instead of their id, there would have been no victims.

Weigel is correct to note that "the Sixties" did not cause the sexual abuse scandal. Nor, it should be added, did the media, as some in Rome have said. The blame rightly belongs to the Catholic Church. As Weigel observes, "a culture of dissent took root in the Catholic Church in the United States," one where "fidelity" was flouted.[95] It is beyond question that no priest could behave badly if he practiced fidelity to his vows and to the teachings of the Catholic Church. Weigel and Father Richard John Neuhaus made this point many times. It cannot be made too often.

Father Greeley and other dissidents like to blame *Humanae Vitae* for creating all the divisiveness in the Church. Weigel agrees, but not for the usual reasons. The 1968 encyclical that reaffirmed the Church's opposition to artificial contraception may have been ignored by the laity, but they did not engage in open rebellion. That was left to nuns and priests. In the aftermath of the rebellion, Patrick Cardinal O'Boyle of the Archdiocese of Washington disciplined 19 Washington priests for what any other organization would call insubordination. But the rebels appealed to Rome and they won: the Vatican ordered O'Boyle to lift his sanctions. What drove the decision was fear of schism. The pope believed that it was better to risk dissent than to see the Church break apart, and it was his hope that when things calmed down, the Church could get back to normalcy. Thus does Weigel dub this the "Truce of 1968."[96]

In reality, the truce was a ruse: radical dissent, publicly expressed, continues to this day. Moreover, the Church has been in de facto schism ever since. Pope Paul VI knew there was something rotten going on when he said in 1972 that "the smoke of Satan" had entered the Catholic Church. It was in this climate that the sexual abuse scandal flourished.

Sexual Abuse Scandal

Once the dissenters saw they could push their agenda with impunity, they sought to conquer the parishes, schools, seminaries, and the various offices of the bishops. For example, under the auspices of the Catholic Theological Society of America, Reverend Anthony Kosnick's book *Human Sexuality* was introduced to seminarians. The 1977 book is riddled with moral relativism, taking a radically nonjudgmental position on contraception, cohabitation, homosexuality, swinging, adultery, and even bestiality. The Catholic Church teaches that there is an objective moral nature to sexual acts, something Kosnick, in terms that can only be described as postmodern, rejects.[97]

Although the book was quickly criticized by the Committee on Doctrine of the United States bishops' conference and was censured by the Vatican in 1979, the most influential association of theologians stood by it. More important, legions of seminarians used it as an assigned text. There is simply no way any priest could swallow Kosnick's moonshine and practice fidelity. But it wasn't just Kosnick's sick book that was used in the seminaries.

In 1990, I appeared on the *Phil Donahue Show* debating the propriety of some human sexuality classes on college campuses, especially those courses that assigned the text *Our Sexuality* by Robert Crooks and Karla Bauer. The authors positively reject the idea that there is any such thing as "deviant sex." Whether the subject is sex with the dead (necrophilia), incest, bestiality, or a fetish like smelling someone's dirty underwear, all of this can be understood as merely "atypical sex." Little did I know that this book was required reading for some seminarians at the time.[98]

These books, and instructional material like them, do not impel otherwise psychologically healthy seminarians to engage in sexually deviant behavior. But they do provide a rationale—a green light, so to speak—to those who are already disturbed, or inclined that way. That's where the real damage is done.

One priest who embodied everything that people like Kosnick, Crooks, and Bauer taught was Reverend Paul Shanley, the infamous pervert from the Boston Archdiocese accused of having sex with everyone ranging from those who just got off their tricycle to those who are ready for a nursing home. There was one proviso—they had to be male.

As theologian Father Matthew L. Lamb has noted, in the same year that the bishops' conference criticized Kosnick's book, Father Shanley was maintaining that "homosexuality is a gift of God and should be celebrated." Moreover, Shanley gave a speech in October 1977 saying there was no sexual activity that caused psychic damage, "not even incest or bestiality."[99] It is indisputable that Shanley had been advocating pedophilia, homosexuality, incest, and bestiality for decades. We know this because the information comes straight from the files kept on him by the Archdiocese of Boston. After this was known, and after Shanley publicly advocated sex between men and boys (he was at the formative meeting of the North American Man/Boy Love Association in 1978), he was promoted to pastor.[100]

The person who got Shanley going was Humberto Cardinal Medeiros. In 1970, three years after accusations of sexual abuse by Shanley were reported to the archdiocese, Cardinal Medeiros appointed him as his "representative for sexual minorities." To be sure, Shanley was not selected at random for this bizarre position. He was selected because he could be trusted to do the job. And he performed with distinction: he lectured around the country on the merits of man-boy sex, incest, and bestiality. When the bishop of Dallas, Thomas Tschoepe, heard Shanley promote pedophilia, he roared laughing, and he did so in front of third- and fourth-year seminarians. We know this from the testimony of Father Joseph Wilson, a courageous priest from Queens, New York.[101]

Thanks to Peggy Moer of the *Wanderer*, we know that Shanley believed there were 34 sexual minorities. No doubt those who exercised their sexual preference by fornicating with corpses were among those whom he ministered to in an official capacity. While this was happening, Shanley served as a chaplain with Dignity, a homosexual group that claims to be Catholic notwithstanding the fact that its members totally reject every Church teaching on sexuality. He was also selected by the United States Catholic Conference (which was the civil arm of the bishops) to serve on the Youth Adult Ministry Board. His role was to educate young people about the plight of sexual minorities (all 34 of them).

In 1979, Cardinal Medeiros put an end to Shanley's "special ministry." This didn't go down too well with the "hippie priest" (as he was called), and so he publicly condemned the cardinal's admonition that gays should abstain from sex. Shanley branded this "virtually useless advice," as only he would know. Aside from losing his special post, nothing happened to Shanley. It is not surprising, then, that ten years later he publicly criticized the revision of two new oaths issued by the Vatican: the Profession of Faith and the Oath of Fidelity. And what did the Archdiocese of Boston do? It excused Shanley from taking the oath.[102]

Shanley did what he did because he was a bad and belligerent man and no one stopped him. No wonder John Cardinal O'Connor once said that while most priests are good men, some are evil.[103] Much the same, of course, could be said about any demographic group, but Catholics expect more from their priests. Be that as it may, what allowed the scandal to unfold was due to two principal groups: molesting priests and their enabling bishops. Without citing the role played by homosexuality, the former is unintelligible; without citing clericalism, the latter makes no sense.

Most gay priests are not molesters, but most of the molesters have been gay. This is indisputable. No, homosexuality does not cause predatory behavior, but when any condition is overrepresented as an explanatory variable, it demands attention. We know, for example, that 81 percent of the victims of priestly sexual abuse have been males, and most have been postpubescent.[104] Indeed, the John Jay Report explicitly concluded that "The majority of alleged victims were post-pubescent, with only a small percentage of priests receiving allegations of abusing young children."[105] Ergo, we are not talking about pedophilia, rather the condition is homosexuality. As for the enabling bishops, a sense of elitism, or unaccountability, is what allowed them to practice such callous indifference.

Clericalism, it needs to be stressed, has nothing to do with ideology, which is why a theological conservative like Bernard Cardinal Law of Boston and a theological liberal like Rembert Cardinal Weakland of Milwaukee had much in common. They also had something else in common: they were forced to resign.

Regarding the bishops, consider the elitism that was at work in Boston and Milwaukee. For example, in 1981, a woman began complaining to the Archdiocese of Boston about the predatory behavior of Shanley. The following year, Auxiliary Bishop Thomas V. Daily (who would later become the Bishop of Brooklyn) wrote to Shanley advising him "not to speak at all when she calls but merely to leave her hanging until she hopefully gets discouraged."[106] In 1984, three Milwaukee parochial school teachers wrote to Archbishop Weakland about the predatory behavior of Reverend Dennis Pecore. Weakland wrote back saying that "any libelous material found in your letter will be scrutinized carefully by our lawyers."[107] The teachers were then summarily fired. In 1988, the Wisconsin Court of Appeals chastised Weakland's response to the teachers as "abrupt" and "insensitive," exactly the kind of attributes associated with clericalism.[108]

It appears, tragically, that at least some of the dissidents have learned nothing. Even today, after all the monstrous deeds of Paul Shanley have been disclosed, he is defended by Sister Jeannine Gramick, his ideological soul mate. Gramick and Shanley go back to the early 1970s, when their joint interest in homosexuality began. In 2005, she wrote a piece in the *National Catholic Reporter* that was sickening. After she made the obligatory comment how she was "horrified" by Shanley's crimes, she got down to her real interest, which was finding a way to rescue the pervert. "At the same time," she wrote, "my heart grieved for this man I had not seen in almost 20 years, but whose principles and whose advocacy for the downtrodden I had applauded for three decades."[109]

When Shanley told her he refused to sign papers to laicize

him, Sister Jeannine exclaimed, "Good!" She asked herself, "What loving family or community would abandon a member because he or she was accused of a heinous crime?"[110] It might also be asked what kind of person would embrace a man who in 1977 said that when an adult and a child have sex, "the adult is not the seducer—the kid is the seducer."[111] One of the crimes Shanley has been accused of is raping a six-year-old in the confessional, just the kind of thing that we would expect from a NAMBLA activist. Fortunately, Gramick's apologia did not go unanswered in the pages of the *National Catholic Reporter.* Maureen Orth (whose husband, Tim Russett, died in 2008) wrote a splendid piece about Shanley in *Vanity Fair* and did the same in the left-wing weekly. She recounted how nine of Shanley's victims whom she interviewed explained how the hippie priest would instruct them to "use my body." Gramick, as Orth pointed out, never spoke to one of Shanley's victims.[112]

The good news is that the scandal has long been over. While the bill came due in 2002 when the *Boston Globe* exposed the Archdiocese of Boston for its serial delinquency, most of the damage was done years earlier: fully three-quarters of all the abuse cases took place between 1960 and 1984,[113] and the data in recent years show that the problem has largely been checked.

So where does this leave the "agents of change"? In 1998, Francis Cardinal George, Archbishop of Chicago, shook lay leaders when he told them that "liberal Catholicism is an exhausted project."[114] Ten years later, *Time* magazine's senior religion writer, David van Biema, was asking, "Is Liberal Catholicism Dead?"[115] To be sure, there will always be those who respectfully challenge the Church to rethink its ways. They are not the problem. The problem lies with those raging Catholics who would like to shove their fanciful *Nothing Sacred* church down the throats of the faithful. They gave it their best shot and they lost, but not before creating much havoc. It's up to the rest of us to clean up the mess they left behind.

CHAPTER 9

Self-Sabotage: Protestantism

The Numbers Don't Lie

"We have figured out your problem. You're the only one here who believes in God."[1] This is how Dave Shiflett begins his book *Exodus: Why Americans Are Fleeing Liberal Churches for Conservative Christianity*. The quotation cited is a remark made by one seminarian to another, the nonbeliever being more representative of the student body than the believer. Which means the guy who believes in God is a freak.

There is something bizarre going on when the average student studying to become an auto mechanic is far more likely to believe in God than the average student studying to become a minister. Not only that, the student of auto mechanics, unlike the divinity student, does not lack for integrity. When I asked Bronwen Catherine McShea about this matter, she provided great insight. McShea is a former Catholic League policy analyst who did her graduate work in theology at Harvard and Yale. "I would say the atmosphere is much more challenging—and marginalizing—to students with strong faith, less because 'belief in God' per se is so rare," she said, "but more because there is a deep-seated opposition to certainty in religious belief." Belief in absolute truth, she added, is regarded as a close cousin to "intellectual fascism."[2] Sounds like mutiny is commonplace in divinity schools.

The mutiny is confined to the mainline denominations, the ones that have been in a rush to assimilate to the dominant culture. A loss of faith does not mark evangelicals or fundamentalists, or Lutherans who belong to the Missouri Synod. What has happened to the secular-leaning mainline denominations has been nicely captured by Walter Russell Mead.

Mead is not being flip when he says that "liberal Protestantism tends to evanesce into secularism: members follow the 'Protestant principle' right out the door of the church."[3] Second, Mead says, "liberal Christians are often only tepidly engaged with 'religious' issues and causes." He cites, by way of example, their interest in the environment or human rights, issues which mesh so well with the secular world that they have little that is distinctively religious about them. Third, Mead cites the liberal Protestant disposition to separate themselves from the Catholic Church on abortion and gay rights, and from Jews on support for Israel, leaving them somewhat ineffectual in the interfaith community. Finally, they are fighting with themselves over gay rights and other issues, weakening them even further.

The numbers don't lie. In the 1970s, somewhere between three-fifths and two-thirds of Americans were Protestants. By 2008, the figure was 51 percent.[4] It was the mainline Protestant denominations—Episcopal, Lutheran, Methodist, and Presbyterian—that took the biggest hit. In general, the more liberal the denomination, the more devastating the loss. For example, the United Church of Christ, which makes the mainliners look orthodox, is losing members at a record pace. No wonder Dr. Richard Land of the Ethics and Liberty Commission of the Southern Baptist Convention has charged that "liberal Protestantism is imploding."[5]

Joseph Bottum, editor of *First Things*, saw what was happening and declared in 2008 that "The death of the Mainline is the central historical fact of our time." He drew his conclusion based on data which showed that "only three Mainline denominations still have enough members to be included among the ten largest churches: the United Methodist Church, the Evangelical Lutheran Church in America, and the Presbyterian Church (U.S.A.)." Worse, all three are still losing members big-time. When considering all of the mainline denominations, the situation is catastrophic. "In other words," Bottum wrote, "less than 8 percent of Americans today belong to the central churches of the Protestants."[6]

Along with this marked decline in membership is a great deal of denominational switching. While most people (72 percent) stay with one religion all their lives,[7] the fact remains that Protestants are a highly mobile group. Even the fabulously successful Rick Warren admits that his "purpose driven" ideas have led to splits in congregations that have adopted his message.[8] When the faithful shop, however, they typically find a home in some other Protestant camp: they are nine times more likely to switch denominations than they are to become Catholics.[9] Among the beneficiaries of this fluidity are evangelicals and smaller Protestant denominations. Those who switch do so either because they find that their church fails to engage them, or seems hypocritical or judgmental (58 percent), or because their new church offers more appealing doctrines (42 percent).

By contrast, the Southern Baptist Convention, which is nothing but orthodox, has posted impressive gains: there are more Southern Baptists than there are Episcopalians, Methodists, Presbyterians, and members of the United Church of Christ combined.[10] The Assemblies of God, a Pentecostal church, is growing at a fast rate, beating out even the Church of Jesus Christ of Latter-day Saints and the Catholic Church; the latter continues to grow largely because of immigrants.[11] Protestants remain the majority religion, but as Walter Russell Mead has observed, it was just two or three decades ago that "the mainline Protestants were the majority of the majority." Now "evangelicals have become the majority of the majority."[12]

Sabotage

It is only just, from a Christian perspective, that those denominations that have lost their moorings should suffer the most dramatic decline in membership. Quite frankly, the mainline denominations have sold out: it is not the Christian faith that they seek to emulate, but secularism. Consider, for instance, that at the same time the Episcopalians were being torn apart over the election of an openly homosexual bishop, Gene Robinson, the Presbyterians in 2003 had assembled in Birmingham, Alabama, to decide what alternative nonsexist terms they could come up with to replace the Christian Trinity of Father, Son, and Holy Ghost. "Mother, Child, and Womb" was one suggestion, as was "Rock, Redeemer, and Friend." Ten years earlier, the Presbyterian Church (U.S.A.) held a conference, cosponsored by the United Methodist Church, the Evangelical Lutheran Church in America, and other mainline churches, where they "reimagined" God as "Our Maker Sophia" and substituted milk and honey for the traditional bread and wine Communion.[13]

This is beyond silly—it is sabotage. No wonder so many mainline Protestants are bailing: the most elite members of their community have abandoned the faith. When Episcopalians gathered in Columbus, Ohio, in 2003 and refused to even consider a resolution affirming that Jesus is Lord, they proved, as Charlotte Allen said, that they are not "a serious Christian church."[14] That is too nice: what these disaffected activists did was to stick their middle finger in the face of the rank and file. Not content to rid themselves of the faith, they are hell-bent on destroying it for everyone else.

"Every Christian group in America right now has or is experiencing cultural battle,"[15] says Deborah Caldwell of Beliefnet. She stresses, however, that division is nothing new to Protestantism. In the nineteenth century, the Methodists split over slavery and became the Northern Methodists and the Southern Methodists. It is true that over the past two centuries, many denominations have split. Father Robert Kaynor, an Episcopalian priest, cites the Congregationalists and Unitarians, Lutherans, Baptists, Methodists, Presbyterians, Holiness churches, and Mormons.[16] In the 1970s, Presbyterians split over the question of women in the church, and virtually all of the mainline denominations are currently struggling over the issues of gay ministers and gay marriage. But as important as these issues are, they still don't touch the heart and soul of Christianity the way the Episcopalians did in Columbus.

"It's not ultimately about civil rights or peace or gender or gay rights, it's ultimately about biblical authority" is the way Susquehanna University professor Jeffrey Mann puts it.[17] The battle over biblical interpretation is not altogether new, but it has reached a climax when some theologians don't even bother to wrestle with biblical exegesis; fidelity to the source is a distraction to postmodernist theologians. Consider, for example, the theologians who comprise the so-called Jesus Seminar. Evangelical leader Al Mohler said it best when he noted that the Jesus Seminar "tells us virtually nothing about Jesus, but a great deal about the liberal scholars who sit around with colored beads, creating a Jesus in their own image." In fact, Mohler insists, "The Jesus invented by the Jesus Seminar is a Palestinian smart aleck who sounds like a cynical and sarcastic intellectual."[18]

And they wonder why few are listening to their secular pronouncements. Historian Thomas Reeves has figured it out: "There's no reason to get up on Sunday morning to go and hear a sermon about AIDS and a God who is nice. I can stay home and read the *New York Times* and get the same message." Reeves, who converted from Protestantism to Catholicism, is not off the mark when he says that in the 1960s liberal Protestantism "became worldly and embarrassed by the Gospels."[19]

One of the first to chronicle what was happening to the Protestant community was Dean Kelley. Writing in the early 1970s, Kelley noted that the more ecumenical the church, the more likely it was to see its rolls decline. Conversely, the more exclusive the church, the more likely it was to witness an increase in membership. Among the big winners were Black Muslims, Mormons, Southern Baptists, Pentecostals (especially the Assemblies of God), Jehovah's Witnesses, and Orthodox Jews. The big losers were the Episcopalians, Presbyterians, Methodists, Unitarians, and Reform Jews. Catholics, Lutherans, and Conservative Jews occupied the middle ground.[20]

Fifteen years later, in 1987, two liberal professors of religion, Wade Clark Roof and William McKinney, concurred with Kelley. "Almost all the churches that retained distance from the culture by encouraging distinctive life-styles and beliefs grew," they said, noting that "those most immersed in the culture and only vaguely identifiable in terms of their own features suffered declines."[21] Sociologist Dean Hoge of Catholic University of America concluded in 1994 that the reason why theologically conservative churches were doing so well had to do with financial sacrifice, personal piety, and personal salvation.[22] In short, they made demands on the faithful, something the more liberal churches wouldn't dare think of doing.

The fact is that the mainline church decline has much to do with the vacuousness of teachings, and this has been going on for over a half century. According to one study, many baby-boomer Protestants grew up in households where either "they had only the vaguest idea what their own parents—or more commonly their fathers—believed" or where "a deep commitment to the tenets of orthodox Christianity" was largely absent from their homes.[23] Some commentators today try to put a happy face on what is happening by noting that there are megachurches like St. Luke's

United Methodist Church in the Orlando suburbs that are posting big numbers, but when the growth is credited to "ministries" like the Canine Crusaders, a pet therapy program, it is foolish to say that this has anything to do with Christianity.[24] The fact is that by 2008 it could be said that "Many major mainline churches are suffering budget shortfalls."[25] Tithing is in decline, and boycotts are growing: local churches are forwarding less money to denominational headquarters "because of disputes over national church policies on divisive issues, such as gay marriage."[26]

Surely one of the factors contributing to "Christianity lite" is the craven need on the part of the White Anglo-Saxon Protestant elite to attain recognition and respect from the secular elite. This is hardly something new. "Liberal Protestants," writes Tom Reeves, "ever eager to be intellectually respectable, often directly or indirectly endorsed the secular world";[27] he was writing about events in the 1920s. Perhaps liberal Protestants tried too hard. "During the 1950s and 1960s," says Franklin Foer, "mainline Protestantism lost its grip on the elite." What happened, he says, was a "courageous act of noblesse oblige," by which he means "the elite had democratized its schools and universities and given them a secular, nondenominational tint."[28] Worse than that was the utter collapse of faith.

In 1963, the first large-scale study of religion was undertaken by Charles Glock and Rodney Stark. What they found was a "New Denominationalism," a fragmentation of the Protestant community. At issue were the core Christian beliefs: many were openly questioning "whether or not there is a God of the sort it makes any sense to worship" and "whether or not Jesus was merely a man." It was clear, even then, that the majority of those who belonged to the United Church of Christ had given up their Christian beliefs.[29] Fast-forward to 2008 and it is not surprising that Barack Obama's religious tutor, Reverend Jeremiah Wright, belonged to this church. He is the kind of clergyman one would expect from a congregation of secularists.

In the 1960s, secularism had invaded the seminaries of the Southern Baptist Convention as well. It was a time when professors were teaching that Lazarus wasn't really dead—he simply fainted. No wonder when *Roe v. Wade* was decided in 1973, the Southern Baptist Convention praised it. It was not until 1978, when a Texas judge named Paul Pressler joined with two biblical writers, Paige Patterson and Bill Powell, that the effort to reclaim the Southern Baptist Convention began in earnest.[30] It has, of course, rebounded nicely, and that's because the liberal saboteurs were shown the gate.

Why do they stay if they no longer believe? Why do they continue to corrupt the divinity schools if they don't believe in the divinity of Jesus? Disillusionment? Anger? Reprisal? Nihilism? All are explanatory variables, but there is something else going on as well: they have a comfortable lifestyle and they know that if they check out, few would be interested in hiring them. Think of it. A religion teacher who is bored with teaching can always pursue another ministry within his congregation, but a religion teacher who no longer believes in God is homeless. So they park themselves in academia, home to many other unhappy campers. If they had any integrity they'd do the manly thing and leave. But they don't.

What many of these former believers are doing is worse than those who are guilty of false advertising: what they are doing is cruel. What other word can be used to describe a Unitarian minister who has lost the faith and yet continues to pose as a hospital chaplain servicing the sick and dying of another religion? It did not matter to her that her patients "longed for greater assurance of an afterlife." What mattered is that she cared. Unfortunately for her patients, she didn't care enough to tell her boss that she no longer had the resources to deliver the expected services.[31]

This Unitarian hospital chaplain is not an anomaly within her own ranks. For Unitarians, belief in God is optional. Indeed, this is one religion where it makes no sense to speak of the faithful since there is no common faith. Jesus, the Trinity, the Apostles Creed, the Virgin Mary, and other Christian beliefs are not what unites Unitarians. Reverend Barbara Wells, a Unitarian minister, opines that what unites them is the "message." And that message is experiential: "They come to our church and they cry or they have that aha experience."[32] Aha. But why do they come to church to cry when they could do it at home?

This is perplexing for Unitarians who actually do believe in God, men like David Burton and Dean Fisher. They are trying to introduce God to their colleagues, but it's a tough sell. According to Burton, "at least half of Unitarians are now atheists." Which leads him to say that "an atheistic church really is an oxymoron," a conclusion that even those who come to church to cry cannot reasonably reject.[33] Indeed, the Unitarian crackup is so far along that in 2003 the First Unitarian Church of Brooklyn literally "celebrated" (their word) the *Roe* decision that legalized abortion on demand.[34]

The following year, some Unitarians were celebrating free love. The Unitarian Universalists for Polyamory was established to promote "the philosophy and practice of loving or relating intimately to more than one other person at a time with honesty and integrity." As Sally Amsbury of Oakland put it, "polyamory is never having to say you've broken up." Sally should know: her sex life includes her husband and two "other significant others." So popular is this form of debauchery that "other significant others" are fondly known as OSOs. In any event, when a Boston spokesman for the Association of Unitarian Universalists was asked about all this, he said that the views of the polyamorists are not necessarily endorsed by the denomination's board of trustees.[35] Which means they probably are.

While it may be easy to dismiss Unitarians as a relatively small and ineffectual group, the same cannot be said of Episcopalians. Although they have lost a lot of members—to the point where there are more Muslims than Episcopalians in the United

States—they still command the attention of all Protestants, as well as those who belong to other faiths. But unless they change course, they will go the way of the Unitarians.

The liberal Episcopalian seminaries have been devastated. In 2008, plans to eliminate the Master of Divinity program at the Seabury-Western Theological Seminary in Evanston, Illinois, were announced; faculty contracts were discontinued in 2009. At about the same time, the Rochester, New York, satellite of Bexley Hall Seminary in Columbus, Ohio, said it had to close, and the Episcopal Divinity School in Cambridge, Massachusetts, had to sell its seven buildings to nearby Lesley University for $33.5 million just to stabilize its finances. Things will only get worse under Rev. Katherine Ragsdale: before she took over as president of the Cambridge school in July 2009, she wrote a piece saying "abortion is a blessing."[36] Overall, the Episcopal seminary system declined by 25 percent between 2005 and 2008, with no end in sight.[37] Things are so desperate that men are being ordained who have never been to seminary.[38]

It may be an exaggeration to say that heresy has been mainstreamed in the Episcopalian Church, but the fact that it is a debatable proposition suggests how far standards have fallen. No institution can survive when termites are welcomed, but this is one lesson the elite in the Episcopalian Church have yet to learn.

Heresy Celebrated

When Bishop James Pike bragged that the "Church's classical way of stating what is represented by the doctrine of the Trinity is . . . not essential to the Christian faith," the only penalty he endured was a silly admonition that he should "consider himself censured."[39] This was a joke, given that Pike, who was dean of St. John the Divine in New York City, was hailed as a hero by some of his fellow bishops. Nothing could tarnish his status—not his alcoholism, his three marriages, or his multiple affairs. Even his role in leading Protestants and Other Americans United for Separation of Church and State against John F. Kennedy—because the Massachusetts senator was a Catholic— failed to tarnish his image.

What seemed to have mattered more to Pike was that he was given celebrity status by New York's secular elite. Indeed, he was just the kind of clergyman that those who believe in nothing adore: Pike rejected the Trinity and original sin, and he scoffed at the Virgin Birth. Not surprisingly, he appeared on the cover of *Time*, and it was no small wonder that he was praised for being "refreshing," "outspoken," and "brilliant."[40] No one doubts that he had an effect. "Sometime after the 1960s," observes Jody Bottum, "everyone in the hierarchy of the Episcopal Church became Bishop Pike—with the perverse effect that Pike's ostensible rebellion turned, at last, into the norm."[41] And it's been downhill ever since.

Since the sixteenth century, Episcopalians have used the Book of Common Prayer as their guiding light. But when the General Convention of the Episcopal Church in the United States convened in 1976, the prayer book was bashed for being too punitive, too preoccupied with "sin." Even though the Book of Common Prayer was not a formal catechism, it still represented orthodoxy, and it was precisely because it did so that dissident bishops hated it. Wild times ensued: after witnessing the slap on the wrist given to Pike for his heresy and the equally lame response to three retired bishops who illegitimately ordained female priests, the elite guard pushed the feminist envelope by canonizing the ordination of women. Bishop Paul Moore of New York took notice and a year later ordained a practicing lesbian. After a brief uproar, he apologized, but in the end he got what the dissidents wanted: the issue of ordaining openly gay persons was now on the table.

After Bishop Pike faded from the news, the Right Reverend John Spong, bishop of Newark, picked up where Pike left off. It's not clear what Christian teaching, if any, Spong believes in, but at any rate we do know that the retired bishop's contribution to the decline of the Episcopal Church is legion. Any clergyman who could write a book titled *Why Christianity Must Change or Die* calling on Christians to reject Christianity in order to save it belongs in the books *Guinness World Records* or *Ripley's Believe It or Not!*

If we can't be sure what Spong believes, we can be certain what he doesn't believe. We know, for example, that he does not believe that God is a supernatural being; he rejects Jesus as the earthly incarnation of God; he denies that Jesus performed miracles; he labels the Virgin Birth pure mythology; he derides the Easter celebration of Jesus rising from the dead; he finds it implausible to believe that Jesus ascended into heaven; and, for good measure, he thinks it ludicrous that the Bible is the word of God. Spong posted his litany of nonbeliefs on the Internet, much to the delight of radical secularists. Dave Shiflett gets it right when he says that Spong was "tolerated and indeed celebrated by his colleagues, and in the media, because he could be counted on for excellent quotations delivered with the certitude he found odious in his theological opponents."[42] The damage he did is not a matter of dispute. Between 1972 and 2005, the Episcopal Diocese of Newark lost nearly 24,000 congregants, or 46 percent of its membership; this was nearly three times the average decline in the Episcopal Church nationwide.[43]

While Pike and Spong are theological deviants, they are hardly alone. In 1991, the General Convention of the Episcopal Church defeated a resolution that would have prohibited its clergy from practicing adultery. Three years later, 71 bishops said they would ordain practicing homosexuals and bless gay unions, even though church policy did not yet sanction such things. At about the same time, Bishop Spong publicly declared St. Paul to be a repressed and frustrated homosexual.[44] And while all this was going on, Gene Robinson, a man who dumped his wife and children to live with another man, was ordained a bishop. He "got married" in 2008 to his pal, boasting, "I always wanted to be a June bride."[45] Unconventionally, the couple decided against a wedding cake and took only two days to enjoy their honeymoon. Perhaps that's because they had been going together for 20 years.[46]

When Robinson was ordained in 2003, I asked a staff member to prepare a report on how this was being received on the editorial pages of the nation's major newspapers. The tally showed there were 14 editorials that strongly praised the decision; five said it was the business of the Episcopal Church to decide; and two were opposed. No newspaper loved it more than the *Los Angeles Times*.

Within the Episcopal Church, Robinson's ordination split the bishops. Those bishops who support him are so upset with their colleagues who are opposed to him that many refuse to take Holy Communion with their peers at House of Bishops meetings in the United States.[47] Now, when the Eucharist is rejected by the clergy as a means of protest, there is no greater testimony to the collapse of faith in the Episcopalian community than this. Their nihilism is unbounded.

Ken Woodward, a veteran contributor to *Newsweek*, says that among Episcopalians, it is estimated that between 30 and 50 percent of the clergy is gay or lesbian in dioceses such as New York and San Francisco. "In these and other cities," Woodward writes, "it is not at all difficult to find congregations in which everyone on one side of the Communion rail is gay while the folks in the pews are split between homosexuals and heterosexuals." So unusual is the situation that Woodward was told by a woman priest that "If my husband needed counseling from a priest, he'd be hard-put to find one that was neither a woman or a gay man."[48] That so many gays should be found in a church that allows the clergy to marry suggests that it is not celibacy per se that accounts for the large number of gay priests in the Catholic Church.

By the summer of 2006, the Episcopal Church was spinning out of control. "Propelling the Episcopal Church in the United States closer to a possible schism with the global Anglican Communion," reported the *New York Times*, "the Episcopal Diocese of Newark nominated a gay priest on Wednesday as one of four men to be considered for bishop." What made this such an in-your-face move was the fact that the nominations came the day after the Archbishop of Canterbury, the spiritual leader of Anglicans the world over, introduced a measure that would require the Episcopal Church to either renounce gay bishops and the blessings of gay unions or forfeit their membership in the Anglican Communion.[49] But it's too late to simply issue a warning: the nutty elite in America is forcing a schism.

In 2008, matters came to a head. Angered over the embrace of practicing homosexuals in their ranks, Anglican conservatives, led by African archbishops, declared they would segregate themselves from their secular-minded colleagues. They maintained, quite reasonably, that too many Anglicans in the United States and Europe were following a "false gospel" that plays fast and loose with Scripture. So they voted to form a new power bloc within the Anglican community.[50]

In 2009, the chasm in the Episcopal Church grew wider. The Anglican Church in North America is the name of the new rival denomination headed by Pittsburgh Bishop Robert Duncan. "We're going through Reformation times, and in Reformation times things aren't neat and clean," Duncan said.[51] The dioceses of San Joaquin, California; Quincy, Illinois; Fort Worth, Texas; and Pittsburgh, Pennsylvania, are the core members of the new province. The gay rights agenda had gotten too out of hand for the religious conservatives to handle.

As a Catholic, it is none of my business what the Episcopal Church does, but I do sympathize with the legions of faithful

Episcopalians who want their church back. The faithful do not deserve to have their religion sabotaged by elitists who are out to upend the church, and this is as true among Catholics as it is Protestants. Indeed, it is one of the reasons why an uncommon alliance of traditionalists across faith communities is happening. We're all fed up with the mutineers on board.

My reservations about questioning the internal decisions made by another religion did not, however, stop me from protesting an obscene depiction of Our Blessed Mother at the Cathedral of St. John the Divine in New York City. No one has a right to blaspheme the mother of Jesus, and it is not an internal matter when it happens publicly. My exchange with the Right Reverend Mark S. Sisk, Bishop of New York, provides good insight into the thinking of the Episcopalian elite.

My involvement began when I learned that Bishop Sisk had received a complaint from someone about the work of Diane Victor; her piece *The Eight Marys* was part of the Season South Africa exhibit at the cathedral. The complainant described Victor's work as follows: "Blood cascading from between her legs, as a wire hanger dangled from her left hand. Another scene had a dog precariously positioned under her raised skirt. Mary then appears as a wash woman with clothespins attached to her naked torso. One final image is a Pieta representation where both are nude and Jesus is lying across Mary's lap with his penis intentionally and prominently as a focal point." In response to this complaint, Bishop Sisk said that the work did not violate the cathedral's criteria. Explicitly, he said that it was not deemed "blasphemous or demeaning to religion."

I reiterated all this in my letter of February 3, 2005, to Bishop Sisk, saying, "I have one question for you: Would you object if an artist portrayed your own mother the way the Virgin Mary was shown in this exhibit?" I then told him I would share his response with the Catholic community. A month later, I received a letter from Thomas P. Miller, who said he was writing on behalf of Bishop Sisk. It was a beauty.

Miller said that "the artist's figures are not meant to be representations of the Holy Mother." So what are they? "They are self-portraits in reference to the artist's own struggle as a woman to come to terms with traditional religious iconography," he said. The art, he stressed, was supposed to express "the dynamic spirit of a democratic South Africa." Somehow I managed to miss that point.

Miller was a master at dishing out the baloney. Just read this paragraph and decide for yourself: "Diane Victor's personal struggle as an artist and as a woman may be difficult to look at, but that very difficulty might serve to remind us of our call to be stewards of divine mercy in a deference to God's judgment. In a Cathedral filled with beautiful and transcendent images, we are reminded that, like Jesus and in Christ's name, we are called to reach out beyond our comfort to the unlovely and unloved. Mary's Song promises that God looks with favor on the lowly, who will be lifted up, as the proud will be scattered and the powerful brought down. In this light, the Victor portraits reach for Mary's advocacy and offer hope even for what is most disturbing among us." Whew!

Why is it that these deranged artists are always struggling? And what explains why she is struggling *as a woman*? Is it a struggle for her to accept her sex? If so, she needs treatment, something any man of the cloth who purports to be troubled by the "unlovely" should have counseled. As for this business about "the Victor portraits . . . offer hope even for what is most disturbing among us," someone needs to tell this struggling artist that nothing is more disturbing than her own work.

I've deliberately saved the best for last. After being told that I didn't quite understand Victor's masterpiece, I was then congratulated: "Your questioning of 'The Eight Marys' has helped us to think more incisively about this important mission and reminded us of the importance of critical dialogue in the arts as well as religion."[52]

A House Divided

The saboteurs in the Protestant community have succeeded to such an extent that it makes no sociological sense to refer to this constellation of denominations as a community. The difference between the mainline denominations and evangelicals, for example, is so profound that the latter have more in common with Roman Catholic traditionalists and Orthodox Jews than they do with the mainliners. This was underscored in 2006 by a huge survey of religion undertaken by Baylor University's Institute for Studies of Religion and the university's department of sociology.

The Baylor scholars found, not surprisingly, that when it comes to religion and politics, evangelicals were by far the most conservative. What was perhaps somewhat surprising—it sure is revealing—is that there is no explanatory value attached to mainline Protestants: in other words, their religion does not inform their politics at all.[53] Looks like their quest for assimilation has been achieved.

Nothing separates evangelicals and the mainline denominations more than abortion. Two-thirds of evangelicals think that abortion should be illegal in most or all cases, compared to 45 percent in the general population.[54] Mainline Protestants are not only tolerant of abortion, the leadership actively promotes abortion rights. Agencies of the Episcopal Church, United Methodist Church, Presbyterian Church (U.S.A.), and the United Church of Christ all belong to the Religious Coalition for Reproductive Choice. The coalition brooks no compromise on abortion, supporting abortion on demand through term and is strongly opposed to any ban on partial-birth abortion.

There are strong differences with regard to support for Israel as well. On the one hand, there is Pastor John Hagee's tireless efforts to raise money for Israel, as well as his annual conference, Christians United for Israel. On the other hand, there is the Jerusalem-based Sabeel Ecumenical Liberation Theology Center, a left-wing group that has long sought to get the mainline denominations in the United States to divest their assets in firms doing business in Israel.

Sabeel works with the World Council of Churches and the United Methodist Board of Global Ministries, as well as other leftist groups, seeking to pressure the Israeli government on the issue of Palestinian rights. And that's because they buy into liberation theology: it paints Israel as an oppressive colonial power that must be defeated. No denomination has bought this hook, line, and sinker more than the elites at the Presbyterian Church (U.S.A.). They have so polarized their church that one expert has said, "The Presbyterian denomination is very divided and facing a potential schism."[55]

The saboteurs have created a mess for the Protestant faithful. Just like their Catholic ideological kin, they have been very successful in tearing things down. That they have nothing constructive to offer is plain to see. And that's because they have infinitely more in common with hard-core secularists than they do rank-and-file Christians.

CHAPTER 10

The Perfect Cultural Storm

Secular saboteurs within the ranks of Catholicism and Protestantism are not going to give up, but they are also not likely to win. The senior citizens who largely comprise this segment of the population need new recruits if their agenda is to be met. While young people may be somewhat indifferent to religion, they are not screaming mad at their churches. And that's where the Catholic dissidents and the Protestant malcontents come up short. Sociologist Ken Sanchagrin was "astounded to see that by and large the growing churches are those that we ordinarily call conservative." Conversely, "the more liberal the denomination, by most people's definition, the more they were losing."[1]

This is good news, but what remains an open question is how the culture war is going to play out in the end. Tensions between religious conservatives and secular activists are nothing new in American history, but today they are at a boiling point. According to Princeton's Robert Wuthnow, who has been tracking the differences between traditionalists and modernists for decades, the social divide is likely to grow.[2] The number of players is relatively small but their social and cultural effects are enormous.

Central to the battle between secularists and traditionalists are issues governing sexuality and the public role of religion.

When these twin areas of contention intersect, they have the makings of the perfect cultural storm. Indeed, it is on this turf that the culture war will be decided, the outcome of which will determine the content of the normative order. Nothing touches the heart and soul of the culture more than sexuality and religion, and nothing mobilizes secular saboteurs to war on the faithful more than challenges to their sexually libertine agenda.

The issue of gay marriage is front and center. How will the right of two men to marry affect religion? According to Anthony Picarello, past president and general counsel of the Becket Fund, "the impact will be severe and pervasive." Indeed, he says, "This is going to affect every aspect of church-state relations." Marc Stern, general counsel for the American Jewish Congress, concurs. Does this mean that churches and religious charities will lose their tax-exempt status if they oppose same-sex marriage? "That," says Stern, "is the 18 trillion dollar question."[3]

What's in play is no small list of concerns. Referring to Stern's observation, Peter Steinfels writes, "He has in mind schools, health care centers, social service agencies, summer camps, homeless shelters, nursing homes, orphanages, retreat houses, community centers, athletic programs and private businesses or services that operate by religious standards, like kosher caterers and marriage counselors."[4] With regard to education, gay marriage will affect religious schools in admissions, employment, housing, and regulation of clubs. Licensing will also be impacted, especially laws affecting psychological clinics, social workers, and marital counselors.[5]

Chai Feldblum is one of the most prolific legal activists in the gay rights arena. The Georgetown University law professor recognizes that laws banning discrimination against gays will continue to burden religious institutions, and though she is sympathetic to such concerns, she says that in a contest between religious liberty and gay rights, the right choice isn't difficult. "I'm having a hard time coming up with any case in which religious liberty should win," she says. For Feldblum, "There can be a conflict between religious liberty and sexual liberty, but in almost all cases the sexual liberty should win because that's the only way that the dignity of gay people can be affirmed in any realistic manner."[6] What is particularly striking about her formulation is that religious liberty is affirmed in the First Amendment, and yet there is absolutely nothing in the Constitution regarding sexual liberty. No matter, Stern is correct to conclude that "this is going to be a train wreck."[7]

To be sure, those out to sabotage America with their secular agenda are pushing hard for a train wreck. They are led, on the intellectual front, by the new atheists: Richard Dawkins, Christopher Hitchens, Sam Harris, and Daniel Dennett. The so-called Four Horseman are fueled by religious hatred and a contempt for the religious traditions that mark Western civilization. Mike Sullivan, president of Catholics United for the Faith, labels them "positively evangelical," noting their aggressive style.[8] Some are beyond the pale. University of Minnesota professor Paul Z. Myers, an atheist who runs in the same circles as Dawkins, showcased his indecency when he intentionally desecrated the Eucharist in 2008.[9] It doesn't get much lower than this.

The ideological fervor of the new atheists blinds them to the positive role religion plays in the promotion of a free society. But not all agnostics and atheists are secularists at heart. Surely Guenter Lewy is not. In the 1990s, this renowned social scientist started a book on secular humanism and moral relativism with the expressed intent of showing how they neither undermined the meaning and significance of human life nor contributed to the erosion of moral values. He ended up unable to support his thesis. Indeed, he came to realize how indispensable religion is to the moral order. "We know of no society anywhere that has managed to build a culture devoid of religion," he wrote. For good reason: "The great universal religions in particular have taught the virtues of disinterested goodwill, social responsibility, and individual integrity, without which no society will flourish."[10]

The new atheists can complain all they want, but they cannot rebut certain verities. "No society has yet been successful in teaching morality without religion," argues Lewy, "for morality cannot be created." Morality, as Lewy observes, "requires the support of tradition, and this tradition is generally linked to religious precepts."[11] He is not easy on secular firebrands, the kind cut from the cloth of the Four Horsemen. He attributes to them a "selfish and hedonistic individualism" that reduces moral issues to civil liberties. "They herald the toleration of destructive behavior as a blow struck on behalf of personal freedom," he says. Worse, "They turn moral relativism into a protective umbrella for all kinds of eccentricities, not to say moral depravities."[12] Lewy, an agnostic, proposes an affirmation of "the most basic moral precepts of the Judeo-Christian tradition,"[13] a prescription that would drive the secular saboteurs right off the cliff.

The militant atheists will stop at nothing, and that is why they must be relentlessly confronted by religious conservatives. As Gertrude Himmelfarb has noted, counterrevolutions are not easy to sustain, though she is encouraged by the "ecumenical spirit" that is "evident in the alliances among traditionalists of all faiths."[14]

Deal Hudson, author of an important book on the growing alliance between traditional Catholics and evangelicals, is also encouraged by the willingness of religious conservatives to put aside their theological differences by joining hands in the culture war.[15] Look what happened in California over the Proposition 8 controversy. Catholics, evangelicals, Mormons, Muslims, Latinos, and African Americans played a decisive role in defending the traditional understanding of marriage, making California the thirtieth state to ban gay marriage by referendum. Moreover, Catholic and Orthodox bishops in Europe held a forum in December 2008 committing themselves to a common defense of marriage and the family. Bosnian Orthodox theologian Vaclav

Jezek spoke for many when he opined that "The family is not the product of a coincidence, but rather the perfect image of communion."[16]

Rabbi Daniel Lapin says it all when he opines that "As long as people share the same moral vision for America's public square, it is less important whether that vision is fueled by Catholic, Protestant, Jewish, Mormon, Buddhist or Moslem faith." What counts is that "We must not allow secularism's high priests to separate us from one another."[17] That is not likely to happen, if only because the stakes are so high that only fringe elements in these religions will balk at an alliance.

If there is one area where traditionalists have an edge, it is in their commitment to having children. The numbers that really count are found in birth rates, and this is a war the secularists are losing. In their green-tinted vision of the world, there are already too many people. Hence, their fondness for contraception and abortion. Not so with religious conservatives: they continue to breed like rabbits.

After looking at the numbers, one poor soul, San Francisco columnist Mark Morford, issued a clarion call to his fellow secularists. The statistics, he said, "are ugly, getting uglier: Despite all divine hope and prayer to the contrary, it looks like baby-happy conservatives are outbreeding liberals by a margin of some 20 to 40 percent." He calls this a "trend," indeed an "onslaught."[18] He's right. Chalk up a big win for religious conservatives. It looks like nature, and nature's God, really is on the side of the angels.

NOTES

Catalyst is the monthly journal of the Catholic League.

Chapter 1: Revenge of the Nihilists

1. Samuel G. Freedman, *Jew vs. Jew: The Struggle for the Soul of American Jewry* (New York: Simon & Schuster, 2000), p. 23.
2. Robert George, *The Clash of Orthodoxies: Law, Religion and Morality in Crisis* (Wilmington, Delaware: ISI Books, 2001), pp. 3-4.

Chapter 2: Multicultural Sabotage

1. S. L. Price and Andrea Woo, "The Indian Wars," *Sports Illustrated*, March 4, 2002, pp. 66-71.
2. Ron Charles, "Jesus in America: His Changing Image," *Christian Science Monitor*, December 23, 2003, p. 18.
3. Dinesh D'Souza, "The Secular Crusade Against Religion," *Catalyst*, January-February 2007. This article was adapted from his book *The Enemy at Home: The Cultural Left and Its Responsibility for 9/11* (New York: Doubleday, 2006).
4. Most surveys say the Christian population in the U.S. is just over or under 80 percent. It is estimated that only 72 percent of Israelis are Jewish. See Tovah Lazaroff, "28% of Israelis not Jewish," *Jerusalem Post*, June 12, 2002, p. 2.
5. Timothy Samuel, Shah and Monica Duffy Toft, "Why God Is Winning," *Foreign Policy*, July 1, 2006.

6. Garry Wills, "A Country Ruled by Faith," *New York Review of Books*, November 16, 2006.

7. For a cogent reply to this idea see M. Stanton Evans, "The Christian History of the U.S. Constitution," *Human Events*, April 19, 1995, pp. 11–13.

8. Ibid.

9. M. Stanton Evans, *The Theme Is Freedom* (Washington, D.C.: Regnery, 1994), p. 34.

10. Ibid., p. 35.

11. *Church of the Holy Trinity v. United States*, 143 U.S. 457, 471 (1892).

12. "Many Americans Uneasy with Mix of Religion and Politics," *Pew Forum on Religion & Public Life*, August 24, 2006, p. 4.

13. "California Courthouse Triggers Big Controversy," *Catalyst*, November 2004.

14. "Jewish Organizations Split Over Pledge Case Strategy," *Forward*, November 14, 2003.

15. Rabbi Daniel Lapin, *America's Real War* (Sisters, Oregon: Multnomah, 1999), p. 14.

16. Don Feder, "Yes—Once and for All—America Is a Christian Nation," *Catalyst*, June 2005.

17. Richard Bernstein, *Dictatorship of Virtue: Multiculturalism and the Battle for America's Future* (New York: Alfred A. Knopf, 1994), pp. 4, 7.

18. William Donohue, "They Made the Right Choice," *Catalyst*, June 2005. See also John Mortimer, *The Oxford Book of Villains* (New York: Oxford University Press, 1992).

19. Joseph Ratzinger and Marcello Pera, *Without Roots: The West, Relativism, Christianity, Islam* (New York: Basic Books, 2006), pp. 78–79. The words quoted are those of Ratzinger.

20. Herbert London, *America's Secular Challenge: The Rise of a New National Religion* (New York: Encounter Books, 2008), p. 3.

21. Jacques Steinberg, "Yale Returns $20 Million to an Unhappy Patron," *New York Times*, March 15, 1995, p. A1.

22. Robert Royal, *1492 and All That: Political Manipulations of History* (Washington, D.C.: Ethics and Public Policy Center, 1992).

23. Diane Ravitch, *The Language Police* (New York: Alfred A. Knopf, 2003), pp. 142-146.

24. Gilbert T. Sewall, *Islam in the Classroom: What the Textbooks Tell Us*, a report by the American Textbook Council, 2008, pp. 24, 27.

25. Ravitch, *The Language Police*, pp. 20-22, 114-115.

26. Stephen L. Carter, *God's Name in Vain: The Wrongs and Rights of Religion in Politics* (New York: Basic Books, 2000), p. 187.

27. James Martin, "An Interview with Camille Paglia," *America*, November 12, 1994.

28. Jason Mattera, "PC Campus: Academia's Top 10 Abuses of 2008," yaf.org, December 2008.

29. "Red Cross Apologizes for Ban on Religious Speech," *Catalyst*, April 2002.

30. Michael Zapler, "The Force Behind Kwanzaa," *Chronicle of Higher Education*, December 14, 1994, p. A7.

31. "Majority OK with Public Nativity Scenes," FoxNews.com (the results were from a Fox News poll), December 9, 2003.

32. Frank Rich, "I Saw Jackie Mason Kissing Santa Claus," *New York Times*, December 25, 2005, Section 4, p. 8.

33. Adam Cohen, "This Season's War Cry: Commercialize Christmas, or Else," *New York Times*, December 4, Section 4, p. 11.

34. Irving Kristol, "On the Political Stupidity of Jews," *Azure*, Autumn 1999.

35. Burt Prelutsky, "The Jewish Grinch Who Stole Christmas," WorldNetDaily.com, December 7, 2005.

36. For a story and pictures of this event see the January-February 2006 *Catalyst*.

37. Rabbi Daniel Lapin, "Merry Christmas is NOT Offensive—Jews Should Protect Religious Freedom for Everyone," TowardTradition.org, November 21, 2005.

38. Jeff Jacoby, "De-Christmasing Christmas," Boston.com, November 30, 2005.

39. "Celebrate Diversity: Celebrate Christmas," *New York Times*, November 28, 2006, p. A23.

40. Don Feder, "Christmas—Going, Going . . . Gone?," Grass topsUSA.com, November 30, 2005.

41. "Many Americans Uneasy with Mix of Religion and Politics," pewforum.org, August 24, 2006, p. 1.

42. "Survey: Americans Believe Religious Values Are 'Under Attack,'" adl.org, November 14, 2008.

43. "New York City School System Discriminates Against Christians," *Catalyst*, January-February 2002.

44. U.S. District Court, Eastern District, *Skoros v. City of New York*, CV-02-6439, February 18, 2004, p. 30.

45. U.S. Court of Appeals for the Second Circuit, *Skoros v. City of New York*, 04-1229-cv, February 2, 2006.

46. See the amicus brief filed by the ADL in the U.S. Court of Appeals for the Second Circuit, *Skoros v. City of New York*, CV-04-1229, p. 9.

47. Interview of Deborah Lauter on Fox News Network, November 21, 2006.

48. "Central Michigan University Repeals Christmas Warnings," *Catalyst*, January-February 2004.

49. "Indiana Law Professor Censors Christmas Tree," *Catalyst*, January-February 2004.

50. "Anti-Christmas Fever Abounds," Catholic League news release, December 14, 2006.

51. "Root Cause of the War on Christmas," *Catalyst*, January-February 2009.

52. Ibid.

53. "How We Beat Wal-Mart," *Catalyst*, December 2005.

54. "Victory Over Wal-Mart; All Demands Met," *Catalyst*, December 2005.

55. "'Merry Christmas' Returns; Culture War Continues," *Catalyst*, November 2006.

56. "Jesus' Tomb Not Found; Cameron's 'Titanic Fraud,'" *Catalyst*, April 2007. See also "'Lost Tomb' Is a Lost Cause" in the same issue. For information on the Discovery Channel's decision, see James Hibberd, "Is Discovery Burying 'Lost Tomb'?," tvweek.com, March 8, 2007.

57. Simcha Jacobovici and Charles Pellegrino, *The Jesus Family Tomb* (San Francisco: HarperSanFrancisco, 2007).

58. William Donohue, "Executive Summary," *Catholic League's 2007 Annual Report on Anti-Catholicism.*

59. *Anderson Cooper 360 Degrees,* CNN, April 2, 2007.

60. "U.S. House Passes Resolution Supporting Christmas and Christianity," a Christian Newswire release by Liberty Counsel, December 12, 2007.

61. John O'Sullivan, "The Sensitivity Trap," *New York Post,* July 7, 2008, p. 21.

62. *Catholic League's 2001 Annual Report on Anti-Catholicism,* p. vi.

63. *Catholic League's 2003 Annual Report on Anti-Catholicism,* p. 18.

64. "Fear Guides Media Response to Cartoons," *Catalyst,* April 2006.

65. "Beheadings, Anyone?," *Catalyst,* April 2006.

66. "Univ. of Oregon Okays Obscene Depiction of Jesus," *Catalyst,* June 2006.

67. *Nightline,* transcript, September 22, 2006.

68. Alex Strachen, "'South Park' a Perfect 10: Creators of Popular Program Continue to 'Rip on Everyone' for 10th Straight TV Season," *Nanaimo Daily News* (British Columbia), October 17, 2006.

69. James Davison Hunter, *Culture Wars* (New York: Basic Books, 1991), pp. 150–151.

70. Nicholas von Hoffman, "Holy Rollers Hell-Bent on Destroying Secular Law," *New York Observer,* May 23, 2005, p. 4.

71. John Dean, "Michelle Goldberg's Study of the Rise of Christian Nationalism, and Its Adherents' Strategy to Use the Courts to Further Their Agenda," FindLaw.com, August 25, 2006.

72. Andrew Sullivan, "My Problem with Christianism; A Believer Spells Out the Difference Between Faith and a Political Agenda," *Time,* May 15, 2006, p. 74.

73. Charles W. Socarides, "How America Went Gay," *America,* November 18, 1995.

74. Rabbi Lapin, *America's Real War,* pp. 39–40.

75. Midge Decter, "The ADL vs. the 'Religious Right,'" *Commentary,* September 1994.

76. Julia Duin, "Jewish Leaders to Devise Strategy," *Washington Times*, December 5, 2005.

77. Abraham Foxman, "The Threat of Islamic Extremism," ADL. org, October 28, 2006.

78. Richard John Neuhaus, "Weird and Wonderful Travels in Evangelicaldom," *First Things*, May 2007, p. 59.

79. Michelle Goldberg, *Kingdom Coming: The Rise of Christian Nationalism* (New York: W. W. Norton, 2006), pp. 6–7.

80. Ibid., p. 23.

81. Ibid., p. 184.

82. Rabbi James Rudin, *The Baptizing of America: The Religious Right's Plans for the Rest of Us* (New York: Thunder's Mouth Press, 2006), p. 3.

83. Ibid., p. 15.

84. Ibid., p. 18.

85. Ibid., pp. 72–73.

86. Sam Harris, *Letter to a Christian Nation* (New York: Alfred A. Knopf, 2006), p. ix.

87. Ibid., p. xi.

88. Ibid., p. 25.

89. Ibid., p. 41.

90. Ibid., pp. 60–61.

91. Ross Douthat, "Theocracy, Theocracy, Theocracy," *First Things*, August-September 2006, p. 23.

92. G. Jeffrey MacDonald, "This Year, Lots of Fireworks Over the Founders' Faith," *Christian Science Monitor*, July 3, 2006, USA Section, p. 1.

93. Stanley Kurtz, "Scary Stuff," National Review Online, April 28, 2005.

94. Nicholas D. Kristof, "A Modest Proposal for a Truce on Religion," *New York Times*, December 3, 2006, Section 4, p. 13.

Chapter 3: Sexual Sabotage

1. Robert George, *The Clash of Orthodoxies*, p. 15.

2. Will Herberg, "What Is the Moral Crisis of Our Time?," *Intercol-*

legiate Review, Fall 1986, p. 9; this is a reprint of the 1968 article by Herberg in the same journal.

3. Leszek Kolakowski, "The Idolatry of Politics," *New Republic,* June 16, 1986, p. 31.

4. See the Catholic League news releases of August 19 and 22, 2002, on *Opie and Anthony* at catholicleague.org. When they were fired, I petitioned the FCC to withdraw my request that WNEW have its license rescinded.

5. John Leo, "Repackaging the Perps," *U.S. News and World Report,* May 17, 1999, p. 14.

6. "National Day of Prayer," larryflynt.com/national_prayer_day.

7. "120 Days of Sodom: Information from Answers.com," Wikipedia, pp. 3-4.

8. Peter Mullen, "Nostalgia for Nihilism," *The Catholic Herald,* May 2, 2008.

9. William Norman Grigg, "The Porn Revolution," *The New American,* June 2, 2003.

10. "Thinkers Behind the Culture of Death," an interview with Donald DeMarco, yourcatholicvoice.org, November 12, 2004.

11. Mullen, "Nostalgia for Nihilism."

12. William Donohue, "Psychology's War on Catholicism," in Nicholas Cummings, William O'Donohue, and Janet Cummings, eds., *Psychology's War on Religion* (Phoenix: Zeig-Tucker, 2009), pp. 129-146.

13. Ibid.

14. Ibid.

15. Dennis Altman, *Homosexual* (New York: Avon Books, 1971), p. 105.

16. Daly's most prominent book was *The Church and the Second Sex* (New York: Harper & Row, 1968).

17. A. C. Grayling, "Greed Can Indeed Be Good," *Financial Times* (Weekend Magazine), April 29, 2006, p. 25.

18. Mead had an affair with Ruth Benedict while engaged to Luther Cressman and an adulterous affair with Edward Sapir. See Joyce Milton, *The Road to Malpsychia: Humanist Psychology and Our Discontents* (San Francisco: Encounter Books, 2002), pp. 23-24.

19. Sue Ellen Browder, "Kinsey's Secret: The Phony Science of the Sexual Revolution," *Crisis*, May 2004, p. 14.

20. Ibid., p. 15.

21. Milton, *The Road to Malpsychia*, p. 221.

22. Joseph Epstein, "The Secret Life of Alfred Kinsey, Sex Researcher," *Commentary*, January 1998, pp. 37–38.

23. Tom Bethell, "Sex, Lies, and Kinsey; Exposing the Father of Child Abuse," *American Spectator*, May 1996.

24. Tom Bethell, "Kinsey as Pervert," *American Spectator*, April 1, 2005.

25. Judith A. Reisman, *Kinsey: Crimes & Consequences*, 2nd edition (Arlington, Virginia: First Principles Press, 1998), pp. 176–177.

26. Milton, *Malpsychia*, p. 222.

27. John Leo, "Apologists for Pedophilia," *U.S. News & World Report*, April 22, 2002, p. 53.

28. Edward Eichel, "Kinsey Has No Clothes," letter to the editor, *Wall Street Journal*, May 6, 1993, p. A11.

29. "SIECUS Sex Education Guidelines," *In Focus* (publication of the Family Research Council), 1995.

30. Dana Mack, "What the Sex Educators Teach," *Commentary*, August 1993, p. 33.

31. Rod Dreher, "The Racist Roots of Pro-Abortionists," *New York Post*, October 10, 1999, p. 20.

32. Ellen Chesler, *Woman of Valor: Margaret Sanger and the Birth Control Movement in America* (New York: Simon & Schuster, 1992), p. 15.

33. Daniel Flynn, *Intellectual Morons* (New York: Crown Forum, 2004), pp. 154–157.

34. Joseph R. Stanton, "History's Blind Spot," *Catholic World Report*, November 1994, p. 63.

35. Robert P. Lockwood, "NARAL, Anti-Catholicism and the Roots of the Pro-Abortion Campaign," *Catalyst*, June 2001; a longer version is available in the Research Papers section of the Catholic League Web site.

36. Ibid.

37. "Abortion Opponents Say Anti-Catholicism Taints Debate," UPI, December 17, 1989.

38. Robert P. Lockwood, "NARAL, Anti-Catholicism and the Roots of the Pro-Abortion Campaign."

39. Ibid.

40. Douglas Martin, "Lawrence Lader, Champion of Abortion Rights, Is Dead at 86," *New York Times*, May 10, 2006, p. A23.

41. "NARAL Welcomes Democrats and Kissling," *Catalyst*, March 2003.

42. "Hugh Hefner's Hollow Victory," *Christianity Today*, December 1, 2003. See also James L. Lambert, "Playboy's Message to America," CatholicExchange.com, June 2, 2003.

43. "New NOW Leader Is Foe of Catholics," Catholic League news release, July 3, 2001; and "Anti-Catholic Bigots Rally to Attack Vatican," Catholic League news release, July 12, 2001.

44. William Donohue, "Pope Protesters a Pathetic Lot," *Catalyst*, November 1995.

45. James Martin, "An Interview with Camille Paglia," *America*, November 12, 1994, p. 10.

46. Bruce Lambert, "Places for AIDS Patients Are Still Scarce," *New York Times*, December 17, 1989, Section 4, p. 6.

47. Private collection. See also Mary Ann Poust and Gerald M. Costello, "Unfair, Unjustified and Offensive," *Catholic New York*, December 14, 1989, p. 3.

48. Ray Kerrison, "Protests Rock St. Pat's," *New York Post*, December 11, 1989, p. 2.

49. Pat Buchanan, "The Desecration of St. Pat's," *New York Post*, December 16, 1989, p. 15.

50. Manuel Perez-Rivas and Ji-Yeon Yuh, "Protest Siege at St. Pat's," *Newsday*, December 11, 1989, p. 2.

51. Kerrison, "Protests Rock St. Pat's."

52. "The Storming of St. Pat's," *New York Times*, December 12, 1989, p. A24.

53. Martin Duberman, "Stonewall: After Many a Summer Endures a Symbol; The Making of a Myth," *Harvard Gay & Lesbian Review*, July 31, 1994, p. 4.

54. Poust and Costello, "Unfair, Unjustified and Offensive."

55. Ibid.

56. See the Don Shewey interview, "Madonna: The Saint, the Slut, the Sensation," *Advocate*, May 7, 21, 1991.

57. The account of the 1994 event is taken from my article "Stonewall at 25," *Crisis*, October 1994.

58. The account of the 1995 event is taken from my article "Gays, Giuliani and Catholics," *Crisis*, September 1995.

59. News as reported by Zachary Margulis and Dave Saltonstall, *New York Daily News*, June 25, 1995, p. 6.

60. See the Frequently Asked Questions regarding NYC Pride, June 22-29, 2008, nycpride.org/faq.

61. Cara Buckley, "Closing Time at a Diner That Never Closed," *New York Times*, June 30, 2008, p. B3.

62. William Donohue, "Gays, Giuliani and Catholics," *Crisis*, September 1995.

63. See the Catholic League news releases on this issue that were issued from September 25 to October 31, 2007, as well as the November and December 2007 issues of *Catalyst*. All are available at catholicleague.org.

64. "Gay Marriage Loses; Protests Turn Ugly," *Catalyst*, December 2008.

65. "Gay Fascists Storm Church," *Catalyst*, December 2008.

66. "Gays Vandalize San Francisco Church," Catholic League news release, January 5, 2009.

Chapter 4: Artistic Sabotage

1. Michael J. Lewis, "Body and Soul," *Commentary*, January 2007, p. 31.

2. "A Show to Hold Your Nose For," *New York Post*, Page Six, July 14, 2008, p. 12.

3. "Los Angeles Museum Hosts Attack on Virgin Mary," Catholic League news release, October 16, 1997.

4. The Tom of Finland Foundation DISPATCH, Summer 1996, available at tomoffinlandfoundation.org. See, too, William Donohue,

"Executive Summary," *Catholic League's 1996 Annual Report on Anti-Catholicism*.

5. *Catholic League's 1996 Annual Report on Anti-Catholicism*, p. 4.

6. *Catholic League's 2006 Annual Report on Anti-Catholicism*, p. 6.

7. "Figurines Show Pope and Nuns Defecating at Napa, California Museum," Catholic League news release, January 4, 2002.

8. *Catholic League's 2007 Annual Report on Anti-Catholicism*, p. 9.

9. "Catholic Bashing on Campus," *Catalyst*, July-August 2008.

10. "Custodian Throws Away Art Exhibit Mistaken for Trash," Associated Press, June 20, 2003; "Garbage as Art—Art as Garbage," blogcritics.org, August 28, 2004.

11. William Donohue, *The New Freedom: Individualism and Collectivism in the Social Lives of Americans* (New Brunswick, New Jersey: Transaction Press, 1990), p. 41.

12. Ibid., p. 40.

13. Roger Kimball, "The Elephant in the Gallery, or the Lessons of 'Sensation,'" *New Criterion*, November 1, 1999, p. 4.

14. "Firestorm of Protest Greets Beastly Art Exhibit," *Catalyst*, November 1999.

15. Ibid.

16. "Donohue on the 'Today' Show," *Catalyst*, November 1999.

17. "Donohue on National Public Radio," *Catalyst*, November 1999; "Donohue at Rally Against the Museum," *Catalyst*, November 1999.

18. "Donohue at Rally Against the Museum," *Catalyst*, November 1999.

19. "Arts, First Amendment Supporters Rally at Brooklyn Museum," People for the American Way news release, October 1, 1999.

20. "William Donohue, "Myths Color 'Sensation' Exhibit," *Catalyst*, November 1999.

21. "Extraordinary Press Conference," *Catalyst*, November 1999.

22. William Donohue, "Myths Color 'Sensation' Exhibit."

23. "Orthodox Union Criticizes Brooklyn Museum Exhibit," Orthodox Union news release, September 27, 1999.

24. "Brooklyn Museum of Art Emits New Stench," *Catalyst*, December 1999.

25. Ibid.

26. *Catholic League's 2001 Annual Report on Anti-Catholicism*, pp. 9–10.

27. Steven C. Dubin, *Displays of Power: Controversy in the American Museum from the Enola Gay to Sensation* (New York: New York University Press, 1999), p. 275.

28. Rob Owen, "'Hornblower' Actor Pleased with Series' Second Part," *Pittsburgh Post-Gazette*, January 20, 2001, p. C6.

29. Erik Piepenburg, "Dysfunctional Since Before It Was Cool," *New York Times*, July 6, 2008, p. AR5.

30. *Catholic League's 2001 Annual Report on Anti-Catholicism*, pp. 50–51.

31. "'Corpus Christi' to Run in Fall; Protest Mounts," *Catalyst*, July-August 1998.

32. "Censoring Terrence McNally," *New York Times*, May 28, 1998, p. A28.

33. The ad was reproduced in the July-August 1998 edition of *Catalyst*.

34. Ibid.

35. Letter by Abraham Foxman to Rick Hinshaw, Catholic League director of communications, July 7, 1998.

36. "'Corpus Christi' to Run in Fall; Protest Mounts," *Catalyst*, July-August 1998.

37. William Donohue, "'Corpus Christi' Is Gay Hate Speech," *Catalyst*, November 1998.

38. "Catholics, Protestants, Jews and Muslims Protest 'Corpus Christi,'" *Catalyst*, October 1998.

39. Robin Pogrebin, "Pickets, Pro and Con, for Play Premiere," *New York Times*, October 14, 1998, p. B3.

40. "Rally Against 'Corpus Christi' a Hit; Critics Pan the Play," *Catalyst*, November 1998.

41. Ibid. See also Pogrebin, "Pickets, Pro and Con, for Play Premiere."

42. "League's Free Speech Assailed," *Catalyst*, November 1998.

43. Two news releases were sent by this ad hoc group, one on June 7, the other on June 8, 1998. They are part of the Catholic League's archives on this issue.

44. Transcript of debate on *New York Close-Up,* New York 1, hosted by Sam Roberts of the *New York Times,* June 3, 1998.

45. William Donohue, letter to Barbara Handman, October 15, 1998.

46. Jason Zinoman, "A Modern Gay-You-Know-Who Superstar," *New York Times,* October 22, 2008, p. C2.

47. Mark Blankenship, "Moments in History, Converging Anew," *New York Times,* October 19, 2008, p. AR8.

48. Clark Hoyt, "The Perilous Intersection of Art and Religion," *New York Times,* November 9, 2008, Section WK, p. 9.

49. Norm Clarke, "Roast Attendees Take Umbrage with Stunt by Penn & Teller," *Las Vegas Review-Journal,* January 17, 2003, p. A3.

50. "Mother Teresa Defamed; CBS Petition Started," *Catalyst,* July-August 2005.

51. Don Shewey, "Madonna: The Saint, the Slut, the Sensation," donshewey.com. The interview first appeared in the *Advocate,* May 7, 21, 1991.

52. "NBC Yields," *Catalyst,* November 2006.

53. "Springer's 'Opera' Comes to Carnegie Hall," *Catalyst,* January-February 2008.

54. Ibid.

Chapter 5: Sabotaged by Hollywood

1. William Donohue, "Jews and Hollywood," *Catalyst,* January-February 2005.

2. Claire Hoffman, "Report Says TV Losing Its Religion," *Los Angeles Times,* December 15, 2006, p. C3.

3. "The Media Assault on American Values," Special Report of the Media Research Center, 2007.

4. Caryn James, "The Unknown Sundance, in Unlikely Places," *New York Times,* February 4, 1996, Section 2, p. 13.

5. Michael Medved, *Right Turns: Unconventional Lessons from a Controversial Life* (New York: Crown Forum, 2004), p. 326.

6. Michael Medved, *Hollywood vs. America* (New York: Harper-Perennial, 1992), pp. 52-55.

7. See the transcript for *The O'Reilly Factor,* October 5, 2006.

8. William Donohue on the MSNBC TV show *Scarborough Country,* December 8, 2004.

9. Ibid.

10. William Donohue, "Jews and Hollywood," *Catalyst,* January-February 2005.

11. Ibid.

12. Ibid.

13. Shmuley Boteach, "American Isn't a 'Christian' Nation," *Jerusalem Post,* February 10, 2005, p. 16.

14. "Editor's Notebook; Brando's Jews," *Forward,* July 9, 2004, p. 8.

15. William Donohue, "Nice to Know What Offends Hollywood," *Catalyst,* September 2006.

16. Ibid.

17. Thomas J. Herron, "Bill Donohue's Catholic League Whacks Culture War," *Culture Wars,* October 2004, p. 20.

18. Thomas J. Herron and E. Michael Jones, "Non-Existent Conspiracy Causes Catholics to Cower," *Culture Wars,* December 2006, p. 37.

19. William Donohue, "Priest," *Catalyst,* May 1995.

20. The *New York Times* ad of April 10, 1995, "What's Happening to Disney?," was republished in *Catalyst,* May 1995.

21. John Cardinal O'Connor's article, "From My Viewpoint," was first published in *Catholic New York*; it was republished in *Catalyst,* May 1995.

22. William Donohue, "There's Anger in the Land," *Catalyst,* May 1995; Don Feder, "Church Catches Hell in 'Priest,'" *Catalyst,* May 1995; Rabbi Daniel Lapin, *America's Real War* (Sisters, Oregon: Multnomah, 1999), pp. 310-311.

23. *Catholic League's 1999 Annual Report on Anti-Catholicism,* pp. x-xi.

24. Ibid. The ad is reprinted in the annual report.

25. "'Dogma' Finally Opens," *Catalyst*, November 1999.

26. *Catholic League's 1999 Annual Report on Anti-Catholicism*, p. xi.

27. Ibid.

28. Ibid.

29. "'Dogma' Finally Opens," *Catalyst*, November 1999.

30. "'Dogma' Petitions Sent to Disney," *Catalyst*, November 1999.

31. Christopher Noxon, "Is the Pope Catholic . . . Enough?," *New York Times Magazine*, March 9, 2003.

32. "Jewish Groups Attack Mel Gibson," *Catalyst*, July-August 2003.

33. William Donohue, "Even Playing Dirty Didn't Work," *Catalyst*, April 2004.

34. "Jewish Groups Attack Mel Gibson," *Catalyst*, July-August 2003.

35. Ibid.

36. Paula Fredriksen, "Mad Mel," *New Republic*, July 28–August 4, 2003.

37. "Mel Gibson's Foes Overheat; Smear Campaign Backfires," *Catalyst*, December 2003.

38. Ibid.

39. Ibid.

40. Joanna Molloy and Corky Siemaszko, "Mel Flick Not Pope's Passion," New York *Daily News*, January 20, 2004.

41. See Peggy Noonan's two columns, "It Is as It Was," *Wall Street Journal*, December 17, 2003, and "'Passion' and Intrigue," *Wall Street Journal*, January 22, 2004. Also, private correspondence, February 7, 2007.

42. Philip F. Lawler, "Is It As It Was?," *Catholic World Report*, March 2004, p. 28.

43. "Pope Approves 'The Passion'; Critics of Mel Confounded," *Catalyst*, January-February 2004.

44. Ibid.

45. William Donohue, "An Open Letter to the Jewish Community," *Catalyst*, March 2004. The letter was dated February 4, 2004, and was sent to prominent Jews nationwide.

46. My letter to Shapiro is dated February 3, 2004; he replied the next day.

47. Koch made his remarks in the New York *Daily News*, March 27, 1998; they were reprinted in *Catalyst*, May 1998.

48. "'Passion' Critics Evince New Puritanism," Catholic League news release, February 24, 2004.

49. "Critics See Porn and S&M in 'The Passion,'" Catholic League news release, March 5, 2004, and "Critics of the 'The Passion' Crackup," Catholic League news release, March 8, 2004.

50. "Critics of 'The Passion' Crackup," Catholic League news release, March 8, 2004.

51. Vatican Spokesman: "'The Passion' Is Not Anti-Semitic," Catholic League news release, March 12, 2004.

52. "Paula Commits Genocide," *Catalyst*, September 2004.

53. "Violence and 'The Passion' (Part Two)," *Catalyst*, June 2004.

54. William Donohue, "Even Playing Dirty Didn't Work," *Catalyst*, April 2004.

55. William Donohue, "Jews and Hollywood."

56. "'Da Vinci Code' Disclaimer Sought in Movie," *Catalyst*, April 2006.

57. Sharon Waxman, "Sprinkling Holy Water on 'The Da Vinci Code,'" *New York Times*, August 7, 2005, Arts and Leisure, p. 2.

58. William Donohue, "'Da Vinci Code' Peddles Lies," *Catalyst*, May 2006.

59. "'60 Minutes' Isn't Fooled," *Catalyst*, June 2006.

60. *The Golden Compass: Agenda Unmasked*, a booklet authored by William Donohue and Kiera McCaffrey and published by the Catholic League, 2007. It is available on the Catholic League Web site, catholicleague.org.

61. Ibid.

62. Ibid.

63. Ibid.

64. Hanna Rosin, "How Hollywood Saved God," *Atlantic Monthly*, December 2007.

65. "Pundits Get It Wrong on Boycott," *Catalyst*, January-February 2008.

66. "Philip Pullman's *His Dark Materials* Film Trilogy in Doubt after Golden Compass Sequel in Limbo," telegraph.co.uk, July 18, 2008.

67. "Bishops Pull 'Golden Compass' Review," *Catalyst*, January-February 2008.

68. William Donohue, "'Angels & Demons': *More Demonic than Angelic*," a booklet published by the Catholic League, 2009. See catholicleague.org. All of the discussion of *Angels & Demons* is based on the booklet.

69. Ibid. See also Thomas E. Woods, Jr., *How the Catholic Church Built Western Civilization* (Washington, D.C.: Regnery, 2005), pp. 4–5.

70. Ibid. See also Rodney Stark, "Catholicism and Science," *Catalyst*, September 2004.

71. Ibid. All of this is in the booklet that I wrote.

Chapter 6: Sabotaged by Lawyers

1. David Limbaugh, *Persecution: How Liberals Are Waging War Against Christianity* (Washington, D.C.: Regnery, 2003), pp. 149–150.

2. Philip Hamburger, *Separation of Church and State* (Cambridge, Massachusetts: Harvard University Press, 2002), p. 252.

3. Robert Cord, *Separation of Church and State: Historical Fact and Current Fiction* (New York: Lambeth Press, 1992). See also William Donohue, "Myths About Church-State Separation," *Catalyst*, November 2004.

4. John T. McGreevey, *Catholicism and American Freedom* (New York: W. W. Norton, 2003), p. 185.

5. Hugo Black, Jr., *My Father: A Remembrance* (New York: Random House, 1975), p. 104.

6. Hamburger, *Separation of Church and State*, p. 449.

7. Ibid., pp. 451–452.

8. T. R. Reid and Marjorie Hyer, "The Catholic Church in America; Lacking the Benefit of State Aid, the Church Struggled and Prospered," *Washington Post*, October 7, 1979, p. 12.

9. Robert Bork, "What to Do about the First Amendment," originally published in *Commentary*, February, 1995; an excerpt was reprinted in the April 1995 edition of *Catalyst*.

10. McGreevey, *Catholicism and American Freedom*, p. 264.

11. Bork, "What to Do about the First Amendment."

12. For a review of Jacoby's book and reference to Noonan's remark, see my article "The Secular Crusade," *Catalyst*, October 2004.

13. Patrick M. Garry, *Wrestling with God: The Courts' Tortuous Treatment of Religion* (Washington, D.C.: Catholic University of America Press, 2006), p. 129.

14. Ibid., p. 22.

15. For a review of Garry's book, see my article "Judicial Jujitsu: How the Courts Treat Religious Liberty," *Catalyst*, July-August 2006.

16. Garry, *Wrestling with God*, p. 22.

17. Ibid., pp. 22–23.

18. William Donohue, *The Politics of the American Civil Liberties Union* (New Brunswick, New Jersey: Transaction Press, 1985), p. 306.

19. Ibid., chapter 4. See also my book *Twilight of Liberty: The Legacy of the ACLU* (New Brunswick, New Jersey: Transaction Press, 1994), chapter 3. There is a 2001 edition in paperback that contains a new afterword.

20. Ibid.

21. Mike Branom, "Judge: Woman Can't Wear Veil in ID Photo," Associated Press, June 6, 2003.

22. "Americans United Washes the Face of a Bigot," *Catalyst*, January-February 2003.

23. Ibid.

24. Charles R. Morris, *American Catholic* (New York: Times Books, 1997), p. 253.

25. "Americans United Washes the Face of a Bigot."

26. Jeffrey Rosen, "Is Nothing Secular?," *New York Times Magazine*, January 30, 2000, p. 42.

27. "Americans United Responds to *The New York Times Magazine* Article on Separation of Church and State," Americans United news release, February 1, 2000.

28. Bruce Felknor, "Questions of Conscience; Religious Bias a No-Show," *Chicago Tribune*, October 17, 2004, p. C1.

29. The Catherine Dent video is available from YouTube.

30. "VMI Dinner Prayer Ruled Unconstitutional," Associated Press Online, April 29, 2003.

31. "California Missions Deserve Federal Funds," Catholic League news release, November 18, 2004.

32. "Las Cruces 'Cross' Logo Protested," *CNSNews*, February 18, 2003.

33. Dimitri Cavalli, "By Process of Intimidation," *Wall Street Journal*, November 17, 2006, p. W15.

34. Interview on *The O'Reilly Factor*, transcript, December 19, 2000.

35. "Americans United Files Litigation Challenging Veterans Administration Bias Against Wiccans," Americans United news release, November 13, 2006.

36. William Donohue, letter to House Armed Services Military Personnel Subcommittee, reprinted in *Catalyst*, July-August 2005.

37. Sandhya Bathija, "Defend the Wall!: Conn. Bishops Rally for Church-State Separation—Sort Of," Au.org, March 11, 2009.

38. Morgan Bergman, "Americans United for Separation of Church and State," *Organization Trends* (a publication of Capital Research Center), December 2002, p. 5.

39. "ACLU and American Atheists Privilege Judaism," Catholic League news release, December 10, 1998.

40. Tim Bryant, "Judge's Order Forces St. Ann to Remove Nativity Scene," *St. Louis Post-Dispatch*, December 10, 1998, p. A9.

41. "Religious Left Group Sponsors Homosexual Film Festival," *CultureFacts* (a publication of the Family Research Council), October 6, 2000.

42. Donohue, *Twilight of Liberty*, pp. 194–197, 207–210.

43. Ryan Underwood, "Wal-Mart Puts 'Christmas' Back into Sales Season," *Tennessean*, November 11, 2006, p. A1.

44. Roger Armbrust, "'Corpus Christi' Rallies a Go," *Back Stage*, October 16, 1998, p. 1.

45. "Arts, First Amendment Supporters Rally at Brooklyn Museum," People for the American Way news release, October 1, 1999. See also "Church Squeamish in Public Marketplace of Ideas," American Atheists news release, September 30, 1999.

46. "Catholic League Quotes on 'Golden Compass,'" *Catalyst*, January-February 2008.

47. "Speak Out for Atheist Free Speech? Support Kathy Griffin, Target of Catholic League Bullying, Emmy Academy Cowardice?," American Atheist news release, September 13, 2007.

48. Catholic League's 2007 *Annual Report on Anti-Catholicism*, p. 4.

49. "AU Bulletin," Americans United for Separation of Church and State, November 2005.

50. Ryan J. Foley, "Federal Judge Clears Use of Religion in Care for Veterans; Dismisses Atheist Group's Challenge," Associated Press, January 10, 2007.

51. Stacy Foster, "Foundation Lobbies Assembly Speaker to End," *Milwaukee Journal Sentinel*, June 19, 2008, p. B5.

52. "Democracy Threatened in Florida," Catholic League news release, June 13, 2008.

53. "Politics and Faith," *New York Post*, August 30, 2000, p. 44.

54. Jonathan Weisman, "Groups Decry Talk of Faith," *Baltimore Sun*, August 30, 2000, p. A1.

55. Julia Duin, "Why Bush Threatens Secularism," *Washington Times*, April 14, 2005, p. A1.

56. Ibid.

57. "AU Comments on Congressional Resolution Supporting 'God Bless America' in Public Schools," Americans United news release, October 16, 2001.

58. "Proposed Christian 'miracle debris' Cross At Ground Zero Unconstitutional, Inappropriate and 'Insulting' said American Atheists," American Atheists news release, June 14, 2002.

59. For a blurb on the book featuring the endorsements see ffrf.org.

60. Philip Terzian, "Atheist's End," *Wall Street Journal*, March 23, 2001, p. W17.

61. John MacCormack, "The Case of the Headless, Handless Corpse," *Dallas Observer*, February 18, 1999.

62. Richard Tregaskis interviewed Madalyn Murray O'Hair in *Playboy*. It was printed in the October 1965 issue and is available at positiveatheism.com.

63. Alan Wolfe, "Among the Non-Believers," *New Republic*, April 12–April 19, 2004, p. 28.

64. "Catholic League Backs 'Justice Sunday,'" *Catalyst*, June 2005.

65. Peter Wallsten, "Battle Over Benches Spills Across Pews," *Los Angeles Times*, April 25, 2005, p. A10.

66. Frank Rich, "A High-Tech Lynching in Prime Time," *New York Times*, April 24, 2005, Section 4, p. 13.

67. "Justice Sunday Reloaded," *New York Times*, August 16, 2005, p. A14.

68. "Roberts' Religion Probed; Catholic Baiting Erupts," *Catalyst*, September 2005.

69. "Ripping Roberts on Religion," *Catalyst*, September 2005.

70. Ibid.

Chapter 7: Democratic Sabotage

1. Geoffrey Layman, *The Great Divide: Religious and Cultural Conflict in American Party Politics* (New York: Columbia University Press, 2001), p. 53.

2. Ibid., p. 104.

3. Louis Bolce and Gerald De Maio, "A 'Prejudice' for the Thinking Classes: Media Framing of the New Religious Divide, Political Sophistication, and the Christian Fundamentalist," paper given at the 2007 Southern Political Science Association annual meeting, New Orleans, January 4–7, 2007.

4. Arthur C. Brooks, *Who Really Cares?* (New York: Basic Books, 2006), p. 43.

5. Ibid., p. 45.

6. Layman, *The Great Divide*, p. 184.

7. Jeane Kirkpatrick, *The New Presidential Elite: Men and Women in National Politics* (New York: Sage, 1976).

8. Louis Bolce and Gerald De Maio, "Our Secularist Democratic Party," *Public Interest*, Fall 2002.

9. Mark Stricherz, *Why the Democrats Are Blue* (New York: Encounter Books, 2007), pp. 4–5.

10. Ibid., p. 98.

11. Michael Gerson, "A Second Home for Religious Voters?," *Washington Post*, November 2, 2007, p. A21.

12. Layman, *The Great Divide*, pp. 114–115.

13. David Carlin, *Can a Catholic Be a Democrat?: How the Party I Loved Became the Enemy of My Religion* (Manchester, New Hampshire: Sophia Institute Press, 2006), pp. 13–14.

14. Layman, *The Great Divide*, pp. 117–118.

15. Galston made his remarks at the May 2006 Pew Forum biannual Faith Angle Conference on Religion, Politics and Public Life. See the transcript "Religion, Moral Values and the Democratic Party," May 22, 2006, at pewforum.org.

16. Layman, *The Great Divide*, p. 107.

17. Bolce and De Maio, "Our Secularist Democratic Party."

18. Steven Waldman, "2004: Convention Blog," beliefnet.com, July 28, 2004.

19. Julia Duin, "Kerry Advisers Tell Hopeful to 'Keep Cool' on Religion," *Washington Times*, June 18, 2004, p. A1.

20. Rachel Zoll, "GOP Looks for More Jewish Votes for Bush," *Durham Herald-Sun*, September 2, 2004.

21. Richard John Neuhaus, "Weird and Wonderful Travels in Evangelicaldom," *First Things*, May 2007, p. 59.

22. E. J. Kessler, "Dems' Talk of 'Values' Seen as Risk with Jews," *Forward*, November 11, 2004.

23. "How the Jews Vote," *Forward*, November 11, 2004.

24. Nathan Diament, "How the GOP Won the Orthodox Vote," *Forward*, November 11, 2004.

25. Louis Bolce and Gerald De Maio, "The (In) Sincere Friends of Religion," *Crisis*, January 2007, pp. 13–14.

26. Louis Bolce and Gerald De Maio, "Secularists, Antifundamental-

ists, and the New Religious Divide in the American Electorate," edited by Matthew J. Wilson, *From Pews to Polling Places: Faith and Politics in the American Religious Mosaic* (Washington, D.C.: Georgetown University Press, 2007).

27. Carlin, *Can a Catholic Be a Democrat?*, p. 57.

28. Garry Wills, *Under God: Religion and American Politics* (New York: Simon & Schuster, 1990), p. 84.

29. William A. Donohue, *Twilight of Liberty: The Legacy of the ACLU* (New Brunswick, New Jersey: Transaction Press, 1994), p. xv.

30. Ibid., p. xii.

31. Ibid., pp. xvi–xx.

32. Layman, *The Great Divide*, pp. 119–120.

33. William A. Donohue, "Clinton's Catholic Problem," *Catalyst*, March 1995; it first appeared in the January 1995 edition of *Crisis*.

34. Ibid.

35. Catholic League news release, July 21, 1993. It was reprinted in the *Catholic League Newsletter*, September 1993.

36. The *Washington Post* editorial appeared August 2, 1993. See "Washington Post Says League Is Right," *Catholic League Newsletter*, September 1993.

37. Donohue, "Clinton's Catholic Problem."

38. Ibid.

39. Ibid.

40. Ibid.

41. "Democratic National Committee Offends Catholics; Terry McAuliffe Implored to Intervene," Catholic League news release, July 31, 2002.

42. "Democratic National Committee Refuses to Drop Kissling," *Catalyst*, November 2002.

43. "Kissling Bares Her Anti-Catholic Stripes; She Further Shames the DNC," Catholic League news release, October 15, 2002.

44. "Democratic National Committee Dumps Catholics for a Free Choice," Catholic League news release, October 28, 2002.

45. "Democratic National Committee Renews Link with Catholics for a Free Choice," Catholic League news release, October 28, 2002.

46. "Democratic National Committee Sponsors Hard-Core Teen Porn," Catholic League news release, October 28, 2002.

47. Letter by Joseph M. Birkenstock to William Donohue, October 28, 2002.

48. Letter by William Donohue to Joseph M. Birkenstock, October 29, 2002.

49. "Democratic National Committee Dumps Porn Site But Keeps Anti-Catholic One," Catholic League news release, October 29, 2002.

50. "Catholic League to DNC: We'll Be Your Worst Nightmare in 2004," *Catalyst*, December 2002.

51. "DNC's New Website Devoid of Anti-Catholic Link," Catholic League news release, April 13, 2004.

52. "Kerry's Religion Outreach Director Quickly Silenced," *Catalyst*, July-August 2004.

53. Amy Sullivan, "The Dems Finally Get Religion," time.com, February 14, 2008.

54. "Kerry's Religion Outreach Director Quickly Silenced."

55. "DNC's New Religion Advisor Wants 'Under God' Out of the Pledge," Catholic League news release, August 2, 2004.

56. "DNC's Religion Advisor Says: 'Love Thy Neighbor' Means Paying Taxes," Catholic League news release, August 3, 2004.

57. "DNC's Religion Advisor Unmasked," Catholic League news release, August 4, 2004.

58. Ibid.

59. "DNC's Religion Advisor Quits," Catholic League news release, August 5, 2004.

60. "Huge Victory Scored; Edwards' Bigots Resign," *Catalyst*, March 2007; for the latter statement in its entirety, see her Pandagon blog site and Kathryn Jean Lopez, "Unholy Hire," National Review Online, February 6, 2007.

61. Ibid. See also McEwan's blog posting of February 21, 2006.

62. McEwan, "On Cunts," shakespearessister.blogspot, November 29, 2006.

63. "John Edwards Tolerates Anti-Catholicism," Catholic League news release, February 8, 2007.

64. "Edwards Blogger Strikes *Again*: They Must Be Fired Now!," Catholic League news release, February 12, 2007.

65. "Campaign Blogger for John Edwards Quits After Outrage Over 'Anti-Catholic' Comments," Associated Press, February 13, 2007.

66. A copy of the ad that was to run appears in *Catalyst*, March 2007.

67. The *New York Times* ad appeared on September 28, 2004. See also "MoveOn.org Slanders Christians," Catholic League news release, September 28, 2004.

68. "Elites Ignite Anti-Christian Hysteria," Catholic League news release, October 28, 2004.

69. "Religious Bigots Explode After Election," Catholic League news release, November 4, 2004.

70. Ibid.

71. "Elites Continue Their Crackup," Catholic League news release, November 8, 2004.

72. "Religion in the 2008 Election: Post-Election Survey," publicreligion.org, November 14, 2008.

73. Eric Gorski, "Obama Results Show Gains in Key Religious Voters," Associated Press, November 6, 2008.

74. Dan Gilgoff, "Newt Gingrich Steps Up Efforts to Mobilize Religious Conservatives," USnews.com, March 20, 2009.

Chapter 8: Self-Sabotage: Catholicism

1. "Religion and Politics," *CQ Researcher*, July 30, 2004, p. 652.

2. "'We Are Church' Referendum Is Huge Failure, Sr. Fiedler Admits," *Wanderer*, November 27, 1997.

3. Virginia Heffernan, "Pope John Paul Appraised As Pope, Not Rock Star," *New York Times*, April 5, 2005, p. A10.

4. Andrew Greeley, "John Paul's Mixed Legacy," beliefnet.com following the pope's death.

5. "A Pope and a Pontificate Full of Contradictions," We Are Church press release, April 2, 2005.

6. Thomas Cahill, "The Price of Infallibility," *New York Times*, April 5, 2005, p. A23.

7. Arthur Jones, "Theologians See, Experience Downside to John Paul II's Papacy," *National Catholic Reporter*, April 18, 2005.

8. William Donohue, "Catholic Dissidents Are Fixated on Sex," Catholic League news release, April 13, 2005.

9. "An Open Letter to Catholic Voters," National Coalition of American Nuns news release, October 22, 2006.

10. E. J. Dionne Jr., "Cardinal Ratzinger's Challenge," *Washington Post*, April 19, 2005, p. A19.

11. Daniel Williams and Alan Cooperman, "Conclave Begins With Day of Ritual," *Washington Post*, April 19, 2005, p. A1.

12. Deborah Caldwell, "Catholics React to the New Pope," belief net.com, April 19, 2005.

13. Bill Tammeus, "Priest's Message: 'Be Liberal,'" *Kansas City Star*, May 14, 2005, p. F12.

14. William Donohue, "Church and State in an Election Year," *Catalyst*, June 2004.

15. Ibid.

16. Ibid.

17. Susan Snyder, "Act of Defiance," *Philadelphia Inquirer*, August 1, 2006, p. A1.

18. Michael Paulson, "Making a Stand for Women Priests," boston.com, July 28, 2006.

19. "Finished Playing by the Rules," *National Catholic Reporter*, December 7, 2007.

20. Andrew Greeley, "Gay Marriages Are Welcome in God's Order," *The Times-Union*, June 22, 1996, p. B10.

21. Andrew Greeley, "Priests Are Happy Without Wives," *Chicago Sun-Times*, December 5, 2007, p. 37.

22. Daniel J. Harrington, S.J., and James F. Keenan, S.J., *Jesus and Virtue Ethics* (New York: Sheed & Ward, 2003).

23. Maximillian A. Pakaluk, "Modern Catholics Play It Fast and Loose with Doctrine," *The Harvard Student*, November 10, 2003.

24. "Memorandum by MCC Staff on Erroneous Testimony on Catholic Teaching at April 28 Hearing in the Massachusetts

Legislature on H. 3190, the Marriage Affirmation & Protection Amendment," macathconf.org/03_memo_on_erroneous_testimony_4 .htm, June 2, 2003.

25. Robert F. Drinan, "Posturing on Abortion," *New York Times*, June 4, 1996, p. A15.

26. Liz Trotta, "Abortion Veto Raises Catholic Groundswell; Clinton Targeted on Partial-birth Ban," *Washington Times*, July 11, 1996, p. A1.

27. Joel Mowbray, "The Anti-Catholic Catholic Group," *Insight on the News*, August 5, 2002, p. 20.

28. Naomi Theodorou, "Hail Frances," *Mother Jones*, May-June 1991, p. 11.

29. William Donohue, "The Real Agenda of Catholics For a Free Choice," *Daily Catholic*, October 10, 2002.

30. Marjorie Reiley Maguire, "Not Catholic," *National Catholic Reporter*, April 21, 1995, p. 18.

31. Lisa Hisel, "Catholicism and Abortion Since Roe v. Wade," *Conscience*, January 31, 1988.

32. Judy Mann, "Conflict," *Washington Post*, May 20, 1983, p. B1.

33. Washington News Section, UPI, June 30, 1986.

34. Lisa Hisel, "Catholicism and Abortion Since Roe v. Wade."

35. Ann Carey, "Disorder Among the Nuns," *Our Sunday Visitor*, April 6, 2008.

36. "Fallen Off Church's Edge," *National Catholic Reporter*, August 22, 2007.

37. Carey, "Disorder Among the Nuns."

38. Ibid.

39. Brian C. Anderson, "How Catholic Charities Lost Its Soul," *City Journal*, Winter 2000, p. 30.

40. Julia Duin, "Virginia Law Eyed in Girl's Abortion; Bishops Alerted to U.S. Probe," *Washington Times*, June 18, 2008, p. A1.

41. For information on the Catholic Charities event, see John Jalsevac, "San Francisco Catholic Charities Hosts 'Who's Who' Crowd of Homosexual Marriage Supporters," lifesitenews.com, June 24, 2008. For information on Newsom, see "Gay Adoption Issue Spurs Bigoted Furor," Catholic League news release, March 15, 2006. Information

on the lawsuit against the Board of Supervisors can be found in the Catholic League news release "Political Assault on Catholics Triggers Lawsuit," April 4, 2006.

42. Joseph A. Varacalli, *The Catholic Experience in America* (Westport, Connecticut: Greenwood Press, 2006), p. 226.

43. "'Strong Language,'" an interview with Michael Novak, *National Catholic Register*, May 11, 2008, p. 12.

44. Richard Ostling, "U.S. Scholars Wonder Whether Pope Benedict XVI Will Take Further Actions Against Dissenters," Associated Press, May 12, 2005.

45. Anne Hendershott, *Status Envy: The Politics of Catholic Higher Education* (New Brunswick, New Jersey: Transaction Press, 2008).

46. Rev. Michael Reilly, "Politically Correct at Boston College," newsmax.com, January 6, 2001. Boston College theologian Peter Kreeft shared the crucifix story with me.

47. Michael Paulson, "Catholic Symbols Stir Diverse Feelings at BC," boston.com, February 12, 2009.

48. John L. Allen, Jr., "Muslim Chaplain Sees Value in Crucifixes," *National Catholic Reporter*, May 14, 2004, p. 10.

49. Carlos Campos, "Prominent Cardinal's Anti-Gay Comment Sparks Protest," Cox News Service, May 21, 2003.

50. "Nothing's Agenda Exposed," *Catalyst*, July-August 1998.

51. "*The Myth of Hitler's Pope*: An Interview with Rabbi David G. Dalin," catholicexchange.com, July 29, 2005.

52. Robert P. Lockwood, "Papal Sin: Structures of Deceit," book review for the Catholic League, June 2000 at catholicleague.org.

53. Lockwood, "*Constantine's Sword*: A Review Article," *Catalyst*, January-February 2001.

54. Joseph Bottum, "When the Swallows Come Back to Capistrano," *First Things*, October 2006, p. 31.

55. "Call to Action: 25 Years of Spirituality and Justice," Call to Action anniversary edition newsletter, October 2001.

56. Ibid.

57. Colleen Carroll, *The New Faithful: Why Young Adults Are Embracing Christian Orthodoxy* (Chicago: Loyola Press, 2002), p. 281.

58. Bob Reeves, "Catholic Group Calls for More Openness," *Lincoln Journal Star*, June 4, 2006, p. 1.

59. S. L. Hansen, "Vatican Rejects Call to Action Appeal," Catholic News Service, ncrcafe.org, February 21, 2007.

60. Tom Roberts, "Retiring Reformers Note New Goals," *National Catholic Reporter*, May 30, 2008, Section G1.

61. "CTA Backs Voice of the Faithful as 4,200 Gather in Boston," *Call to Action News*, September 2002.

62. Tom McFeely, "Voice of the Faithful? Lay Organization Under Renewed Fire for Promoting Dissent," catholiconline, September 8, 2006.

63. Father Brian McSweeney, "Speakers Questioned," letter to the editor, *Catholic New York*, December 2003, p. 27.

64. Ibid.

65. Tom McFeely, "Voice of the Faithful?"

66. "Seal of the Confessional Under Attack; Voice of the Faithful Member Is Responsible," Catholic League news release, January 24, 2003. The VOTF member was Anne Coughlin, who lobbied to end the exemption in New Hampshire. The Catholic League side prevailed but not without a fight.

67. "VOTF Respond to Catholic League New York Times Ad and Calls on Bishops to Be Accountable NOW," Voice of the Faithful news release, June 8, 2006.

68. "Spin Without End in Abuse Scandal," *National Catholic Reporter*, June 16, 2006.

69. William Donohue, "Spin in Abuse Scandal," letter to the editor, *National Catholic Reporter*, July 14, 2006, p. 19.

70. Delfin Vigil, "Catholic Group Convenes to Change the Church," *San Francisco Chronicle*, October 10, 2005, p. B1.

71. Dan Tepfer, "New Leader of Voice of the Faithful Hopes to Improve Dialogue with Diocese," Connecticut Post Online, July 16, 2006.

72. Paul Lakeland, "Vocational Crisis," *Commonweal*, February 24, 2006, p. 26.

73. Peter Feuerherd, "Priests Offer Mediation for Bishop, Laity," *National Catholic Reporter*, May 19, 2006.

74. Chuck Colbert, "Voice of the Faithful Members Profiled," *National Catholic Reporter*, March 10, 2006.

75. James Vaznis, "Catholic Lay Group Assesses Strengths, Flaws," boston.com, October 24, 2005.

76. Father Bill Pomerleau and Lynne Sullivan, "Voice of the Faithful Facing Financial, Membership Crisis," Catholic News Service, May 29, 2007.

77. "Voice of the Faithful Strategic Plan: 2008–2010," Voiceofthe faithful.org, first posted in 2008.

78. Kevin McLaughlin, "Robinson Speaks Out: Bishop Defies Cardinals to Speak on Sex and Power," *National Catholic Reporter*, May 30, 2008, Section G1.

79. "Cardinal Mahony Bars Australian Bishop with 'Doctrinal Difficulties' from Archdiocese," catholicnewsagency.com, May 19, 2008.

80. On September 15, 2008, Voice president Dan Bartley wrote a letter to Boston Archbishop Sean Cardinal O'Malley, who is the Chairman of the Bishops' Committee on Clergy, Consecrated Life and Vocations, making the case for an end to priestly celibacy. It was published on the Web site of VOTF.

81. Deal Hudson, "The Catholic Left Meets in Philadelphia," inside catholic.com, July 15, 2008.

82. "Victory in Connecticut," *Catalyst*, April 2009.

83. Tom Monahan, "5,000 Angry Protesters Descend the Capitol," Msnbc.com, March 13, 2009.

84. "Bill Giving Laity Control of Parish Finances Killed in Connecticut," Catholic News Service, March 11, 2009.

85. John L. Allen, Jr., "Vatican Denounces Fr. Roger Haight's Book, Bars Him From Teaching," *National Catholic Reporter*, February 18, 2005, p. 10.

86. "Statement of the Board of Directors: With Respect to the Notification Issued by the Congregation for the Doctrine of the Faith Concerning the Book, *Jesus: Symbol of God,* Rev. Robert Haight, S.J., and Prohibiting Fr. Haight from Teaching Catholic Theology," April 1, 2005.

87. Cindy Wooden, "Vatican Action Against U.S. Jesuit is Not Definitive, Order Says," Catholic News Service, January 5, 2009.

88. Call to Action ad on its National Conference, *National Catholic Reporter*, July 19, 2002, p. 10.

89. James Carroll, "An Ex-Priest Calls for Vatican Reforms to Stem a Church Revolt," *People*, October 15, 1990, p. 52.

90. Peter Steinfels, "Bishops and Liberals Split on Agendas," *New York Times*, November 11, 1991, p. A10.

91. Jay McNally, " 'We Are the Church' Referendum Is Huge Failure, Sr. Fiedler Admits," *Wanderer*, November 27, 1997, p. 6.

92. David Morrison, "We Are Church: 'It Seemed Like a Good Idea,' " *Our Sunday Visitor*, December 7, 1997, p. 21.

93. George Weigel, *The Courage to Be Catholic: Crisis, Reform, and the Future of the Church* (New York: Basic Books, 2002), p. 62.

94. Joyce Milton, *The Road to Malpsychia: Humanistic Psychology and Our Discontents* (San Francisco: Encounter Books, 2002), pp. 138–145.

95. Weigel, *The Courage to Be Catholic*, p. 67.

96. Ibid., pp. 68–72.

97. Anthony Kosnick, *Human Sexuality: New Directions in American Catholic Thought* (New York: Paulist Press, 1977), p. 88.

98. Robert Crooks and Karla Bauer, *Our Sexuality* (Redwood City, California: Benjamin Cummings, 1990). When I appeared on the Donahue show, the book was already in its fourth edition; there are now 10 editions of this textbook. For evidence of its use in seminaries, see Michael S. Rose, *Goodbye, Good Men: How Liberals Brought Corruption into the Catholic Church* (Washington, D.C.: Regnery, 2002), p. 100.

99. Father Matthew L. Lamb, "Theological Malpractice," nationalreview.com, October 3, 2002.

100. Enrique Rueda, *The Homosexual Network* (Old Greenwich, Connecticut: Devin-Adair, 1982), pp. 313–314.

101. William Donohue, "A Crisis of Faith," *Catalyst*, June 2002. See also Leon J. Podles, *Sacrilege: Sexual Abuse in the Catholic Church* (Baltimore, Maryland: Crossland Press, 2008), p. 129.

102. Ibid.

103. John Cardinal O'Connor, "'Priest' and Real Priests," *Catholic New York*, April 6, 1995, p. 7.

104. For a fair reading of this subject see Kevin Cullen, "National Review Board Report; More Than 80 Percent of Victims Since 1950 Were Male, Report Says," *Boston Globe*, February 28, 2004, p. A1.

105. "The Nature and Scope of the Problem of Sexual Abuse of Minors by Catholic Priests and Deacons in the United States," A Research Study Conducted by the John Jay College of Criminal Justice, February 2004, Section 4.2.

106. Pam Belluck, "Scandals in the Church," *New York Times*, April 26, 2002, p. A22.

107. Dave Umhoeffer, "Scandal Casts New Light on Weakland's Statements," *Milwaukee Journal Sentinel*, May 26, 2002, p. A1.

108. Ibid.

109. Jeannine Gramick, "Finding Empathy for Shanley," *National Catholic Reporter*, January 14, 2005.

110. Ibid.

111. William Donohue, "When Guidelines Are Not Enough," *Catalyst*, July-August 2002.

112. Maureen Orth, "Gramick's Charity to Shanley Is More Than He Deserves," *National Catholic Reporter*, January 14, 2005.

113. Jerry Filteau, "Poll Finds Many Catholics Unaware of Church Steps to Prevent Abuse," catholicnews.com, May 18, 2007.

114. Paul Elie, "The Patron Saint of Paradox," *New York Times Magazine*, November 8, 1998, p. 44f.

115. David van Biema, "Is Liberal Catholicism Dead?," time.com, May 3, 2008.

Chapter 9: Self-Sabotage: Protestantism

1. Dave Shiflett, *Exodus: Why Americans Are Fleeing Liberal Churches for Conservative Christianity* (New York: Sentinel, 2005), p. xii.

2. Private correspondence, Bronwen Catherine McShea to Bill Donohue, November 17, 2006.

3. Walter Russell Mead, "God's Country?," *Foreign Affairs*, September-October 2006.

4. "U.S. Religious Landscape Survey," Pew Forum on Religion and Public Life, 2008, p. 18.

5. Land's comments were made at a Pew Research Center forum on September 26, 2006. See the transcript, "God's Country? Evangelicals and U.S. Foreign Policy."

6. Joseph Bottum, "The Death of Protestant America," *First Things*, August-September, 2008, pp. 25–26.

7. Cathy Lynn Grossman, "God and Gays: Churchgoers Stand Divided; the Faithful Face Difficult Choices," *USA Today*, June 13, 2006, p. 1D.

8. "Strategy for Church Growth Splits Congregants," Associated Press, September 5, 2006.

9. George Gallup, Jr., and D. Michael Lindsay, *Surveying the Religious Landscape: Trends in U.S. Beliefs* (Harrisburg, Pennsylvania: Morehouse Publishing, 1999), p. 19.

10. Walter Russell Mead, "God's Country?"

11. "Assemblies of God Grow Most in 2005," *Akron Beacon Journal*, April 8, 2006.

12. Mead's comments were made at the Pew Center forum of 2006 where Land made his remarks.

13. Charlotte Allen, "Liberal Christianity Is Paying for Its Sins," *Los Angeles Times*, July 9, 2006, p. M3.

14. Ibid.

15. John M. Powers, "Mainline Churches Face Great Divide," *Insight on the News*, January 5, 2004, p. 27.

16. Dawn Baumgartner Vaughan, "No Change Expected in Where, How People Pray," *Herald-Sun*, April 2006, p. B4.

17. John M. Powers, "Mainline Churches Face Great Divide."

18. Shiflett, *Exodus*, p. 123.

19. Mike Aquilina, "Self-Inflicted Wounds," *Our Sunday Visitor*, March 9, 1997, p. 8.

20. Dean Kelley, *Why Conservative Churches Are Growing* (New York: Harper & Row, 1972), pp. 88–90.

21. Wade Clark Roof and William McKinney, *American Mainline*

Religion (New Brunswick, New Jersey: Rutgers University Press, 1987), p. 4.

22. Thomas C. Reeves, *The Empty Church: The Suicide of Liberal Christianity* (New York: Free Press, 1996), p. 32.

23. Benton Johnson, Dean R. Hoge, and Donald A. Luidens, "Mainline Churches: The Real Reason for Decline," *First Things*, March 1993, p. 16.

24. Mark I. Pinsky, "Lifeline for Mainliners," *USA Today*, May 19, 2008, p. A11.

25. Greg Garrison, "Few Churchgoers Tithe, Study Says," Newhouse News Service, May 14, 2008.

26. Ibid.

27. Reeves, *The Empty Church*, p. 107.

28. Franklin Foer, "Beyond Belief," *New Republic*, December 29, 2003–January 5, 2004, p. 22.

29. Finke and Stark, *The Churching of America*, pp. 226–228.

30. Dave Shiflett, *Exodus*, pp. 120–121.

31. Ibid., p. 62.

32. Carol M. Ostrom, "Unitarians Making a Strong Pitch," *Seattle Times*, September 29, 1990, p. A16.

33. Dave Shiflett, *Exodus*, p. 59.

34. Rod Dreher, "Celebrating *Roe*," National Review Online, January 20, 2003.

35. Don Lattin, "Polyamorists Say They Relate Honestly to Multiple Partners," *San Francisco Chronicle*, April 20, 2004, p. B1.

36. Randy Sly, "From New President of Episcopal Divinity School: 'Abortion is a Blessing,' " *catholic.org*, April 2, 2009.

37. G. Jeffrey MacDonald, "Episcopal Seminaries Face Uncertain Finances, Future," Religion News Stories, May 15, 2008, religionnews.com.

38. Such is the case of Garret Keizer, a contributing editor of *Harper's* magazine. See his article "Turning Away from Jesus: Gay Rights and the War for the Episcopal Church," *Harper's*, June 2008, pp. 39-50.

39. Dave Shiflett, *Exodus*, p. 39.

40. Tom Landess, "An American Dilemma," *Chronicles*, July 2006, p. 21.

41. Bottum, "The Death of Protestant America," p. 28.

42. Dave Shiflett, *Exodus*, pp. 48–49.

43. John Chadwick, "Episcopalians Face up to Decline; Newark Diocese Seeks Dynamic New Bishop," *The Record*, December 9, 2005, p. A1.

44. Thomas Reeves, *The Empty Church*, p. 20.

45. Keith Fournier, "Male Episcopal Bishop Wants to Be a 'June Bride,'" catholiconline, December 11, 2007.

46. Kevin Eckstrom, "10 Minutes with . . . Gene Robinson," Religion News Service, May 21, 2008.

47. Garret Keizer, "Turning Away from Jesus: Gay Rights and the War for the Episcopal Church," p. 40.

48. Kenneth L. Woodward, "Courting Schism," *Commonweal*, September 12, 2003, p. 10.

49. Tina Kelley, "Gay Episcopal Priest Named As Possible Newark Bishop," *New York Times*, June 29, 2006, p. B1.

50. Dina Kraft and Laurie Goodstein, "Anglican Conservatives, Rebelling on Gays, Will Form New Power Bloc," *New York Times*, June 30, 2008, p. A6.

51. Laurie Goodstein, "Episcopal Split as Conservatives Form New Group," *New York Times*, December 4, 2008, p. A1.

52. The letter I wrote to Bishop Sisk appeared in the March 2005 edition of *Catalyst*, "Artist Defiles Virgin Mary: Episcopal Bishop Offers His Blessings." For the bishop's response, written by Miller, see "Episcopal Bishop Responds," *Catalyst*, April 2005.

53. "American Piety in the 21st Century: New Insights to the Depth and Complexity of Religion in the U.S.," *The Baylor Religion Survey*, September 2006, pp. 14, 24.

54. Jeffrey L. Sheler, "Nearer My God to Thee," *U.S. News & World Report*, May 3, 2004, p. 59.

55. Ronald R. Stockton, "Presbyterians, Jews and Divestment: The Church Steps Back," *Middle East Policy*, Winter 2006.

Chapter 10: The Perfect Cultural Storm

1. Laurie Goodstein, "Conservative Churches Grew Fastest," *New York Times*, September 18, 2002, p. A22.

2. Hanna Rosin, "Beyond Belief," *Atlantic Monthly*, January 1, 2005.

3. Maggie Gallagher, "Banned in Boston; The Coming Conflict between Same-Sex Marriage and Religious Liberty," *The Weekly Standard*, May 15, 2006.

4. Peter Steinfels, "Will Same-Sex Marriage Collide with Religious Liberty?," nytimes.com, June 10, 2006.

5. Gallagher, "Banned in Boston."

6. Ibid.

7. Steinfels, "Will Same-Sex Marriage Collide with Religious Liberty?"

8. Mike Sullivan, "The Threat of the New Atheism," *Catalyst*, July-August 2008.

9. "Minnesota Prof Pledges to Desecrate Eucharist," Catholic League news release, July 10, 2008. See scienceblogs.com/pharyngula for the various posts by Myers on his pledge.

10. Guenter Lewy, *Why America Needs Religion: Secular Modernity and Its Discontents* (Grand Rapids, Michigan: William B. Eerdmans, 1996), p. 134.

11. Ibid., p. 133.

12. Ibid., p. 138.

13. Ibid., p. 146.

14. Gertrude Himmelfarb, *One Nation, Two Cultures* (New York: Alfred A. Knopf, 1999), p. 143.

15. Deal W. Hudson, *Onward, Christian Soldiers* (New York: Simon & Schuster, 2008).

16. "Catholics and Orthodox Unite to Defend Family," zenit.org, December 15, 2008.

17. Rabbi Daniel Lapin, *America's Real War* (Sisters, Oregon: Multnomah, 1999), p. 355.

18. Mark Morford, "A Call for Progressive Breeders to Bed Down Already," *San Francisco Chronicle*, September 29, 2006, p. E9.

ABOUT THE AUTHOR

WILLIAM DONOHUE has been the president of the Catholic League for Religious and Civil Rights since 1993. Founded in 1973, the League works to safeguard the religious freedom and free speech of Catholics in America. Trained as an educator, Donohue began his teaching career at St. Lucy's School in New York's Spanish Harlem and went on to teach sociology at La Roche College in Pittsburgh. He holds a PhD in sociology from New York University.